OLD COOK BOOKS
An Illustrated History

Author's Note:
All prices quoted with dollar equivalents were correct at the time of going to press.

Dates given in parentheses after the title of any work indicate that the book in question was published in that year but carries no date of issue on either the title-page or elsewhere.

By the same author:
The Collector's Book of Books
The Collector's Book of Children's Books
The Collector's Book of Detective Fiction
The Collector's Book of Boys' Stories

OLD COOK BOOKS
An Illustrated History

by
Eric Quayle

Photographs by Gabe Monro

A Brandywine Press Book
E. P. Dutton
New York

This book was edited and produced by
THE BRANDYWINE PRESS, INC.
Clarkson N. Potter, President

Design and Production by Helga Maass
Margaret M. Madigan, Editor
Typography by David E. Seham Associates, Inc.

Published, 1978, in the United States by E. P. Dutton,
a Division of Sequoia-Elsevier Publishing Company, Inc.,
New York, and simultaneously in Canada by Clarke, Irwin & Company
Ltd., Toronto and Vancouver

For information contact: E. P. Dutton,
2 Park Avenue, New York, N.Y. 10016

Library of Congress Catalog Card Number: 78-68399
ISBN: 0-87690-283-2

10 9 8 7 6 5 4 3 2 1
First Edition

For Jean,
who was once
my own Mrs. Beeton

CONTENTS

Chapter One

BOILED BOAR AND SUCKING PIG

The art of cookery stretches back in time to primordial man. It is as old as his first great scientific discovery—the knowledge that he had harnessed fire and made it a servant to do his will.

Together with Man's use of the earliest rudimentary methods of kindling flame came his awareness that cooked food often tasted better than raw. A bloody hunk of fresh-killed meat, accidentally or experimentally dropped into the crackling flames of the open fire at his cave's mouth, led to his realization that the flesh of animals, birds, and fishes was tenderized and rendered vastly more palatable when subjected to prolonged heat. Hooked out from the embers by an antler or smoking stick, it provided the first cooked meal prepared for human consumption. Cookery, the subtle art of rendering food appetizing and more attractive for eating, dates back to that sizzling episode. The aroma lingers as it is wafted by imagination back to us through hundreds of thousands of years of time.

Aeons were to pass before the first crude recipes for the preparation of food were painstakingly written on skins of parchment and vellum. Yet the basic rules of culinary good behavior were already being laid down, later to be etched in the traditions of the family and tribe. Rules and methods that endured for centuries were memorized, and were passed on orally and by example to succeeding generations struggling to exist in environments hostile to human survival. The most economical use of the available food and its short-term preservation by cooking were some of the earliest lessons learned, and how to tenderize a leg of bison without at the same time charring it to a cinder, or the broiling of the tribal steak of elk, came as naturally to Stone Age woman as the preparation of a mixed grill to her modern counterpart.

Thousands of years later came the first written recipes that we know of, preserved on the baked clay tablets of Ancient Egypt. These simple directions and rules of good husbandry, the time for seed sowing and harvesting the crops, and the culinary uses to which herbs and spices could be put, as well as the seasoning and cooking of the fish and game animals hunters brought back from the field, were the guides known and used in the days of the pharaohs. But it is to the times of the Roman Empire that we turn for recipes in experimental use today, and for the basic guidelines still displaying their influence in many present-day cookery techniques.

Visitors to the excavated ruins of the Roman town of Pompeii and Herculaneum can still inspect kitchens, complete with pots and pans of half-cooked food, standing almost exactly as they were on the catastrophic day of August 24, 79 of the Christian Era, when the great eruption of Vesuvius overwhelmed both cities. It was only when the first sytematic excavations began in the 1760s, excavations that have continued almost without a break until the present day, that the hundreds of inscriptions and writings on the walls of houses and public buildings once more came to light. Amongst these, scrawled on the lintels of fireplaces and on kitchen walls, were the recipes used by Pompeiian cooks close on 2,000 years ago.

It is by an analysis of these, and from the writings of a likable character of the name of Apicius, that we know much of the culinary habits of the wealthier classes of Romans during the supremacy of their far-flung Empire. The name Apicius appears to have been given to at least three celebrated Roman gluttons, famed for their bacchanalian orgies, in which eating and drinking took pride of place even over sexual frolics. The first lived about 92 B.C., the second about A.D. 14, and the third about the middle of the first century A.D. It is the second of these gustatory gladiators who concerns us here, for his name is linked with some of the earliest cookery recipes to survive in manuscript form.

M. Gavius Apicius is reported by more than one contemporary author to have written books on cookery during the reign of the Emperor Tiberius. A number of amusing anecdotes are told about his feats of trenchership, and we are indebted to Seneca for the account of his melancholy death. Having spent a vast fortune, mainly on food and drink and the entertaining of like-minded gourmandizers, he awoke one morning with an elephant-sized hangover gained during the revels of the previous night. Disconsolately totting up what was left of his fortune, he was apparently horrified that, out of a total of some hundred million *sesterces,* he was now down to his last million. Later that day, Seneca informs us, "with the prospect of starvation before him," he poisoned himself.

To bibliographers, and not less to collectors of old cook books, Apicius and the works attributed to him have posed many problems. The task of unscrambling the confusion of interwoven texts contained in the earliest manuscripts which bear his name has been long and difficult. In the catalogues of booksellers and auctioneers his name is often wrongly given as "Apicius Coelius," due to errors of nineteenth-century scholarship. This error of attribution occurred because of a misinterpretation of a Latin abbreviation by bibliographers working on a manuscript of cookery recipes housed in the Vatican Library, Rome. This often consulted and famous manuscript has, on the first folio, which acts as a title, the letters API CAE.

As Barbara Flower and Elisabeth Rosenbaum pointed out in their *The Roman Cookery Book,* 1958, these letters were believed to have been an abbreviated form of the author's name, and several later versions expanded them to the full "Apicius Coelius." Modern scholarship now shows this to be an error, and that the author's name is almost certainly Marcus Gavius Apicius.

The Vatican manuscript is the work of an unknown compiler who lived in the fourth or early fifth century, as E. Brandt proved in his *Unter-suchungen zum Römanischen Kochbuch,* 1927. This well-meaning scribe, whose name we will never know, based his collection of recipes mainly on older manuscripts giving lists of Apicius's dishes and menus; but he then zealously padded out the work with culinary formulas taken from a variety of exotic sources. Many he extracted from Apuleius's well-known book on agricultural practices and guides to domestic science, while others came from manuscripts written in Greek and devoted to rules governing a healthy diet. He gave no indication to his readers of what he had done, so Apicius was credited with dozens of meals and recipes unknown in the palaces of ancient Rome.

During the Middle Ages, many manuscripts devoted to aspects of cookery and the carving of meats were in circulation, nearly all of which seem to have stemmed from the Vatican codex. So, as one might expect, the earliest cookery books we know of were based on the same source. Just over forty years after the invention of printing by movable metal type, the first of these made its appearance, being issued with two differing aspects of title and publisher. *Apicius de re Quoquinaria,* 1498, was issued by Guillermus le Signerre, of Milan; and exactly the same book appeared a few months later as *Appicius Culinarius,* 1498, under the imprint of Joannes de Legnano. Textually both issues are identical. The second edition, published as *De Re Coquinaria* (about 1500), under a Venice imprint, was edited by Blasius Lanciloti, as a quarto of thirty-two leaves, to which he added a further eight leaves devoted to *Grammatica et Rhetoribus Claris Libellus* by Suetonius. This two-part second edition of the earliest printed cookery book now changes hands at auction at over $3,500, and if a copy of the far rarer first edition of 1498 came on the market it could well fetch ten times that figure. A third edition was published in 1503.

Collectors of moderate means may well have to be content with the first translation into English, published as *Cooking and Dining in Imperial Rome,* 1936, issued in Chicago. This translation was by J. D. Vehling, a professional cook, who approached his task with sleeves rolled up as he tested the various recipes in his kitchen. Unfortunately, his understanding of the old Latin text did not match his skill as a cook, and the work is full of the most grotesque errors of translation. Many of these have been pointed out by Barbara Flower and Elisabeth Rosenbaum, and it is to their work, as well as several earlier Latin texts, that I am indebted for many of the recipes given below. They based their own translation on the Latin text given by G. Giarratano and F. Vollmer, published by Teubner, Leipzig, in 1922.

The amount of strong-smelling herbs and spices which Apicius heaped into many of his dishes seems to indicate that the natural taste of the fish or meat needed disguising in order to make it palatable. The difficulty of keeping such food untainted, especially during Italian summers, may well have led to the seeking out of herbs capable of wrapping up unpleasant odors and tastes, which, although rendered harmless by cooking, did little to stimulate the appetites of the diners. In fact, in some of his more ambitious recipes, Apicius tips in so many spices and sauces that no single flavor can be distinguished. At the end of one of these culinary bouquets the author proudly declares that, in his opinion, ". . . no one sitting at the table will have any idea what he is eating!"

There were critics of the amount of seasoning in the food of ancient Rome long before Apicius's day. Titus Maccius Plautus (c. 254 B.C. to 184 B.C.), poked fun at the cooks of the period in his play *Pseudolus,* making one of his characters, also a cook, complain:

"I certainly don't ruin dinners by over seasoning, the way most other cooks do. Some have the impertinence to serve you up whole fields of spices in their dishes. These are the men who call cows their friends, and season the herbs in your food with yet more herbs. They pile in coriander, fennel, onion, horse-parsley, and the sharpest and most pungent of garlic. They serve up sorrel, beetroot, and stringy spinach, then pour into this concoction a pound of asafoetida, before pounding up mustard so strong their eyes weep tears. When they season their masters' dinners they don't use spices but screech-owls, then wonder why there are complaints that they feel their intestines being eaten alive! Some of the herbs they use are fearful to speak of, let alone eat. In fact, I tell you that there are men who eat herbs the cows of the fields refuse."

When a Roman entertained his guests the meal usually consisted of three main divisions, much as we have in the present day. The starter or *hors d'oeuvre,* was called *gustum* or *gustatio;* the main meat course, *mensae primae;* and the sweet or dessert, *mensae secundae.* Flasks of a dry wine mixed with honey, called *mulsum,* nearly always accompanied the meal, together with a wide selection of other wines and spirits. Factory-made sauces, such as the extremely popular *liquamen,* for which the towns of Pompeii and Leptis Magna were famous, were available on the table, and had also almost certainly been used in the preparation of many of the dishes served. An advertising inscription on a jar discovered intact in Pompeii, told the reader that it was "Best strained liquamen: prepared in the factory of Umbricus Agathopus." In format and taste, *liquamen* could be compared with our own present-day Worcestershire sauce, and in many dishes took the place of salt.

A hostess in Imperial Rome, planning a dinner party for guests of importance, often seemed to go out of her way to have her cook serve dishes containing exotic and outlandish ingredients. In the manner of her present-day counterpart, she apparently took pride in mystifying and surprising friends of her husband and their wives as to the contents of the appetizing meal she had set before them. Knowing, as we do from Apicius's recipes, their real ingredients, it would be a courageous and highly disciplined diner who today would light-heartedly plunge his fork in his steaming platter of first-century food prepared Roman style and then chew unconcernedly to the final swallow. Blissful ignorance of the fact that he was masticating boiled parrot or toying leisurely with stuffed dormice might well bring warm congratulations on an excellent meal to his host and hostess. But the answer to the fatal question, "What was that delightful main course, by the way?,"

could well cast a cloud over an otherwise enjoyable evening. On such occasions, 'tis folly to be wise.

Yet this is only a reflection that each country and every age have dishes they consider delicacies that would be viewed with the utmost suspicion and even revulsion by those foreign to that particular land or period. Frogs' legs and large snails, an epicurean delight in France, awake no similar response when brought to the vast majority of English tables. And some of the once universally popular old English dishes set out in detail in later chapters, may now have a strange and sometimes far from pleasing countenance to the later generations who read this book. The reverse would probably be just as true.

In early cook books it was apparently assumed that the cook using a recipe would be a professional well versed in the quantities needed to ensure success and in the timing of the cookery process. No quantities or measurements of any kind are given to guide the reader, and the methods to be employed in cleaning and scaling the fish, or preparing the various cuts of meat or game in other recipes, are left to the skill of the cooks, whose daily task it was to prepare food for their masters' tables.

Tablecloths were commonly in use at the tables of persons of substance in Britain long before the Norman conquest in 1066. Knives, drinking-horns, bowls, and dishes, were suitably laid on the board, and attendants kneeled to serve the meat and game on long iron spits.

The Roman recipes set out below, although we may today approach many of them with considerable trepidation, have all been sampled and tested by teams of students and their historical advisers without apparent ill-effects. Often those sitting hungry and impatient waiting for their hosts to serve an unusual Roman delicacy were not informed of its exact nature until after their plates were once again clean. Experience had taught that this was a necessary precaution. One can only wonder where, in twentieth-century London, these researchers into Roman culinary history obtained some of the main ingredients.

Recipes from Imperial Rome

BOILED BOAR

8 gallons sea water	1 boar
2 pounds rock salt	3 sprigs laurel
1 hard-boiled hen's egg	Mustard
2 gallons red wine	Vinegar

After boar is prepared for cooking, prepare the sea water. Pound up the rock salt in a mortar, then mix with the sea water and stir with a stick until the boiled hen's egg will float on it. Add the wine to the mixture, then heat in a large vessel until boiling. Boil the boar in the liquid, adding the sprigs of laurel. When tender, remove from pan and skin the boar. Serve on a central platter with salt, mustard, and vinegar, with:

BOILED BOAR SAUCE

Mix ground pepper, dill seed, thyme, with a cup of crushed rocket seed,* the whole moistened with white wine. Crush green herbs, sprigs of mint, onion, with ground hazel-nuts or ground toasted almonds. To these add a mixture of honey, vinegar, and dates made into a paste, then thinned with extra wine; then color the sauce by the addition of *defrutum* (red wine boiled until much of the liquid has evaporated), *liquamen* and olive oil. The whole mixed well together, and allowed to stand for several hours before being served as relish with the boiled boar.

ROAST KID OR LAMB

Cut up the kid or lamb into conveniently sized pieces, and put in pan with finely-chopped onion, ground pepper, coriander (the fruit of which is carminative and very aromatic), cumin (a plant resembling fennel, also aromatic), *liquamen*, olive oil, and wine.

*Seed of rocket-cress or roquette.

All these ingredients should be pounded in a mortar to render fine. When kid or lamb is cooked, add corn flour to the gravy to thicken. Sprinkle with pepper and serve with mint and parsley.

STUFFED SUCKING PIG

Remove the entrails of the piglet, but leave inside what you think is the best of the offal. Take finely-ground pepper, lovage [the herb *Ligusticum Levisticum*], origan, plucked small birds such as larks if available, and a sheep's brain. Moisten all these with *liquamen,* add two hen's eggs, and make a mash of all ingredients.

Bake the piglet until brown, then stuff with mixture as above, fastening the belly shut with wooden skewers. Hang in a basket in a boiling cauldron until tender. Remove and drain, taking out skewers so that juice can run out.

Place hot on a central platter, sprinkle well with pepper, and serve.

STUFFED DORMICE

Gut and clean plump dormice, two for each guest. Make a stiff stuffing of minced pork and the minced meat of other dormice. Pound this with pepper, asafoetida, pine-kernels, and *liquamen.* When stuffed, sew up the mice, place in a shallow pan and cook in a slow oven.

BOILED ELECTRIC EELS

Boil the electric eels in a large pan until tender. Make a sauce of yolk of eggs, honey, *liquamen,* wine and olive oil. To this add finely-chopped parsley, mint, origan, pepper, lovage, and a seasoning of pepper.

Serve the eels with the sauce, then sprinkle with hot raisins.

SMOKED BOILED STOMACH

Well empty a pig's stomach, then clean and scour with vinegar and salt. Rinse with water, then stuff until nearly full with the following mixture:

Minced pork, into which three pig's brains (skinned and freed from stringy matter) are well beaten up. Add six raw eggs, pine kernels, and powdered pepper. Blend this mixture with the following sauce: aniseed, ginger, a little rue, ground pepper, lovage, asafoetida, all pounded in a mortar to which *liquamen,* wine, and a little oil, are poured.

Blend both mixtures together, then fill the stomach nearly full. Seal ends, and place in large pan of boiling water, having first lightly pricked it with a needle so that it does not burst in the heat. When about half cooked, remove from the pan and hang over fire smoke until it is heavily colored. Boil again until thoroughly cooked.

Slit open with a knife and serve portions in *liquamen* and chopped garlic.

PLAIN ROAST MEAT

Cook meat in oven until tender. Sprinkle with salt, and serve with liquid honey, lightly covering.

GRILLED WOMB

The womb must be from a sterile cow. Soak well in brine overnight after cleaning and rinsing. Roll in bran, then lightly grill on hot stove. Serve with *liquamen,* pepper and spiced wine.

BOILED PARROT

Pluck the parrot, then wash and truss the drawn bird. Place in pan and well cover with water, to which may be added vinegar and a little dill.

When partly cooked, make a bouquet of leek and coriander and boil with the bird.

While the parrot is cooking, put pepper, caraway seed, coriander, rue, asafoetida, and mint in a mortar and pound to a paste. Moisten with vinegar, add dates well shredded.

Remove parrot from pan, and use water remaining to thin the sauce. Thicken with corn flour.

Pour thickened sauce over the bird and serve immediately. The same recipe can be used for flamingo.

TO PRESERVE BIRDS IN HOT WEATHER

To prevent birds not immediately needed for food from going bad in warm or hot weather it is advisable to boil them for at least five minutes with their feathers on.

Do not attempt this until their guts have been drawn, either through the gullet or from the rear end.

Chapter Two

BOKES OF COKERY

The Romans took pride in devising new and unusual methods of preparing even the most humdrum of everyday meals; but for centuries after the final defeat and overthrow of their empire there is little evidence that culinary techniques made any significant progress. The cookery of food during the Middle Ages was usually crude in the extreme, and the few manuscripts containing recipes and bills of fare show a regression from the often high standards set in Roman times.

In Medieval days, the banquets and feasts enjoyed in the castles and fortresses of Europe that we have note of depended for their success almost entirely on the ravenous appetites and unrefined palates of the unwashed mobs that thronged the rough-hewn tables. They relished quantity, and the details we have of the massive roasts of oxen and smoking cauldrons of bubbling stew indicate that the quality of the fare was of secondary consideration. Tender and appetizing meat and vegetables and ladles of succulent stew were bonuses not given at every such gathering. The over-filling of empty bellies and the immediate allaying of pangs of hunger by the quickest means available were the prime objectives of the sweating cooks and the minions who dished out the helpings. These were maxims fearfully observed, for their own skins were often at stake, and the wrath of a half-filled mob clamoring for more was a hazard none of the kitchen staff dared to incur.

Subtle craftsmanship in cookery—indeed, any sign of exacting care and time-consuming artistry in the preparation of food—was often looked upon with dark suspicion. These were sinister times, and there were too many well-authenticated tales of violent illnesses and acutely painful deaths after eating at the tables of seemingly friendly hosts to allow any relaxation of vigilance. Dining out was a hazardous business; but the risk was lessened if you were careful to partake only of the same joints and drink from the same tankards as the rest of the assembled company. There was safety in

The parting guest. An engraving by F. Gradmann of one of the survivors of a gargantuan medieval feast.

numbers, and the massive haunches of beef or venison at which fifty or more could hack and carve their fill, and the communal stewpot holding fifty gallons of steaming ingredients as diverse in character as the land could provide, enjoyed a popularity that survived for several hundred years. And in the rude huts of the yeomen and serfs the lowly ate as much as they could whenever they could, and grimly survived the intervals in between.

Throughout Europe, the main concern when plenty of food was available, especially free food, was to eat until you could eat no more. After reading details of the gargantuan feasts held to celebrate victory in battle, or to mark the long looked for return of a feudal lord to his castellated fortress, one marvels at the almost unlimited capacity for food and drink the eager guests at these revels displayed. Relays of leather-aproned cooks sweated

A supper of larks. An illumination from a late-fifteenth-century manuscript showing a wealthy young man dining on platefuls of larks and other singing birds.

Friday lunch in the home of a twelfth-century nobleman, as depicted in an illuminated manuscript of the period.

far into the night to provide an overfill, their bucket-sized ladles hurrying from smoke-blackened cauldrons to fill the steaming dishes. Anything even remotely edible had been tossed into these same cauldrons as rows of heavy iron pots and kettles of food simmered for days in smoke-filled kitchens. In the background, the spits turned with their heavy carcasses, dripping with fat, before glowing fires of heaped-up logs.

When the revels commenced, immense quantities of food and strong drink were consumed at a single sitting, the plates being scooped clean in greasy handfuls as each new course arrived. Quart-sized pots and leather blackjacks of wine and ale were up-ended with monotonous regularity, until at last the session of four or five hours of solid eating and drinking began to take their toll. The less stalwart were the first to go, as many collapsing across the tables as slid beneath them. Great pride was taken in being the last to submit, but finally the last euphoric handful of grossly distended carousers would heave unsteadily to their feet. Those still able to stagger manfully through the prostrate and spread-eagled ranks of their fellow revelers belched their uncertain way back to straw-filled beds and the oblivion of sleep, leaving the debris of a once-proud feast to be scavenged by the dogs.

The cook and his wife. Albrecht Dürer's drawing of a well-fed cook, made c.1510.

Death claims the cook. An engraving by Matthieu Merian for the 1744 edition of *The Dance of Death*, published at Basle under the title *Todten Tanz*.

Next day, after a night and morning of snoring oblivion, there were the sick-making sights and smells of a head-splitting morning-after to be endured by those forced to crawl out of bed to relieve the demands of nature. Preparations for the next night of revelry would be well advanced before the last of the casualties of the previous feast had regained consciousness and was fit to face the sight of food and drink again. Then it was back into the fray, for one never knew how long the good times would last, and he was a fool who didn't eat his fill while the good God provided.

Modern taste would condemn as distinctly unedifying one aspect of these gormandizing marathons. Frequent use was made of emetics! Once sated with food and drink and approaching the condition where it was just impossible to push any more down the ever-open throat, it was often the practice to deliberately induce vomiting. Once the worst of the retching had subsided and the stomach had been almost completely voided you waded back into the fray loudly demanding more!

The use of emetics was common as far back as Roman days, and the practice continued, especially amongst the well-to-do, until well into the eighteenth century. Emetics were not only a regular accompaniment at every feast and banquet, but were often an intrinsic part of everyday life during the Middle Ages and much later. Mustard and water, or copious draughts of common salt and water, were a cheap and common method of inducing instant and repetitive vomiting. The genteel resorted to more subtle agents; they delicately sipped from miniature wine or cordial glasses sweetly scented emetics taken in minute finger-raising doses. Within seconds the shoulders were heaving, leaving one white-faced and a little unsteady, but with the capacity for a fresh load of whatever the crowded table was able to provide.

It was by these evacuatory means that seemingly unbelievable amounts of solids and liquids were temporarily tucked away. The uneasy stomach was no sooner crammed with food and awash with drink than it was abruptly emptied. An hour or two later it was once again forced to submit to similar indignities. One can only dimly imagine the monumental hangovers our forebears weakly encountered the afternoon after the night before. But, in times of plenty, it was not only socially acceptable to gorge, but a principal pleasure in an all too short life whose middle-age dangers only a minority could expect to encounter.

It was the dawning of the Renaissance, and the gradual turning away from many of the more brutish pleasures, that translated cookery from the trough-filling artisanship of the Middle Ages into the refined artistry that was later to achieve expression in the culinary delicacies of the French courts. The cultured simplicity of early Italian cooking seems first to have been introduced into France by Catherine de Medici (1519 to 1589). Within a few decades these methods had been modified and improved by famous chefs whose names are immortalized in the titles of their exotic-sounding dishes.

Long before Catherine de Medici became Queen of France, the first printed cookery books were in circulation in England. It was in 1476 that William Caxton (c.1421 to 1491), set up the first printing press in England at Westminster, later publishing and printing some eighty books, many of them his own translations of famous French legends and romances. There were no cookery books amongst his list, and it was some nine years after the

This is the boke of Cokery

The "title page" of the earliest known cookery book printed in English: *The Boke of Cokery*, 1500, printed by Richard Pynson. (By permission of the Marquis of Bath, Longleat House.)

death of the master printer that the first work of this nature to be printed in English made its appearance.

The Boke of Cokery, 1500, is known only by a unique copy, now in the library of Longleat House, Warminster, Wiltshire, the seat of the Marquis of Bath. The colophon tells us that it was "emprynted without temple barre by Rycharde Pynson," who came to England during the lifetime of William Caxton, and learned the art of printing as one of his apprentices. Pynson came from Normandy, became a naturalized Englishman, and died in 1530; by which time he had printed well over three hundred books. It was his rival in trade, Jan van Wynkyn, known as Wynkyn de Worde, who inherited Caxton's printing business; Pynson having long since set up his own workshop at Temple Bar, London.

In his *Boke of Cokery,* Pynson not only gave his readers a variety of recipes to choose from, heading this section "The Calender of Cokery," but set out details of as many historical royal feasts as he could muster. Whether he carried out the necessary research himself, or, as seems more likely, used the services of some unknown expert in such affairs, remains a mystery, but he undoubtedly made good use of an early manuscript of recipes now at Holkham Hall, Norfolk. Due to his efforts we know that "The Feast of King Harry the Fourth to the Spenawdes and Frenchmen when they had jousted in Smythe Felde," was composed of three courses of exotic game and meats, a typical list reading:

Creme of almondes; larks, stewed potage; venyson; partryche rost; quayle; egryt; rabettes; plovers; pomerynges; and a leache of brawne wythe batters.

As recipes for a "Festes Ryall" or for use in a "Pryncy's householde or certaine other Estates housholde," he set out lists to delight and amaze the princely guests, and the barons, knights, and gentlemen-at-arms,

The final page of *The Boke of Cokery,* 1500, showing the colophon of Richard Pynson and some notes made in a contemporary hand. (By permission of the Marquis of Bath, Longleat House.)

do therto clowes maces prunes raysyns of corans & gynger mynced grete: than sette the potte on the fyre & styre it well togyder & put the pylottes in the potte & lete theym haue one boylle or two & coloure it rawdell hewe and salte it and serue it.

¶ For to make Buknade.

¶ To make Buknade: take vele smalle chopped & vele perboylled: than gader vp the flesshe and clense the brothe through a streyner & putte it in a pot & sette it on the fyre & put therto onyons mynced and pouder of peper pouder of clowes & canell & whan it boyleth put in the flesshe: than take rawe yolkes of egges in a bolle & caste therto of the hote brothe & medle it well togyder and in the settynge dowe put in the eggis & styre it togyder and gyue it a lytell colour of saffron and salte it and serue it.

¶ For to make charmerchande.

¶ To make charmerchande: Take coostes of moton chopped and putte theym in a fayre potte and sette it vpon the fyre with clene water and boyle it welle: and thanne take percely and sage and bete it in a morter with brede and drawe it vppe with the brothe and put it in the potte withe the fresshe flesshe and lette it boyle welle togyder: and salte it and serue it.

¶ For to make Jusselle syngle.

¶ To make Jusselle syngle: take fresshe brothe of flesshe and sette it on the fyre in a potte: do therto sage leues broken in two or in thre peces and percely and coleur thy brothe: than take egges and grated brede & medle theym togyder: and whan the potte boyleth put the comande to the brothe & salte it and styre it tyll it crudde: and whan it cruddeth gader it togyder with a scomer and alaye it with a lytell ale and salte it and serue it.

¶ For to make Comyne.

¶ To make Comyne: take almonde mylke & set it on the fyre: than take amydon that is stept and put therto poudre of comyne and lete it boile well & stue it ... and put therto suger or hony and coloure it wih saffron and than salt it and lete it be rennynge: and if ye wyl haue it standynge take rawe yolkes of egges well beten and put it in the potte at the syttynge downe and leske it in disshes and cast on a drege made wythe harde yolkes of egges/ suger mynced gynger clowes maces & serue it.

¶ For to make Chekyns in sauce.

¶ To make Chekyns in sauce / take chekyns and choppe them in for comons/ but for a lorde take hoos

b ii

Two pages of recipes from *The Boke of Cokery,* 1500, the earliest cookery book printed in English. (By permission of the Marquis of Bath, Longleat House.)

that a feudal lord could expect to entertain in the opening decade of the sixteenth century. Illustrations of pages from Pynson's book are on pages 24 to 26. A translation into modern English of one example reads:

FOR TO MAKE FISH POTAGE IN EGG SAUCE

To make fish potage in egg sauce. Take loaches and clean, scale, and wash them. Fry them in oil. Take dates, raisins or currants and breadcrumbs, all beaten together in a mortar. Add red wine to your own taste and set it to the fire to boil. Add powdered pepper, cloves, and prunes fried white in oil, and raisins of Cyprus currants.

Colour thy potage in saffron and salt it. Stir in a little vinegar mixed with garlic and ginger.

Place thy fish in this and pour on thy syrup and serve it forth in the same manner used for loaches.

What reception Pynson's *Boke of Cokery* received from the favored few who were able to sample his recipes in the early days of the sixteenth century we shall never know. The life of even a modern cookery book is comparatively short, and we must applaud the happy combination of circumstances that allowed a single copy of this earliest of English cookery books to survive to the present day. Every other copy of the edition printed in 1500 has long since disappeared into the mists of time.

The same good luck enabled a single copy of the first edition of *The Boke of Kervynge,* 1508, to find its ultimate resting place in the University Library, Cambridge. Printed by Wynkyn de Worde, its popularity is indicated by the several new editions that made their appearance during the following hundred years, the last being published as late as 1613. The single copy known of the second edition, dated 1513, and now in the British Library, tells us, in a series of text headings, the correct terms and deportments for those serving and preparing food:

Termes of a Kerver [*carver*]
The Names of Wynes
For to make Ypocras [*Hippocras, a cordial drink made of wine flavored with spices*]
To laye the Clothe
To wrappe your Soveraynes Brede stately [*master's bread*]
The Kervynge of Flesshe, and Servyce
Sauces for all maner of Fowles
Feestes and Servyce from Eester unto Whytsondaye
Of the skin and wholesomeness of certain Birds
Kervynge of Fysshe
Sauces for all maner of Fysshe
The Chamberlayne
Of the Marshall and the Ussher

Under the heading "Termes of a Kerver," we are advised that the terms to be used for the carving and preparing of different types of meat, game, and fish, vary considerably, and it is ignorant to speak of "carving" a deer or a goose or a chicken. Translated into modern spelling, Wynkyn de Worde tells us that we must:

Break that deer	Thigh that pigeon
Lift that swan	Chine that salmon
Sauce that capon	String that lamprey
Spoil that hen	Splat that pike
Unlace that cony	Side that haddock
Disfigure that peacock	Tame that crab
Mince the plover	

As a first course to celebrate the Feast of St. Michael, continuing until "Chrystynmasse," the butler is instructed that he must serve "potage, befe, motton, bacon, or pestelles of porke." Or with "goose, capon, mallarde [*wild duck*], swanne, or fesande [*pheasant*], as it is before sayd, with tartes, or bake metes, or chynes of porke. The goose & swanne may be cut as ye do other fowles that have hole feet [*webbed feet*] or elles as your lorde or your lady wyll aske it." Few dishes were thought more appetizing than freshly caught lamprey, and he gives as a recipe:

FRESSE LAMPRAYE BAKE

Open the pastry, then take whyte brede, and cut it thynne, & lay it in a dysshe, & with a spoon take out gelentyne, & lay it upon the brede with red wyne & poudre of synamon. Then cut a gobbet of the lampraye, & mynce the gobbet thynne, and laye it in the gelentyne. Then set it upon the fyre to hete.

FRESSE CRABBE BAKE

Take a crabbe, breke hym a-sonder into a dysshe, then make ye shell clene. Put in the crabbe-mete agane, tempre it with vynegre & pouder, than cover it with brede, and sende it to the kytchyn to hete. Set it before your lorde, and breke the grete clawes, and laye them in a disshe.

It was an earlier version of the first of these two recipes which tradition states ended the life of King John, who died of a "surfeit of lampreys." Historically, it seems more likely that he gorged himself on peaches and beer pillaged from a Cistercian abbey, and later succumbed to a violent attack of dysentery.

At least as interesting as the actual recipes given in *The Boke of Kervynge* are the rules and instructions set out for the various household servants. Those detailed for the chamberlain are particularly forthright:

The chamberlain must be dylygent & clenely in his offyce, with his head combed . . . and that he have a clene sherte, breches, petycote, and doublet. He must brusshe his hose within & without, & see his shoes and slyppers be made clene. At morne when your lorde wyll arise, warme his sherte by the fyre, & see ye have foot shete made in this manner. Fyrst set a chayre by the fyre with a cuysshen, an other under his fete, then sprede a shete over the chayre, and see there be redy a kerchefe and a combe. Then warme his petycote, his doublet, and his stomachere & then put on his hose & his shoes or slyppers, then stryke up his hose manerley, & then tye them up. Then lace his doublet hole by hole, & laye the clothe aboute his necke and combe his hede. Then loke you have a basyn & an ewer with warme water, and a towell, and wasshe his handes. Then kneel upon your knee & aske your lorde what robe he wyll were, & brynge him such as he commandeth & put it upon hym; then do his girdle aboute hym, & take your leve manerley.

Loke there be a good fyre brennynge bryght, & see the hous of easement be swete & clene, & the privy borde covered with a grene clothe and a cuysshyn. Then see there be down or cotton for your lord's wiping. And loke you have basyn, & ewer with water, & a towell for your lorde.

Then take off his gowne, & brynge him a mantell to kepe hym from colde. Then brynge hym to the fyre, & take off his shoes & his hose, & combe his hede. Sprede downe his bedde, laye the head shete and the pyllowes, & when your lorde is to bedde, drawe the curtynes round hym. Dryve out his dogge or catte, & loke there be basyn and urinall set nere your lorde. Then take your leve manerley that your lorde may take his rest merryly.

Such works formed the basis on which rules of deportment for servants in princely households were drawn up by their imperious masters, and set standards for courtly manners for many years to come. Their influence on contemporary upper-class life was certainly as profound as any modern work on etiquette and good manners, and dictated the fashion of gracious living and the entertainment of one's friends amongst the privileged coterie who could afford to conform.

In the same tradition came *A Boke for to Lerne a Man to be Wyse in Buyldyng of his Howse for the Helth of His Body*, 1540, by Andrew Boorde (1490? to 1549). But it is his famous *A Dyetary of Helth* (1542?) which concerns us here. Although not a cookery book within the strict meaning of the term, it is the first work to set out rules for a healthy diet (for those with the means to afford it), and "treateth of wylde fowl, tame fowle, byrdes, of frutes (and fyrst of fygges), of herbes and of a general dyet, for all manner of men and women, being sycke or hole." Dr. Boorde, once a parish priest but now known as "Merry Andrew" to his friends, was by this time making an

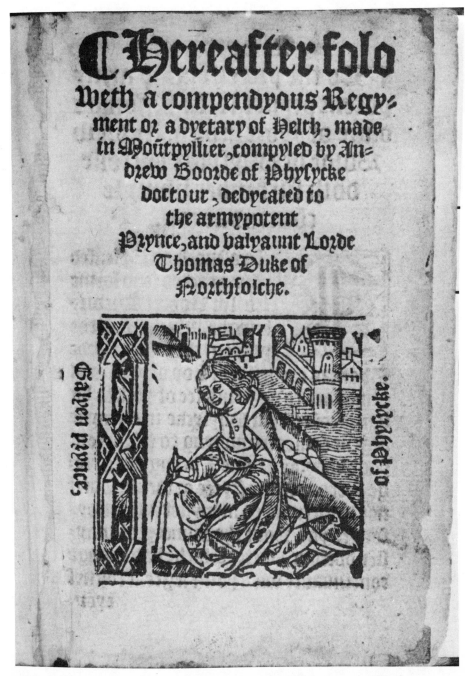

Title page of Andrew Boorde's *A Dyetary of Helth*, 1542 (?), the first work to set out rules for a healthful diet.

enviable living as a physician and purveyor of health foods in Fleet Street, London; although he had more than once been accused of scandalous behavior and loose living. He is alleged to have attributed his extreme virility and undoubted success with the ladies to a balanced diet in which oysters and figs played a prominent part. Later came his *Boke of Berdes,* a satirical work dealing with the beard as a masculine ornament. Unfortunately, soon after its publication, Boorde became so incapably drunk in the house of a Dutch friend that he fouled his own extensive whiskers while sleeping it off. Next morning the hardened accretion proved immovable: Boorde's beard had to be cut off close to his chin, a fact the punsters of the period never allowed him to forget.

His *Dyetary of Helth* passed through at least four editions before the end of the sixteenth century, much of its popularity stemming from the many ingenious dietary methods he revealed by which male virility could be improved and erections prolonged. The common artichoke was his favorite recommended aphrodisiac, and must have led to a considerable run on this scarce vegetable for several seasons. Mixed with rocket seed, the effect was alleged to be dramatic. "Eat them at dyner," he advised his readers, "they doth increase nature, and doth provoke a man to veneryous actes!"

Unfortunately, there were an unlucky few on which this sovereign remedy for keeping one's end up did not immediately work, and Boorde devoted a whole chapter to those he designated with a compassionate eye as "melancholy men." For them the diet was strict:

> Melancholy is colde and drye: wherefore melancholy men must refrayne from fryde meate, and meate whych is ower salte. And from meate that is sowre and harde of dygetyon, and from all meate whych is burnt and drye. They must abstayn from immoderate thurste, and from drynking of hot wines and grosse wine, as red wyne. And use these thyngs: cowe mylke, almond mylke, yokes of rere eggs. Boyled meate is better for melancholy men that rosted meates whych do engender good blode, and meates that whyche be temperately hote, be goode for melancholy men. And so be all herbes whyche be hotte and moyste. These thyngs followyng do purge melancoly: quyckebeam, senna, sticados, harts-tongue, mayden-hair, borage, organum [marjoram], suger and whyte wyne.

Once having thoroughly purged melancholy, a generous helping of rocket seed and artichoke would have its usual dramatic and uplifting effect, with the one-time enforced celibate made "merry wyth much venery." This was Dr. Boorde's specific for nearly all masculine ills, and one he seems to have constantly resorted to himself, to an extent that caused so much scandal in his home town of Winchester that the "three loose women" he kept in his rooms there were "openly punished in the greate churche and stretes of that city."

His *Breviary of Healthe* appeared in 1547; but within a month or two of its appearance Boorde was arrested and thrown unceremoniously into the Fleet Prison on a charge of permitting "boggery" in Winchester, together with an assorted array of sexual malpractices that would make headline news in the Sunday newspapers even today. Merry Andrew indignantly denied the charges, but there was no escape. He resigned himself to death and made his will on April 1, 1549. He died in Fleet soon afterward, probably of the "syckness of the Prysons," so at least he cheated the executioner. As Merry Andrew, his effigy was erected as an Aunt Sally or cock-shy by fairground stallholders for several centuries after his death, the name giving a new phrase to the English language.

Among the imitators of Boorde's dietary works was *The Boke of Nurture for Men Servants and Children* (1545?) by Hugh Rhodes, a work containing many new recipes and methods of preparing food for the table. *A Proper Newe Booke of Cookerye*, 1558, was published anonymously; and was followed by *A New Boke of the Natures of All Wines*, 1568, by William Turner, the first book in English treating of the appreciation and knowledgeable choosing of wines for the table and cellar.

Some few of the best foreign works were translated, notably *Epulario; or, The Italian Banquet*, 1598, culled from a Venetian book of 1549. It is here that the nursery rhyme *Sing a Song of Sixpence* traces its antecedents, for *Epulario* gives precise instructions for the "making of Pies that Birds may be alive in them, and fly out when it is cut up." This was meant to be the *pièce de résistance* of a successful sixteenth-century dinner party, the highlight of a memorable evening. There seems to have been one obvious snag that was completely overlooked by the well-meaning compiler of the recipe. Frightened blackbirds (or any other of our feathered friends, from owls to wrens) temporarily enclosed beneath a warm pie-crust, are far more likely to leave tangible marks of their extreme displeasure within the

Preparing dinner in a sixteenth-century kitchen, by Pieter van der Borcht. The semi-automatic spit was worked by weights in the manner of a long-case clock.

dish than display any tendency to burst brightly into song. In fact, a blithely eaten spoonful of the pie's contents after the hasty evacuation of its avian prisoners would dispel the diner's appetite for at least the remainder of that particular meal. One can only wonder if any of the book's more enterprising readers actually tried it out.

Not more than a handful of other cookery book titles have come down to us with sixteenth-century imprints. How many have disappeared without trace we shall never know, but we can presume that nearly every household of any size had its collection of prized hand-written recipes that were handed on from mother to daughter and added to by later generations.

In printed books, we know of *The Treasurie of Commodious Conceites and Hidden Secrets,* 1573, by John Partridge, which he described in later editions as *The Good Huswive's Closet of Provision.* It was a popular work in Elizabethan days, giving rules of good deportment as well as culinary recipes. By 1640 it had passed through twelve separate editions, the earliest complete survivor being dated 1584. Thomas Dawson produced *The Good Huswife's Jewell,* 1584, with a second part being issued the following year.

The century that had promised so much with the daring publication, way back in 1500, of Pynson's *Boke of Cokery,* closed on a rancid note. In the last year of the old regime, Henry Buttes produced his one and only book. He called it *Dyets Dry Dinner,* 1599. One can only wonder what those who loved the fleshpots, such as the by now successful playwright William Shakespeare, thought of such a dehydrated offering.

Chapter Three

DELIGHTES FOR LADIES

If the culinary literature of the sixteenth-century ended on a rather dry and acrid note, that of the seventeenth proclaimed the news of the good times ahead. Within a month or two of the commencement of this fresh and exciting chapter in the history of human progress and enlightenment, and only three years before the death of England's Queen Elizabeth, a tribute to the womanhood of Britain was paid in most endearing terms through the publication of ''a fragrant little volume'' dedicated to their pleasure and delight.

Its author was Sir Hugh Plat (or Platt) (1552 to 1608?), a wealthy landowner whose enthusiasm for horticulture and experimental gardening techniques had led to an outlay of capital that would have pauperized many a lesser man. Being extremely fortunate in his choice of parents, he had enjoyed an easy and well-favored life from his earliest days. His father was Richard Plat, a well-to-do London brewer who had amassed a considerable fortune attempting to slake the thirst of a grateful populace; while his mother was Alice Birchells, daughter of a family of Cheshire landowners. Richard Plat's country estate was at Aldenham, Hertfordshire, and it was there that young Hugh grew to manhood. Amply provided for by his father, he disdained to practice at the Bar, although he had graduated B.A. at Cambridge before becoming a member of Lincoln's Inn. Almost from the time he left university, he seems to have devoted his considerable talents of inventiveness and experimentation to botanical and culinary affairs.

Discovering improved methods of farming became his fascination, and he was soon engaged in costly experiments that were, he hoped, one day to revolutionize agricultural practice in Britain. His partial success in raising new strains of heavy-cropping wheat and barley led him to publish a number of pamphlets on modern farming methods and good husbandry. These included a work extolling the benefits to be derived from the liberal use of animal manure, published under the unlikely-sounding title of *The Jewel House,* 1594.

He was wealthy enough to be able to take his lack of commercial success with equanimity, and at the age of forty-seven his interest in what today would be called "nature foods" led him to devise several new and appetizing recipes. He later told his readers that he used as a basis for his dishes only such foods which were "sweet, fresh and durable," and within a few months he was addressing himself in flattering terms to the ladies of

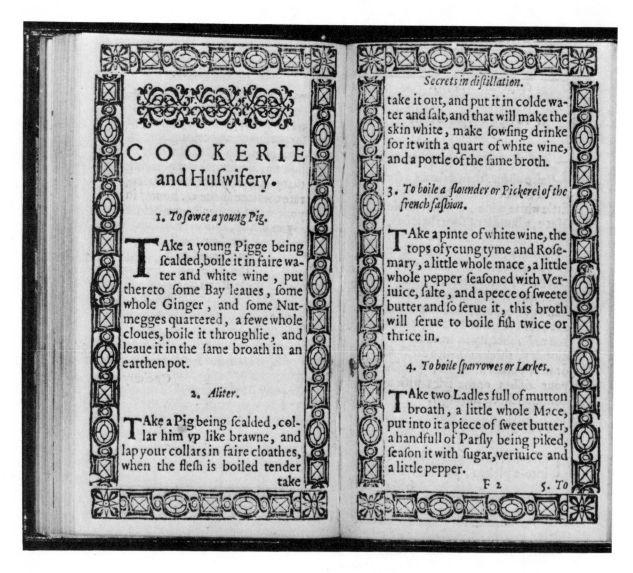

COOKERIE and Huſwifery.

1. To ſowce a young Pig.

Take a young Pigge being ſcalded, boile it in faire water and white wine, put thereto ſome Bay leaues, ſome whole Ginger, and ſome Nutmegges quartered, a fewe whole cloues, boile it throughlie, and leaue it in the ſame broath in an earthen pot.

2. Aliter.

Take a Pig being ſcalded, collar him vp like brawne, and lap your collars in faire cloathes, when the fleſh is boiled tender take

Secrets in diſtillation.

take it out, and put it in colde water and ſalt, and that will make the skin white, make ſowſing drinke for it with a quart of white wine, and a pottle of the ſame broth.

3. To boile a flounder or Pickerel of the french faſhion.

Take a pinte of white wine, the tops of ycung tyme and Roſemary, a little whole mace, a little whole pepper ſeaſoned with Veriuice, ſalte, and a peece of ſweete butter and ſo ſerue it, this broth will ſerue to boile fiſh twice or thrice in.

4. To boile ſparrowes or Larkes.

Take two Ladles full of mutton broath, a little whole Mace, put into it a piece of ſweet butter, a handfull of Parſly being piked, ſeaſon it with ſugar, veriuice and a little pepper.

F 2   5. To

Two pages of Sir Hugh Plat's *Delightes for Ladies,* 1600, showing the wood-engraved ornaments with which he embellished the margins of the first edition.

England, whom he described, viewed from a culinary standpoint, as "true Lovers of Art." He commenced his book with the news that he loved and admired each and every one of them, and laid it at their feet in the words of his preface:

> . . . now my pen and paper are perfum'd,
> Rosewater is the inke I write withall:
> Of sweetes the sweetest I will now command,
> To sweetest creatures that the earth doth beare:
> These are the Saints to whome I sacrifice
> Preserves and conserves both of plum and peare.

Delightes for Ladies, to Adorne Their Persons, Tables, Closets, and Distillatories, With, Bewties, Banquets, Perfumes, and Waters, 1600, printed in London by Peter Short, probably at the author's expense, is itself a delight to examine and read. The text of the little book is enclosed in tastefully designed ornamental borders selected by Hugh Plat to bring joy to the eyes of his female readers, as he hoped the recipes he gave them would bring pleasure to their husbands. Its success appears to have been immediate, a new edition, dated 1602 (and at one time thought to be the first), soon followed, and a further eight separate editions made their appearance by 1636.

The grape harvest, October 1584, on the Rhein. An illustration from *Hierampelas,* 1585, by Georg Horn, an early German cook book.

In his preface to the work, Plat summarized the book's contents with an epistle in verse to gladden his ladies' hearts:

> *Let pearcing bullets turne to sugar balls,*
> *The Spanish feare is husht and all their rage.*
> *Of marmelade and paste of Genoa,*
> *Of musked sugar I intend to wright,*
> *Of Leach, of Sucket, and Quidinea,*
> *Affording to each Ladie, her delight.*
> *I teach both fruites and flowers to preserve,*
> *And candie them, so Nutmeg, Cloves, and Mace;*
> *To make both marchpane paste, and sugred plate,*
> *And cast the same in formes of sweetest grace*
> *Each bird and foule, so moulded from the life,*
> *And after cast in sweet compounds of Arte,*
> *As if the flesh and forme which Nature gave,*
> *Did still remaine in every lim and part.*
> *When crystall frost hath nipt the tender grape,*
> *And cleane consum'd the fruits of every vine,*
> *Yet heere behold the clusters fresh and faire,*
> *Fed from the branch, or hanging on the line,*
> *From Wallnut, small nut, and the Chestnut sweet,*
> *Whose sugred kernels lose their pleasing taste,*
> *Are heere from yeere to yeere preserved meet,*
> *And made by arte with strongest fruits to last:*
> *Th' artichoke, and th' Apple of such strength,*
> *The Quince, Pomgranate, with the Barberie,*
> *No sugar us'd, yet, colour, taste and smell,*
> *Are heere maintain'd and kept most naturally.*
>
> *For Ladies closets and their stillatories,*
> *Both waters, ointments and sweet smelling bals,*
> *In easie tearmes without affected speech,*
> *I heere present most ready at their calls.*
> *To teach and find each secret I doe strive.*
> *Accept them well, and let my wearied Muse*
> *Repose her selfe in Ladies laps awhile.*
> *So when she wakes, she happely may record,*
> *Her sweetest dreames in some more pleasing stile.*

He divided the book into four separate parts, heading them: "The Arte of Preserving, Conserving, Candying, &c"; "Secrets in Distillation"; "Cookerie and Huswiferie"; and "Sweete Powders, Oyntments, Beauties, &c." All make fascinating reading today, many of his recipes and formulas tempting the reader to experiment in the manner laid down by their long-forgotten Elizabethan innovator.

A selection given in the order of the author's chapter headings reveals the amount of ground he attempted to cover in one small twelve mo-size book, and perhaps shows why the work enjoyed such popularity during the early part of the seventeenth century:

TO MAKE A MARCHPANE [MARZIPAN]

Take two pounds of Almondes beeing blanched and dryed in a sieve over the fire. Beate them in a stone mortar, and when they be small mix with them two pound of sugar being finely beaten, adding two or three spoonfuls of Rosewater, and that will keep your almonds from oiling.

When your paste is beaten fine, drive it thin with a rowling pin, and so lay it on a bottome of wafers. Then raise up a little edge on the side, and so bake it. Then ice it with Rosewater and sugar, then put it in the oven againe, and when you see your ice is risen up and drie, then take it out of the Oven and garnish it with prettie conceits, as birds & beastes being cast out of standing moulds.

Sticke long comfits upright in it, cast bisket and carowaies in it, and so serve it. Gild it before you serve it. You may also print off this Marchpane paste in your moulds for banquetting dishes.

And of this paste our comfit makers of this day make their letters, knots, Armes, escocheons, beasts, birds, and other fancies.

TO PRESERVE ORENGES AFTER THE PORTUGALL FASHION

Take Orenges and core them on the side and lay them in water. Then boile them in fair water till they bee tender, shift them in the boiling water to take away their bitternesse. Then take sugar & boile it to the height of sirup as much as will cover them. And so put your Orenges into it, and that will make them take sugar. If you have 24 Orenges, beate 8 of them till they come to paste, with a pounde of fine Sugar, then fill every one of the other Orenges with the same. And so boile them againe in your sirup: then there will bee marmelade of Orenges within your Orenges, and it will cut like an hard egge.

TO MAKE ALMOND BUTTER

Blanch your almonds, and beat them as fine as you can with faire water, two or three houres, then straine them through a linnen cloth. Boile them with Rosewater, whole mace and annis seedes, till the substance bee thicke.

Spread it upon a faire cloth, dreining the whey from it; after let it hang in the same cloth some fewe houres, then straine it and season it with Rosewater and sugar.

CLUSTERS OF GRAPES KEPT TILL EASTER

Clusters of grapes hanging upon lines within a close presse will last till Easter.

If they shrinke you may plumpe them upp with a little warme water before you eat them. Some use to dip the endes of the stalkes first in pitch: some cut a branch of the Vine with everie cluster, placing an apple at each end of the branch: now and then renewinge those apples as they rot, and after hanging them within a presse or cupboard, which would stand in such a room (I suppose) where the grapes might not freeze: for otherwise you must bee forced now & then to make a gentle fire in the roome, or else the grapes will rot and perish.

A SCOTTISH HANDWATER

Put thyme, Lavender, and Rosemary confusedly together. Then make a lay of thicke wine Lees in the bottome of a stone pot, upon which make another lay of the said herbs, and then a lay of Lees, and so forward.

Lute* the pot well, and bury it in the ground for 6 weekes. Distill it, and it is called Dames water in Scotland. A little thereof put in a bason of a common water maketh very sweete washing water.

TO MAKE A POLONIAN SAWSEDGE [Sausage]

Take the fillets of a hog, chop them very small with a handful of red sage, season it hot with ginger and pepper, and then put it into a great sheepes gut. Then let it lie three nights in brine; then boile it and hang it upp in a chimney where fire is usually kept, and these sawsedges will last one whole year.

They are good for sallades: or to garnish boyled meates, or to make one relish a cup of wine.

HOW TO KEEP FRESH SALMON A WHOLE MONTH IN HIS PERFECT TASTE AND DELICACIE

First seeth** your Salmon according to the usual manner, then sinke it in apt and close vessels in wine vinegar with a branch of Rosemarie therein.

By this means Vintners and Cookes may make profit thereof when it is scarce in the markets, and Salmon thus prepared may bee profitably brought out of Ireland and sold in London or elsewhere.

*Lute: a tenacious clay or cement used to make the stopper in the pot airtight.

**Seeth: to boil

Rotten fish. Shopping in Paris in the mid-seventeenth century. An illustration from *La Ville de Paris*, 1655, by Le Sier Berthod.

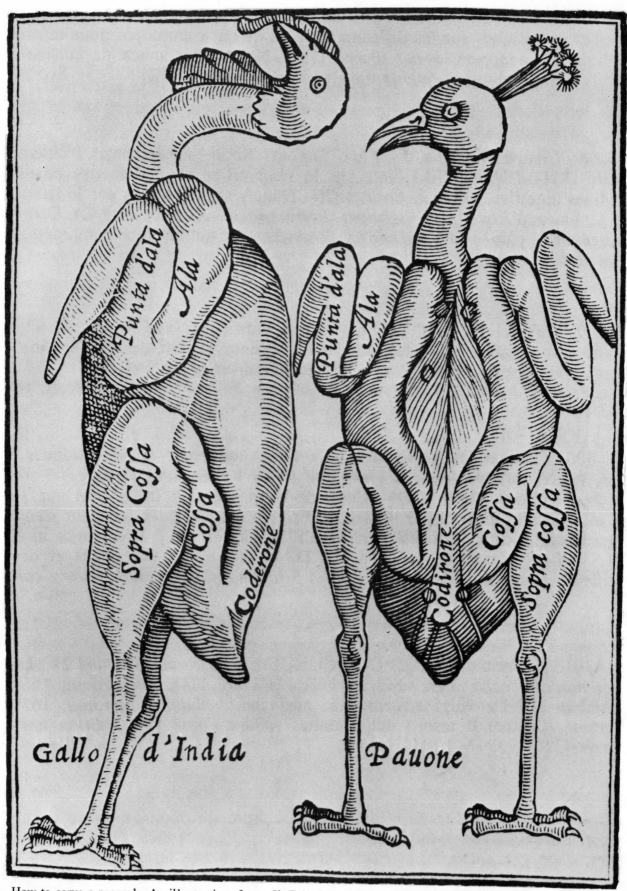

How to carve a peacock. An illustration from *Il Trinciate*, 1593, by Vincenzo Cervio, a famous sixteenth-century Italian cook book.

CLOUTED CREAME

Take your milke being new milked; and presentlie set it upon the fire from morning untill the evening. But let it not seeth: and this is called my Ladie Young's clouted creame.

FLESH KEPT SWEET IN SUMMER

You may keepe veale, mutton, or venison in the heat of summer nine or ten daies good, so as it bee newly and faire killed, by hanging the same in an high and windie roome.

And therefore a plate cupboard full of holes, so as the winde may have a through passage, would be placed in such a roome to avoide the offence of fly-blowes. This is an approved Secret easie and cheape, and very necessary to bee knowne and practiced in hot and tainting weather. Veale may be kept ten daies in bran.

TO TAKE AWAY SPOTS AND FRECKLES FROM THE FACE

The sappe that issueth out of a Birch tree in great abundance, being opened in March or Aprill, with a receiver of glass set under the boring thereof to receive the same, doth performe the same most excellently and maketh the skin very cleare. This sap will dissolve pearl, a secret not known unto many.

SKINNE KEPT WHITE AND CLEARE

Wash the face and body of a sucking child with brest milke, or cowe milke, or mixed with water, every night, and the childes skinne will wax faire and cleare, and resist sunburning.

TO COLOUR BLACKE HAIR PRESENTLY INTO A CHESTNUT COLOUR

This is done with oyle of Vitrioll: but you must doe it verie carefully not touching the skin.

HOW TO GATHER AND CLARIFIE MAY-DEWE

When there has fallen no raine the night before, then with a cleane and large sponge, the next morning you may gather the same from sweet herbs, grasse, or corne. Straine your dewe, and expose it to the sunn in glasses covered with papers or parchment prickt full of holes. Straine it often, continuing in the sunne, which will require the best part of the summer.

Some recommend May-dew gathered from Fennell and Celandine, to be most excellent for sore eyes, and some commend the same (prepared as before) above Rosewater for preserving of fruits, flowers, &c.

HOW TO COLOUR THE HEAD OF HAIRE INTO A CHESTNUT COLOUR IN HALFE AN HOURE

Take one part of lead calcined with sulphur, and one part of quicklime. Temper them somewhat thin with water, lay it upon the haire, chafing it well in, and let it drie one quarter of an houre or thereabouts.

Then wash the same off with faire water divers times, and lastly with sope and water, and it will be a very naturall haire colour. The longer it lyeth upon the haire the browner it groweth. This coloureth not the flesh at all; and yet it lasteth verie long in the haire.

All these delights must have been appreciated by the ladies of the day for the light relief they gave from the cares of a troubled world. Contrasted with the picture of English domestic life given to us in the *Verney Memoirs* written at that time, *Delightes for Ladies* fully achieved the promise of its title. The Verney family papers reveal a sobering picture of the day to day life of a gentlewoman in charge of a large household in the early part of the seventeenth century:

They brewed and baked, churned and ground their meal; they bred, fed, and slew their own beeves and sheep at their own doors. Their horses were shod at home, their planks were sawn, their rough ironwork was forged and mended. Accordingly the mill-house, the slaughter-house, the blacksmith's, carpenter's and painter's shops, the malting and brewhouse, the woodyard full of large and small timber, the sawpit, the outhouses full of odds and ends of stone, iron, bits of marble, carved woodwork and logs cut for burning—the riding house, laundry, the dairy with a huge churn turned by a horse, the stalls and sties for all manner of cattle and pigs, the apple and root chamber, show how complete was the idea of self supply and independence of trade of every kind in the country houses of the time.

The stew ponds provided fish for fast days; a decoy provided a supply of wild fowl; hunting provided venison; and hawking game birds. Cattle were killed in the autumn and salted down for winter use.

Much of the superintendence of all this fell to the lot of the lord, save when he was absent at the wars, or attending to his country business; but the lady had much to do (and all when her lord was away). The spinning of the wool and flax, the fine and coarse needlework, the embroidery, the cooking, the curing, the preserving, the distillery, were all superintended by the lady; and left little time for idle dreaming.

The lady of the manor, like her lord, led a strenuous and active life. When the men were away they acted for them in their numerous and endless lawsuits—it was a quarrelsome and rapacious age. They leased their farms, they found a market for the crops; they kept the money in strong chests concealed in mysterious hiding places, and they wrote long and interesting letters to the absent ones, full of business and news.

They ruled their households, occasionally it must be confessed with a rod or iron.

The well-deserved popularity of Sir Hugh Plat's little book with the fair sex led to several anonymous imitations couched in much the same terms. *A Closet for Ladies and Gentlewomen, or, the Art of Preserving, etc.,* appeared in 1602, and passed through more than ten editions before 1640, its sales at least equaling *Delightes for Ladies.* And the manuscript transcripts of Plat's recipes and household hints, sent to friends and relatives far and wide, must have been legion at a time when printed books were still a most expensive luxury.

Very few of the many cookery books which must have been printed during the reigns of James I and that of his successor Charles I have survived to the present day. Some we know of only because of their registration in the rolls of the Stationers' Company, no single copy surviving to the present day. Their use and popularity meant that they were literally "read to death," finally dropping to pieces on some seventeenth-century flagged kitchen floor to disappear from the culinary annals without further trace. *A New Booke of Cookerie,* 1615, by John Murrell, escaped by a happy chance the fate of its contempories, and a single example of the first edition is safely housed in the Bodleian Library, Oxford. Murrell apparently learned his trade abroad, having traveled extensively in France, Italy, and the Low Countries, with whose methods of cookery he seemed intimately acquainted. He is remembered for being the first to reveal to the British housewife the art of ornamental cookery, and, as a sideline, advertised for sale many of the bread and gingerbread molds he talked about in his books. And it was from Murrell that we gain the first flavor of French cooking, an influence that was to play such a dominant part in the subsequent history of the art. "An excellent and much approved beverage," he tells his readers, "especially for those sicke and ill, seeks the addition of many white snails. . . ."

He enlarged subsequent editions of the same work, the definitive version of which he entitled *A Delightfull Daily Exercise for Ladies and Gentlewomen, Whereby is Set Foorth the Secrete Misteries of the Purest Preservings in Glasse and other Confectionaries, as Making of Breads, Pastes, Preserves, Suckets, Marmalades, Tart Stuffes, Rough Candies, with Many Other Things Never Before in Print, Whereto is Added a Book of Cookery by John Murrell, professor thereof,* 1617. His preamble to the work describes it as being "all set forth according to the now new English and French fashion."

There seems little doubt that John Murrell was one of the first freelance professional cooks and advisers on culinary affairs. He taught the art of ornamental cookery, sold marzipan and bread molds, and advertised pots and pans and cooking utensiles for sale at his establishment or through the offices of the publishers of his books. *Murrels Two Books of Cookerie and Carving,* 1623, was advertised as being for "the fifth time printed" early in 1638; but many of his earliest works in this field have disappeared without trace. With these works, and the instructions in Continental cookery

LE PASTISSIER FRANÇOIS.

A Amsterdam,
Chez Louys et Daniel Elzevier. A°. 1655.

Le Pastissier François, 1655, one of the most sought-after productions of the famous Elzevier Press run by Daniel and Louis Elzevier in Amsterdam.

techniques he gave to fee-paying classes in London and elsewhere, he introduced novel and exotic dishes that enlivened the homespun fare of the seventeenth-century English kitchens. Many of the later practitioners of the art who followed in his footsteps owed Murrell a debt of gratitude, but of his later history and subsequent fate we know nothing.

Within a decade it had become the fashion for wealthy landowners and those close to the Court to have their head cooks trained in the preparation of French and Italian dishes. Young trainee cooks were sent to France with all expenses paid, to serve apprenticeships under master chefs resident at the French Court or in noble households. Years later, in the prefaces of recipe and cook books issued under their own (now distinguished) names, more than one paid tribute to the years of training in the culinary arts which they had received while serving under Continental masters. Many also acknowledged the generosity of their wealthy English patrons who had made possible their long stay abroad.

The most important figure amongst seventeenth-century English cooks to benefit in this way was undoubtably Robert May (c.1588 to 1687), author of *The Accomplisht Cook, or the Art & Mystery of Cookery,* 1660. Born and bred in the kitchen, he came from a family of country-house chefs, ''my Father being a Cook, under whom in my Child-hood I was bred up in this Art.'' In his preface to the second edition, dated 1665, he told his readers that he was dedicating the work ''To the Master Cooks, and such young Practitioners of the Art of Cookery, to whom this Book may be useful.'' He went out of his way to apologize to those in the profession who might think he had basely divulged trade secrets to the public at large, thus destroying much of the mystery surrounding the exotic sauces and Continental dishes their patrons paid them so well to produce:

> To all honest well intending Men of our Profession or others, this Book cannot but be acceptable, as it plainly and profitably discovers the Mystery of the whole Art; for which, though I may be envied by some that only value their private interests above Posterity and the publick good, yet God and my own Conscience would not permit me to bury these my Experiences with my Silver Hairs in the Grave: and that more especially, as the advantages of my Education hath raised me above the Ambitions of others, in the converse I have had with other Nations, who in this Art fall short of what I have known experimented by you my worthy Country men.

Despite having learned his trade there, May only grudgingly gave the master chefs of France the praise he must have known so many of their dishes, sauces, and concoctions deserved. He now lived and worked with English cooks, and to praise the foreigner too highly would have undermined his own popularity at home and exacerbated the jealousies and envious hostility such a work was bound to produce amongst experts in the same field. He was careful to mute his praises and mollify his compatriots in English kitchens by a culinary sideswipe at his former tutors in Paris:

> . . . the French by their Insinuations, not without enough of Ignorance, have bewitcht some of the Gallants of our Nation with Epigram Dishes, smoakt rather then drest, so strangely to captivate the Gusto, their Mushroom'd experiences for Sauce rather than Diet, for the generality howsoever called *A-la-mode,* not worthy of being taken notice of.

Nevertheless, Robert May was determined to slip in many of the best recipes he had learned with so much toil and trouble abroad:

As I live[d] in France, and had the Language, and have been an eye-witness of their Cookeries as well as a Peruser of their Manuscripts and Printed Authors; whatsoever I found good in them I have inserted in this Volume.

His book starts with a bang, so to speak, beginning with a memorable pyrotechnical set piece that must have taxed the labors of a small army of undercooks and serving maids, as well as that of all the skills of the master himself:

TRIUMPHS AND TROPHIES IN COOKERY, TO BE USED AT FESTIVAL TIMES

Make the likeness of a Ship in Paste-board, with the Flags and Streamers, the Guns belonging to it of Kickses. [*Kickshaws: a word derived from the French quelque chose, and meaning a comfit or gew-gaw modeled in marzipan, in this case shaped as cannons.*] Bind them about with packthread, and cover them with coarse paste proportionable to the fashion of a Cannon with Carriages. Lay them in places convenient as you see them in Ships of war, with such holes and trains of powder that they may all take Fire.

Place your Ship firm in the great Charger; then make a (sea of) salt round about it, and stick therein egg shells full of sweet water. You may by a great Pin take all the meat out of the egg by blowing, and then fill it up with the rose-water.

Then in another Charger have the proportion of a Stag made of coarse paste, with a broad Arrow in the side of him, and his body filled up with claret-wine.

In another Charger at the end of the Stag have the proportion of a Castle with Battlements, Portculices, Gates and Draw-Bridges made of Paste-board, the Guns of Kickses, and covered with coarse paste as the former. Place it at a distance from the ship to fire at each other. The Stag being placed betwixt them with egg shells full of sweet water (as before) placed in salt.

At each end of the Charger wherein is the Stag, place a Pye made of coarse paste, in one of which let there be some live Frogs, in the other some live Birds. Make these Pyes of coarse paste filled with bran, and yellowed over with saffron or the yolks of eggs. Gild them over in spots, as also the Stag, the Ship, and Castle.

Bake them, and place them with gilt bay-leaves on turrets and tunnels of the Castles and Pyes. Being baked, make a hole in the bottom of your pyes, take out the bran, put in your Frogs and Birds, and close up the holes with the same coarse paste, then cut the Lids neatly up. To be taken off the Tunnels, being all placed in order upon the Table.

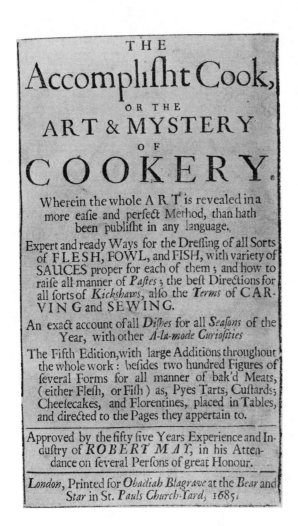

THE
Accomplisht Cook,
OR THE
ART & MYSTERY
OF
COOKERY.

Wherein the whole ART is revealed in a more easie and perfect Method, than hath been publisht in any language.

Expert and ready Ways for the Dressing of all Sorts of FLESH, FOWL, and FISH, with variety of SAUCES proper for each of them; and how to raise all manner of Pastes; the best Directions for all sorts of Kickshaws, also the Terms of CARVING and SEWING.

An exact account of all Dishes for all Seasons of the Year, with other A-la-mode Curiosities

The Fifth Edition, with large Additions throughout the whole work: besides two hundred Figures of several Forms for all manner of bak'd Meats, (either Flesh, or Fish) as, Pyes Tarts, Custards; Cheesecakes, and Florentines, placed in Tables, and directed to the Pages they appertain to.

Approved by the fifty five Years Experience and Industry of ROBERT MAY, in his Attendance on several Persons of great Honour.

London, Printed for Obadiah Blagrave at the Bear and Star in St. Pauls Church-Yard, 1685.

The fifth edition of Robert May's famous cook book. The first edition was dated 1660.

Before you fire the trains of powder, order it so that some of the Ladies may be persuaded to pluck the Arrow out of the Stag, then will the Claret-wine follow, as blood runneth out of a wound.

This being done with admiration to the beholders, after some short pause, fire the train of the Castle, that the pieces all of one side may go off, then fire the trains of the Ship as in a battel.

Next turn the Chargers; and by degrees fire the trains of each other side as before.

This done, to sweeten the stink of powder, let the Ladies take the egg shells full of sweet waters and throw them at each other.

All dangers being seemingly over, by this time you may suppose they will desire to see what is in the pyes; where, lifting the lid off one pye, out skip some Frogs, which make the Ladies skip and shreek. Next after the other pye, whence come out the Birds, who by a natural instinct flying at the light, will put out the Candles. So that what with the flying Birds and skipping Frogs, the one above, the other beneath, will cause much delight and pleasure to the whole company.

At length the Candles are lighted, and a banquet brought in, the Musick sounds, and every one with much delight and content rehearses their actions in the former passages. These were formerly the delights of the Nobility, before good Housekeeping had left England, and the Sword really acted that which was only counterfeited in such honest and laudable Exercises as these.

Robert May was born as early as 1588, and this extravagant Elizabethan set-piece for some royal banquet was almost certainly remembered from the days of his youth. It was then that his father held sway over the cathedral-size kitchens of a nobleman's household, where banquets for a hundred or more guests were heralded by the fireworks and exploding pie crusts of culinary extravaganza of the style detailed above, "before good House-keeping had left England. . . ." But having divested himself of the nostalgia of the Good Old Days, May was careful to inform his readers that his book was meant for all classes, not just for the rich. Talking about his recipes, he declared that: "I have so managed them for the general good, that those whose Purses cannot reach to the cost of rich Dishes, I have descended to their meaner Expenses, that they may give . . . a handsome and relishing entertainment in all seasons of the year, though at some distance from Towns or Villages."

He was as good as his word, and *The Accomplisht Cook* contained recipes for all tastes and length of purses. Typical of the dishes in Section I, headed "Perfect Directions for the *A-la-Mode* ways of dressing all manner of Boyled Meats" are the following:

TO BOIL A CHINE OF MUTTON

Boil it in a fair glazed pipkin [*a small earthenware pot*]. Being well scummed, put in a faggot of sweet herbs, as Time, Parsly, sweet Marjoram, boundhard and stripped with your Knife. And put some Carrots cut like small dice, or cut like Lard, some Raisins, Prunes, Marigold-flowers, and salt.

Being finely boiled down, serve it on sippits [*pieces of toasted or fried bread*]. Garnish your dish with Raisins, Mace, Prunes, Marigold-flowers, Carrots, Lemons, boil'd [bone] Marrow, &c.

TO MAKE AN OLIO PODRIDA

Take a Pipkin or Pot of some three Gallons, fill it with fair water, and set it over a Fire of Charcoals. Put in first your hardest meats, a rump of Beef, Bolonia Sausages, neat's tongues—two dry, two green—boiled and larded.

About two hours after the Pot is boil'd and scummed, put in Mutton, Venison, Pork, Bacon: all the aforesaid in Gubbins, as big as a Ducks Egg, in equal pieces. Put in also Carrots, Turnips, Onions, Cabbidge, in good big pieces, as big as your meat; a faggot of sweet herbs, well bound up, and some whole Spinage, Sorrel, Burrage, Endive, Marigolds, and other good Pot-Herbs a little chopped; and sometimes French barley, or Lupins green or dry.

Then a little before you dish out your Olio; put to your pot, Cloves, Mace, Saffron, &c.

The next have divers Fowls, as first—

A Goose, or Turkey; two Capons, two Ducks, two Pheasants, two Widgeons, four Partridges, four stock Doves, four Teals, eight Snites [*Snipes*], twenty four Quails, forty eight Larks.

Boil these aforesaid Fowls in water and salt in a pan, pipkin or pot, &c.

Then have Bread, Marrow, Bottoms of Artichocks, Yolks of hard Eggs, Large Mace, Chesnuts, boil'd and blancht, two Colliflowers, Saffron.

And stew these in a pipkin together, being ready clenged with some good sweet butter, a little white wine and strong broth.

Some other times for variety you may use Beets, Potato's, Skirrets, Pistaches, Pine Apple seed, or Almonds, Poungarnet, and Lemons.

Now to dish your Olio. Dish first your Beef, Veal, or Pork; then your Venison, and Mutton, Tongues, Sausage, and Roots over all. Then next your largest Fowl, Land-Fowl, or Sea-Fowl, as first, a Goose, or Turkey, two Capons, two Pheasants, &c. &c. Then broth it, and put on your pipkin of Colliflowers, Artichocks, Chesnuts, some sweet-breads fried. Yolks of hard Eggs, then Marrow, boil'd in strong broth or water, large Mace, saffron, Pistaches, and all the aforesaid things being finely stewed up, and some red Beets over all, slic't Lemons, and Lemon peels whole, and run it over with beaten butter. For the garnish of the dish make [bone] marrow pies.

This famous seventeenth-century Olio Podrida was the commencement of a feast for a community of hungry people, the sort of highly-spiced "hotchpotch," to quote the meaning given in the *Oxford English Dictionary*, served at Christmas or to celebrate the successful garnering of the harvest. In his menus, Robert May set out his own recommended bill of fare for Christmas Day, without revealing how many the massive courses were supposed to serve. He had apparently aimed to satisfy an average community of a gentleman's household, family, and servants, including all sitting "below the salt."

A BILL OF FARE FOR CHRISTMAS DAY

Oysters
A collar of brawn
Stewed Broth of Mutton marrow bones
A grand Sallet
A pottage of Caponets

Whats wouldst thou view but in one face
all hospitalitie the race
of those that for the Gusto stand,
whose tables a whole Ark comand
of Natures plentie wouldst thou see
this sight, peruse Mays booke, 'tis hee.

Portrait frontispiece of the author, in Robert May's *The Accomplisht Cook,* 1660.

A breast of veal in stoffado
A boil'd partridge
A chine of beef, or surloin roast
Minced pies
A jegote of mutton with anchove sauce
A made dish of sweet-bread
A swan roast
A pasty of venison
A kid with a pudding in his belly
A steak pie
A haunch of venison roasted
A turkey roast and stuck with cloves
A made dish of chickens in puff paste
Two bran geese roasted, one larded
Two large capons, one larded
A Custard

THE SECOND COURSE FOR THE SAME MESS

Oranges and Lemons
A young lamb or kid

Two couple of rabbits, two larded
A pig souc't with tongues
Three ducks, one larded
Three pheasants, one larded
A Swan Pye
Three brace of partridge, three larded
Made dish in puff paste
Bolonia sausages, and anchoves, and pickled oysters in a dish,
        with mushrooms and Caviare
Six teels, three larded
A Gammon of Westphalia Bacon
Ten ploves, five larded
A quince pye, or warden pye
Six woodcocks, three larded
A standing Tart in puff-paste, preserved fruits, Pippins, &c
A dish of Larks
Six dried neat's tongues
Sturgeon
Powdered Geese
Jellies

Not all May's bills of fare and recipes were as ambitious as those he concocted for feast days, and many of his dishes called only for easily available ingredients that would suit the pockets of the less wealthy among his readers. Others he ingeniously contrived for times of the year when certain foods were out of season or unobtainable in the ordinary course of household business. He even contrived an eggless dish that reminds one of austere war-time recipes; but they were never quite like this:

TO MAKE A CUSTARD WITHOUT EGGS

Take a pound of almonds, blanch and beat them with rose-water into a fine paste, then put the spawn or row of a Carp or Pike into it, and beat them well together, with some cloves, mace, and salt, the spices being first beaten with some ginger.

Strain them with some fair spring water, and put into the strained stuff half a pound of double refined sugar and a little saffron.

When the paste is dried and ready to fill, put into the bottom of the coffin some slic't dates, raisins of the sun stoned, and some boiled currans.

Fill them and bake them. Being baked, scrape sugar on them.

Be sure always to prick your custards or forms before you set them in the oven.

If you have no row or spawn, put rice flour instead thereof.

As a final tribute to Robert May, I print a recipe dear to his heart, and which he headed with a deal of obvious pride:

TO MAKE AN EXTRAORDINARY GOOD CAKE

Take a half a bushel of the best flour you can get, very finely searsed, and lay it upon a large Pastry board. Make a hole in the midst thereof, and put to it three pound of the best butter you can get; with fourteen pound of currans finely picked and rubbed, three quarts of good new thick cream warm'd, two pound of fine sugar beaten, three pints of good new ale; barm, or yeast; four ounces of cinamon fine beaten and searsed, also an ounce of beaten ginger, two ounces of nutmegs fine beaten and searsed.

Put in all these materials together and work them up into an indifferent stiff paste. Keep it warm till the oven be hot, then make it up and bake it.

Being baked an hour and a half ice it: take four pound of double refined sugar, beat it, and searse it, and put it in a deep clean scowred skillet the quantity of a gallon. Boil it to a candy height with a little rose-water, then draw the cake, run it all over, and set it in the oven, till it be candied.

All the later editions of May's *Accomplisht Cook* contained prefaces dated from Soleby*, Leicestershire, a hamlet (now known as Shoby) about five miles west of Melton Mowbray. It was here that May served as chef to the Englefield family for nearly a quarter of a century, until his death as a very old man about 1687. The last edition issued with a preface written during his lifetime was dated 1685, a year in which the master cook celebrated his ninety-seventh birthday surrounded, let us hope, by a wide circle of children, grandchildren, and great-grandchildren. The actual date of his death is unrecorded; but his most appropriate epitaph is to be found beneath the frontispiece of his most famous book. The portrait shows him as a surprisingly young-looking and contented man of seventy-one (see illustration, page 50) with a tribute penned below:

> *What! wouldst thou view but in one face*
> *all hospitalitie, the race*
> *of those that for the Gusto stand,*
> *whose tables a whole Ark command*
> *of Natures plentie, wouldst thou see*
> *this sight, peruse May's booke, 'tis hee.*

*Also known as Shouldby, and Sholeby.

Chapter Four

THE CLOSET OPENED

No culinary bibliographer worth his salt would think of closing the chapter on seventeenth-century cook books without first paying tribute to the memory of that likable rascal Sir Kenelm Digby (1603 to 1665).

Ex-naval commander and privateer, court intriguer and double-agent, he reformed sufficiently to attempt a series of learned treatises on religious controversies and scientific affairs. He was destined to suffer the fate common to many authors, that of being remembered, not for the works of hopeful importance on which years of labor had been lavished, but for literary trivialities that made an instant appeal to his fellow men. In Digby's case his literary immortality stems from a manuscript cook book he compiled for his own amusement. It was certainly not intended for publication.

Life was far from easy in his younger days. His father, Sir Everard Digby, recently converted to Roman Catholicism, lost his head over the Gunpowder Plot. He left his wife and two young sons to live in comparative poverty on a meager patrimony in Buckinghamshire, after dying bravely on the scaffold.

It was in the heart of the Buckinghamshire countryside that young Kenelm spent his youth. In his teens he fell deeply in love with the daughter of their then near neighbor Sir Edward Stanley. Venetia Stanley was three years his senior and already experienced in the ways of a wicked world. But she pledged her undying troth to young Kenelm as she waved him good-by as he left for service abroad in the commission of his King's affairs. After three years intriguing for James I, Digby went back home, to make the disconcerting discovery that his teen-age sweetheart had been pregnant, three times, in the service of a wealthy London gallant, Sir Edward Sackville. She was still his mistress, and doing very well on an allowance of £500 a year.

S.ʳ KENELM DIGBY.

An engraving after Van Dyck's portrait of Sir Kenelm Digby, from the original in Kensington Palace.

Even a newly acquired knighthood, conferred by a grateful sovereign, did little to smooth Sir Kenelm's dented ego, but it certainly helped to renew the flame of Venetia's interest. Such are the wiles of woman that within a few months she had her erstwhile lover once again on his knees before her.

In 1625 they were married, their first child of the Kenelm alliance being born in October of the same year. It was a match that became the subject of one of the minor scandals of the day. The fact that Venetia's husband and Sir Edward Sackville, now Earl of Dorset, remained close and intimate friends was the main cause of gossip, especially when it was discovered that Venetia was still in receipt of her well-earned allowance of £500 a year. Dorset was wealthy, while Sir Kenelm's patrimony amounted to only £300 a year. Both men had the deepest affection for the lovely Venetia, whose wit and intelligence more than matched her beauty, so the arrangement was satisfactory to both sides. Within months the scandal faded and the gossip waned, but the allowance continued for as long as Venetia survived.

Digby's restless ambitions led to the raising of funds to fit out two small men-of-war, and in these he led a daring expedition to harass the French and Flemish. The adventure culminated in an audacious raid on their ships in the Syrian port of Scanderoon, later immortalized in countless ballads and rhymes. The complete success of Kenelm's expedition, despite the cries of anguish from London traders who feared a loss of custom, did much to restore his personal fortunes at home, at least in a social sense. For a time he and his wife lived a happy life of quiet domesticity.

After the death of his beloved Venetia, Digby was inconsolable. Henceforth he lived much of his life abroad, mostly in Paris, where he was credited, during and after the Civil War, with intriguing on behalf of both sides in the conflict. Some historians allow him the benefit of the doubt, saying his seeming friendship with Cromwell and the Roundheads was merely a front to hide his Royalist sympathies. He may well have acted as a double-agent, for he was well received at Court in England after the restoration of Charles II in 1660.

His ancestoral estates were at long last his own again, and from that time onward he devoted himself to science and the arts. Many of his scientific exploits and experiments were no more than alchemy, with the pursuit of the transmutation of base metals into gold high on his list of priorities. The magic of a Sympathetic Powder, credited with the power of healing gangrenous wounds at a distance of several miles, tarnished his scientific reputation when it obstinately failed to work and each and every patient died in distressing circumstances. Nevertheless, Sir Kenelm was one of the founder members of the Royal Society, and many of its most distinguished intellectuals met and dined at his house in Covent Garden. There, you were quite as likely to meet the favorite evangelist of the moment, religious fanatics of all kinds, astrologers, occultists, alchemists, and as many charlatans as men of true worth.

In his prime, the handsome Sir Kenelm Digby had played the part of a swashbuckling cavalier to perfection. He made the acquaintance of many men of letters, including Ben Johnson and Edward Hyde (afterward Earl of Clarendon). The latter described him as being "exceptionally handsome, with a winning voice, a flowing courtesy and civility, and such a volubility

A kitchen in Germany, 1673. Taken from a dated seventeenth-century doll's house, now in the Bethnal Green Museum, London.

of language as surprised and delighted.'' But in later years the pleasures of the table and good eating wrecked havoc with his figure. Puffing and blowing and a martyr to gout, it now took two stalwart retainers to help him mount his horse. Dropsy and the stone finally put an end to his affairs on Earth, the remnants of his fortune being distributed amongst his closest friends to the total exclusion of his surviving sons and daughter.

Some three years after his father's death, John Digby decided that the sheaf of culinary recipes and formulae for wine- and ale-making which had been left in manuscript amongst Sir Kenelm's papers deserved publication. Dozens of dishes that had particularly tickled the palate of his father's rotund and well-fed frame had been carefully noted down over the years, together with hundreds of recipes for making wines and ales of every type. After sorting and editing the manuscript, John Digby commissioned a copperplate engraving as a portrait frontispiece, taken from the oil-painting by Sir Anthony Van Dyke at that time hanging in Kensington Palace. The book was published under the imprint of H. Broome, at the Star in Little Britain, London, and soon established itself as one of the most popular cookery and wine-making books of its age.

The Closet of the Eminently Learned Sir Kenelm Digby Kt, Opened: Whereby is Discovered Several Ways of Making Metheglin, Sider, Cherry

Wine, etc. Together with Excellent Directions for Cookery—also for Pre-serving, Conserving, Candying, etc., 1669, has long been a collector's piece.

Among many recipes of interest, is one giving directions for making tea. Although this is the first printed recipe that mentions what was to become Britain's national beverage, tea drinking in England had been indulged in by those close to court circles since the time of the Restoration. On September 25, 1660, Samuel Pepys noted in his diary: "I did send for a cup of tee (a China drink) of which I never had drunk before. . . ." If Pepys enjoyed his cup, one doubts if it tasted anything like the brew with which Sir Kenelm Digby tempted his readers:

TEA WITH EGGS

To near a pint of the infusion, take two yolks of new-laid eggs, and beat them very well with as much fine sugar as is sufficient for this quantity of liquor.

When they are well incorporated, pour your Tea upon the Eggs and Sugar, and stir them well together. So drink it hot!

This drink is cordial to health when you come home from attending business abroad, and are very hungry, and yet have not conveniency to eat at once a competent meal. You will find this presently dissolveth and satisfieth all rawness and indigence of the stomach, and flyeth suddenly over the whole body and into the veins, and strengtheneth exceedingly, and preserves one a good while from the necessity of eating.

In these parts, we let the hot water remain too long soaking upon the Tea, which makes it extract into itself the earthy parts of the herb. The water is to remain upon the Tea, no longer than the while in which you can say the *Misere* psalm very leisurely. . . .

Bright orange in color, and emitting an undefinable odor slightly reminiscent of softly-boiled eggs, this was a mixture that would almost certainly induce nausea in the stereotyped tea-drinkers of today. It would take more than the whole Book of Psalms to pacify the recipient.

Whether the title of the book was the author's own choice or that of his son is not known. It was almost certainly borrowed from similar titles used in earlier works by other writers, such as *A Closet for Ladies and Gentlewomen, or, The Art of Preserving*, 1602, mentioned earlier; *The Ladies Cabinet Opened*, 1639, often reprinted; and the popular *The Queen's Closet Opened*, 1655, which appeared over the initials of a mysterious Mr. W. M. This latter work contained a portrait frontispiece of Queen Henrietta Maria (1609 to 1669) the estranged consort of the late King Charles I, and apparently made its appearance with her willing consent. The author described himself as being "one of her late servants" and almost certainly served as chef in her kitchens in France. *The Queen's Closet Opened* was still in print as late as 1696, when what was described on the title page as the "10th edition" made its appearance. That Sir Kenelm knew and had read the work there can be little doubt, for he spent several years in France and was a friend and confidant of the exiled Queen.

One of the many recipes Digby brouht home from Paris was that of a pottage with which he often started the day. The formula was obtained from the same chef who attended Queen Henrietta Maria, who was by this time a very stout lady whose breakfast would today suffice for a full-scale dinner.

PORTUGAL BROTH
(As made for the Queen)

Make very good broth with some lean of Veal, Beef and Mutton, and with a brawny Hen or young Cock. After it is scummed, put in an Onion quartered (and if you like it, a clove of Garlick). Add a little Parsley, a sprig of Thyme, and as much Mint, a little Balm; some coriander seeds well bruised and a very little Saffron; a little salt, pepper, and a Clove. When all the substance is boiled out of the meat, and the broth very thick and good, you may drink it so. Or, pour a little of it upon toasted bread thin sliced, and stew it until the bread have drunk up all the broth, and then add a little more and stew. So you may add a little by little, that the bread may imbibe it and swell; whereof, if you drown it at once, the bread will not swell and make so good a jelly.

And thus you have a good *potage*.

Sir Kenelm's liking for soups and pottage led him to include a number of recipes he had devised himself. These were served as appetizers before one settled down to the serious business of breakfasting in gentlemanly style with the friends who dropped in before luncheon was ready to be served. Such rituals often lasted several hours, and were the occasion for much intellectual conversation and highly seasoned gossip of the town. To arrive late was to miss the pottage, but with the consolation of several courses to follow.

ENGLISH POTTAGE

Make a good strong broth of Veal and Mutton. Strain out the meat, and put in the broth a fat Capon or Pullet. If it be too fat, parboil it a little less it oil the broth. Then put it in the broth; and when it has boiled therein a little, put in some grated bread, a bundle of mixed sweet herbs, two or three blades of Mace, and a peeled onion. When it is ready to be served up, take the yolks of six eggs, beat them very well with two or three tablespoonfuls of White Wine. Then take the Capon out of the broth, and thicken the broth with the Eggs. And so dish it up upon the Capon, and toasts of White bread, or slices, which you please. And have ready boiled the marrow of two or three bones, with some tender white boiled Endive, and strew it over the Capon.

Quite a starter for the day! With at least another three courses to come, plus two other separate meals to look forward to before supper closed the culinary accounts until tomorrow! Other light-hearted pleasures of seventeenth-century life, were obviously well down the scale of prime essentials from the pleasures of mealtimes in the Digby household. When Sir Kenelm found time from giving detailed instructions to his chef, he busied himself amongst the bottles and vats in his capacious cellars at Covent Garden. It was here that the fermenting vats of many a future hangover lay waiting his experienced eye and sensitive nose, to be bottled and corked in a glory of contrasting tastes and colors that would grace his table at feasts to come. Most of his wines were homemade, and certainly all of his beer and ale.

Possibly his own favorite recipe for the drink he loved so well is headed as being ''composed by Myself out of Sundry Recipes.'' The quantities he stipulated must have been sufficient to warm the cockles of his heart, and that of the many guests he entertained, through the long winter months and most of the summer too!

METHEGLIN

In sixty gallons of water, boil ten handfuls of sweet briar leaves, Eyebright, Liverwort, Agrimony, Scabious, Balm, Betony, Strawberry-leaves, Burnet, each four handfuls. Of Mint, Angelica, Bayes and Wild-thyme, Sweet Marjoram, each two handfuls. Six eringo roots.

When the water has taken the virtue and goodness out of the herbs and roots, let it settle and the next day pour off clear. In every three gallons of it boil one of honey, scumming it well and putting in a little cold water now and again to make the scum rise. Add also some white of eggs.

When it is clear scummed, take it off and let it cool; then work it with Ale yeast.

Turn it up and hang it in a Bag, with Ginger, Cinnamon, Cloves and Cardamon. And as it worketh over, put in some strong Honey-drink warmed. When it works no more stop it up.

Metheglin was a popular and much appreciated drink, credited with medicinal powers. It orginated from the recipes given for the making of Welsh mead, and many of the seventeenth-century taverns had their own jealously guarded recipes. *The Closet Opened* contains well over a hundred different versions for making this one drink alone, labeled as ''Lady Hungerford's Metheglin,'' ''The Leige,'' ''The Antwerp,'' and as many as Kenelm could extract from private sources and the tavernkeepers he met on his journeys.

Sir Kenelm Digby died, as he would have wished, of a surfeit of good living. Gout and the stone finally brought him low, and it is recorded that he set out for Paris a few days before his death in a determination to have one final fling before he closed his eyes. But it was in his own house at Covent Garden that he died on June 11, 1665, just a few months before the outbreak of the Great Fire of London, a fire which utterly destroyed Christ Church, Newgate, scarring and blackening the tomb where he lay buried beside his beloved wife, Venetia.

What was left of his fortune he stipulated should be distributed amongst the well-fed circle of friends who had been his companions in many a gargantuan orgy of overfeeding. His son, John Digby, whom Sir Kenelm left unmentioned in his will, remarked bitterly that it appeared that his inheritance had been literally eaten away. After editing his father's work, the son permitted himself a single final line of comment to *The Closet Opened*. As a grace to salt Sir Kenelm's rich collection of savory repasts, John Digby wrote to his readers, with the irony of his own situation well in mind: "Fall to, therefore, and much good may it do thee!"

Chapter Five

FIRST CATCH YOUR HARE

In the comparatively contented atmosphere, engendered by the peaceful conditions at home and the news of resounding military successes abroad, that ushered in the reign of good Queen Anne, literary and artistic talents flourished. The stage witnessed brilliant successes and these were mirrored in the world of literature and in the outstanding talents displayed by the artists and craftsmen of the age. Yet it was an epoch of low political and personal morality in which corruption and the abuse of high office were in complete contrast to the exemplary personal and private life of the queen.

Public interest in the Court over which she ruled was intense, and was tinged with a personal sympathy for the misfortunes of a queen who had lost in infancy every one of her seventeen children. Court and palace news was the immediate gossip of the day and any tit-bit of inside information was devoured with a relish that has continued into modern times.

It was at this propitious moment that a distinguished and upper-class cookery book made its appearance. Its aristocratic title at once made clear to its would-be readers that its contents were far removed from the thumbed and dog-eared recipes that acted as the standby for greasy-fingered cooks who satisfied the needs of country squires and the lesser landed gentry. To these minions laboring to fill the bellies of middle-class appetites it made no apology. It was not concerned with everyday needs; its intent was to reveal the secrets of the royal tables and the exotic and costly dishes lovingly devised to tempt the palates of the kings and queens of England.

Royal Cookery; or, the Compleat Court-Cook, 1710, was the forerunner of many such personal revelations by long-serving employees in the British Royal Household. Later titillations from less ingenuous hands

A
RECEIPT

To make an

Oat-meal Pudding.

OF Oats decorticated take two Pound,
    And of new Milk enough the fame to drownd;
Of Raiſins of the Sun, ſton'd, Ounces eight;
Of Currants, cleanly pick'd, an equal Weight;
Of Sewet, finely ſlic'd, an Ounce, at leaſt;
And ſix Eggs, newly taken from the Neſt:
Seaſon this Mixture well, with Salt and Spice;
'Twill make a Pudding far exceeding Rice:
And you may ſafely feed on it like Farmers,
For the Receipt is Learned Dr. *Harmer's*.

A

A

A recipe in verse taken from *Poetical Miscellanies*, 1704, originally edited by John Dryden.

achieved a more sophisticated approach, usually revealing more intimate affairs than mere table plans and details of majestic appetites and princely gluttony. But, in its day, *Royal Cookery* made fascinating reading for the social gossips. What the Queen had daintily picked over at dinner in 1705 was absorbingly interesting to the eighteenth-century society gossip or housewife. Morsels of culinary news gleaned from present day royal menus exert a similar attraction on a substantial section of readers of the social columns of newspapers and glossy magazines here today. In this respect the public appetite remains as keen as ever.

Descriptions of ". . . the magnificent entertainments at Coronations and Instalments, of Balls, Weddings, etc., at Court; as likewise City Feasts . . ." provided edifying gossip after the political scandals and well-publicized moral lapses that winked their way through the coffeehouses and taverns of the metropolis. As a bonus, *Royal Cookery* was also able to boast that its pages contained "the choicest Receipts in all the several branches of Cookery. . . ." The reader was assured that the printed recipes for "the making of Soops, Bisques, Olios, Terrines, Surtouts, Puptons, Ragoos, Forc'd Meats, Sauces, Patties, Pies, Tarts, Tansies, Cakes, Puddings, Jellies, etc. . . ." had all graced the royal tables at one or other of the Queen's palaces of St. James's, Kensington, Hampton Court, or Windsor. The highest fashionable appetite was revealed for all to try and imitate, and a detailed inventory of the royal preference in food and drink was given in recipes of the choicest and most costly dishes the Royal Kitchens could provide.

The author of *Royal Cookery* was Patrick Lambe (1648? to 1709). Man and boy, he had spent a lifetime in the service of British monarchs, having been appointed "youngest child of pastry" in March, 1662, under Charles II. Son of a yeoman cook, he had been born to the art of cookery and knew no other trade. For the rest of his life he served the kings and queens of England, being promoted in 1685, the year of Charles II's death, to the coveted rank of "2nd Master Cook and Yeoman of the Pastry." This carried a salary of £130 per annum, plus free board and lodgings, the best of royal food, and all the lawful and unlawful perquisites that accrued from such an enviable position.

James II confirmed his status, and further promoted the forty-year-old Patrick Lambe to "First Master Cook in the King's Kitchen" in 1688. Ambition could soar no higher! From that time onward Lambe was the most powerful and influential figure in the vast warren of interconnected kitchens that supported the palace of Whitehall. Despite jealousies, he retained his rank under William and Mary, being sworn in again on the accession of Queen Anne. He was still lording it over a vast army of underchefs and dependent minions at the time of his death in 1709, leaving the completed manuscript of his one and only book to be published posthumously. Abel Roper, his friend and executor, corrected the text and saw it through the press of Stationers' Hall printer John Morphew.

It was not long before *Royal Cookery* set the fashion in culinary affairs for those who could afford to follow its extravagant advice. The chefs in charge of the kitchens of the wealthiest aristocrats and landowners in the early part of the eighteenth century were soon designating their dishes for the larger banquets as being "after Queen Anne's fashion." Few others could possibly afford to emulate the vast spreads of exotic and costly foods which Lambe so often called for in his book of royal recipes.

Typical of his side dishes, placed ready in case the course then proceeding failed to make sufficient appeal, was Lambe's meat loaf of pigeons. Its preparation must have occupied the talents of a skilled under-chef for most of a working day, and its ingredients, often called for out of season, would have taxed the ingenuity of any but the best provisioned larders. The garnish of ragoût (described here as "ragoo") was a thick French stew of gravied meat that would equate with our present-day casserole type of dish. It was a favorite on its own, but was more often used for enriching and adding body to a recipe like this:

PUPTON OF PIGEONS

To make this little dish you may take six pigeons (or more if you have a mind to make a bigger dish). Singe and blanch them when you have trussed them well; then fry them in a little Butter or Hog's lard, being first larded with small lardons [*slices of fat bacon*]; then put them in stewing with a little Broth or Gravy.

When they are almost tender, put to them two sweet breads cut in large bits and fry'd, a handful of Morils and Mushrooms well pick'd and wash'd, and twelve chestnuts blanched.

Put all this together, then take a Sauce-pan with a quarter of a pound of Butter, a small handful of Flower, and two whole Onions. Brown it over the Fire with a pint of Gravy, put in your ingredients aforesaid, having first seasoned them with Pepper, Salt, and Nutmeg.

Let it stew so that most of your ragoo sticks to your Meat, then set it off the Fire a-cooling. Take a Patty-pan or Sauce-Pan and butter the Bottom and Sides. Then cut four or five slices of Bacon as long as your Hand and as thin as a Shilling. Place them at the Bottom and Sides of your Pan at an equal distance, then place over it a Quantity of forc'd Meat about half an inch thick, as high on the sides of your Pan as you think will be needed to hold your Pigeons and Ragoo. Then pour in your cold Ragoo, and the Pigeons place with their breasts to the Bottom of the Pan, because the Bottom side is turned up when it goes to Table.

Then take out your whole Onion, Bacon, and Cloves that was in your brown Gravy over the fire, and squeeze in a whole lemon. Place your Pigeons with the Breasts to the middle of the Pan, and your Ragoo betwixt your Pigeons at an equal Distance. Cover it all over with the same forc'd Meat an inch thick, and close it well round the Sides. Smooth it well with your Hands and with Egg, strew on it a little grated Bread, and bake it an Hour before you have occasion to use it. Then loose it from the sides of your Patty-pan or Sauce-Pan with your Knife, put it on your Mazarine or little Dish, wherein you intend to serve it, and turn it upside down clearly.

If it is well baked it will stand upright, like a Brown Loaf.

Squeeze over it an Orange, lay round it fry'd Parsley, putting the Sauce in the middle. So serve it.

The pupton, or molded meat loaf, was a favorite seventeenth-century dish, still popular in the first quarter of the eighteenth century by which time it had degenerated into a glorified meat pudding. Lambe told his readers that he served puptons to the Royal Household "of Partridges and Quails, Turtle-doves and Buntings, and Larks and Moor Fowl." It was often followed by one of his famous fish dishes, in this case a seasonable delicacy:

DRESSED SALMON IN CHAMPAIGN WINE

Wash clean a large salmon, cut it in slices and take off the skin. Take out the middle bones and cut each slice as needed. Place them in a Sauce-pan and season them with Salt, Pepper, an onion stuck with a Clove, a bunch of Herbs and half a Bay-leaf. Add a piece of fresh Butter, a little grated Bread, some Truffles and Mushrooms. Then pour over half a bottle of Champaign Wine, and set the Sauce-pan on a stove with a well-kindled Fire. When the liquor is wasted to the degree you need, bind it with a Cray-fish cullis [*a boiled broth of cray-fish, strained and partially clarified*].
Dish it up handsomely and serve it warm to Table.

This is one of the earliest recipes we know of that makes use of the newly invented champagne wine as one of its ingredients. The champagne imported from France in the early years of the eighteenth century already bore some slight resemblance to the sparkling wine we know by that name today. Although historians of the social scene have pronounced that it was probably "as red as burgundy and as flat as port," in fact, champagne had already paled to "the colour of a partridge's eye" by the time that Lambe's book appeared. Thanks to the tireless experimentation of the monk Dom Perignon, the wine was well on the way to attaining the heady effervescence that popped the corks and frothed the glasses in the gay old Georgian days.

The first edition of *Royal Cookery,* 1710, if complete with its thirty-six plates (mostly folding), is now worth in the region of $600, but much depends on the book's condition. The second edition, with forty plates and dated 1716, now commands about $400; while the third edition, dated 1726, is worth about half this amount. This latter issue appeared again in 1731, still with the words "Third Edition" on its title page, but it must, of course, be classed as the fourth.

Patrick Lambe was the foremost exponent of *haute cuisine,* high-class cooking at its most extravagant, with no thought of the time and labor involved in preparing even the simplest sauces. Mountains of costly meats and spices were used to produce one small dish for the private table of the Queen, while in one of his recipes four contrasting types of meat and three sorts of game birds were used to make less than two quarts of rich gravy. By the time of his death in 1709 he had more than earned the title of "King of Royal Cooks."

Preparing dinner for Dr. Johnson. An incident during Johnson's and Boswell's tour of Scotland in 1773, pictured by Thomas Rowlandson.

His book set a fashion that many chefs in the more distinguished of Britain's aristocratic households were quick to exploit. One of the most successful of these was John Nott, who described himself as "Cook to his Grace the Duke of Bolton." He was one of the first writers in this field to employ an alphabetical sequence to his recipes, calling his book *The Cook's and Confectioner's Dictionary; or, the Accomplished Housewife's Companion,* 1723 (second edition 1724). He addressed his introductory remarks "To all good Housewives":

Worthy Dames,
Were it not for the sake of Custom, which has made it as unfashionable for a Book to come abroad without an Introduction, as for a Man to appear at Church without a Neckcloth, or a Lady without a Hoop-petticoat, I should not have troubled you with this. . . . We, indeed, may say with the Psalmist, The Lines have fallen to us in pleasant Places, since, by the disposition of God, and good Providence, our Lot has been cast in his happy Island of Great

Britain, which like another Canaan, may properly enough be call'd, A Land flowing with Milk and Honey; so richly is it stor'd with Flesh, Fowl and Fish, in an admirable Variety; esculent Roots, Herbs, &c. for Sauces and Sallets; Fruits, as well for making Wines and other potable Liquors (which, well ordered, are not inferiour to those brought to us from foreign Countries) as well as for furnishing Deserts at Banquets: and, in a Manner, with all Things necessary, not only for the support of Life; but also for the gratifying of the most sensual Appetite: that no neighbouring Nation can boast of a Superiority, nay, not even pretend to compare with us, as to an Equality.

After this patriotic outburst, he went on to admit that "though God sends us Meat, yet the Devil does Cooks." Therefore, he told his readers:

. . . to prevent this Inconvenience, I have taken upon me to collect a great Variety of Receipts, or Directions, for ordering these Things with which the most celebrated Artists; and also the nicest and most curious Dames and Housewives our Country has produced; as also, for the Entertainment of the more Curious, have inserted many Receipts, according to the Practice of the best Masters in the Arts of Cookery and Confectionary of France, Italy, Spain, Germany, and other Countries.

He assured his readers that he could "without Vanity say, it is the richest in Variety, and so the compleatest Book, or its Kind, yet extant." In this statement he was probably correct, for his thick octavo volume ran to over 660 unnumbered pages, set out nearly 2,000 different recipes, and finished with what he proudly described as "a copious alphabetical Index." Nott's compilation was the first to arrange all recipes alphabetically, and the number of editions it passed through within the space of the next decade was a tribute to this handy and convenient arrangement. It found favor, as he hoped it would, with "not only British Housewives, but Cooks, &c. in Taverns, Eating-Houses, and publick Inns. . . ."

Many of the recipes he printed were admittedly culled from earlier or foreign sources, but their appearance in *The Cook's and Confectioner's Dictionary* gave them a permanent place in the pages of British cookery books for generations to come. His soups and possets were especially well liked and acted as models for the many imitations that followed.

PEAS-SOOP

Take a Leg of Beef, boil it, make strong Broth. Let it stand till it is cold; then put into it a couple of Quarts of hull'd Peas, and an Onion stuck with Cloves. Boil them very well, season the Soop very highly with Salt, Pepper, Spice, and all sorts of savoury Herbs such as are used in Soops, as a large Leek, Spinage, Sorrel, Lettuce, and Roots, and bits of Bacon cut into the Dish.

Add also crisp'd Bacon, crisp'd or toasted Bread, forc'd Meat Balls and a pint of good Gravy.

Lay in the middle of the Dish eight roasted larded Pigeons. Garnish with crisp'd Bacon and toasted Bread.

MEAT SOOP

Take a Knuckle of Veal, a Scrag End of a Neck of Mutton, and a piece of coarse Beef.

Boil all these to Rags in Water, season'd with Salt, whole Pepper, and an Onion. When the goodness is all boil'd out of the Meat, strain the Liquor and set it over a Stove in a stew Pan, with Cloves, Mace, and a little Lemon-peel. When it is boil'd a little, put in a Pint of strong Claret, and having fry'd a piece of lean Beef on purpose, squeeze out the Gravy into the stew Pan, and add three or four Anchovies. Boil Ox-palates very tender, then cut them into Dice. Add also Veal sweet Breads, Spinage, Endive, Lettuce, and what other Herbs you fancy.

Then make thin Toasts of French Bread, lay the sweet Breads and the Ox-palates over the Toasts, lay a Fowl boil'd with the Breast stuff'd with forc'd Meat in the middle of the Dish. Pour the Soop over all, and serve it up.

COVENT-GARDEN POSSET

Boil a Quart of Cream, put in a Nutmeg quartered, and a quarter of an Ounce of Cinnamon.

Let it boil till it tastes of the Spice, and keep it always stirring that it may not burn.

Beat the Yolks of eight Eggs up with a little cold Cream, and put them into the hot Cream over the Fire, and keep it stirring till it begins to boil.

Then take it off, and stir it till it is indifferent cold. Then sweeten it with Sugar to your Palate; then sweeten a quarter of a Pint of Sack*, or better, and make it ready to boil. Then pour it into a Bason, and pour the Cream to it, holding it as high as you can to make it froth, which is the Grace of the Posset.

Umbles were sometimes the choicest bits of game offal, and sometimes the not-so-choice liver and lights. The latter thus constituted one of the cheapest meat dishes it was possible to procure. Samuel Pepys in his *Diary,* speaks of being fed umble pie "the meanest dinner!," and it is from this savory working-class dish that our oft-quoted saying, "Eating humble pie" has stemmed. "Disguise it as you will, flavor it as you will, call it what you will, umble-pie is umble-pie, and nothing else," wrote James Russell Lowell with an amount of feeling that bespoke the dinner-table disappointments of expectant youth; while Anthony Trollope, in his *Doctor Thorne,* 1858, spoke of the comparative or superlative degree of obsequiousness as being "not only humble but umble." Our present-day steak-and-kidney pie is the up-graded luxurious version of this seventeenth- and eighteenth-century poor man's standby.

Sack: a white wine imported into Britain from Spain and the Canaries.

UMBLE PIE

Cut the Umbles in small pieces, and cut fat Bacon in small pieces. Mix them together, and season them with Salt, Pepper, and Nutmeg. Strip some Thyme, and mince some Lemon, and mix them; you may lay Suet minced in the bottom.

Fill your Pastry, cover them with thin Slices of Bacon, and a good Quantity of Butter. Let it be well soaked in the Oven, and when it is bak'd, beat up Butter with Claret, Lemon, and stript Thyme.

Pour it into your Pastry and serve it up hot.

One final recipe which must have laid many a strong man low: John Nott guaranteed to "fast cleanse the bowels of such as be costive." Its immediate explosive effect meant that the draught could only be downed while actually sitting firmly on the privy, or closet-house . . . "if privy or closet-house there be."

PURGING ALE

Take garden Scurvey-Grass, Burdock-Roots bruised, and blew Currants, of each half a Pound.

Of Rhubarb slic'd, and Horse-Radish roots, scrap'd, each an Ounce and a half. The Roots of Monks-Rhubarb, sharp-pointed Dock, of each three Ounces and a half. Of Mechoacan, and Senna, three Ounces and a half. Coriander-Seeds, Carraway-Seeds, Annis-Seeds, and Daucus-Seeds, bruis'd, of each an Ounce and a half; with three Oranges sliced.

Put all these Ingredients into a Canvas-Bag, with a Stone in it, and hang it in three Gallons of new Ale, and let them work fierce together.

In three Days time it will be drinkable: take a Pint for a Morning's draught.

There must have been very few survivors.

In the meantime a young London housewife was coping with the ever-expanding problems of rearing and feeding her rapidly growing family, an experience which was to stand her in good stead when she finally discovered enough free time to collect together her treasured recipes for the cook book that was to bring her national fame.

She was born just a few months before the great Patrick Lambe took to his bed for the last time, the marriage of Isaac and Hannah Allgood being blessed with yet another mouth to feed on March 24, 1708. Young Hannah, named after her mother, grew up to be a strapping wench whose physical attractions made quite certain that she would never be short of suitors. She was married before she reached the age of seventeen to an up and coming young solicitor named Peter Glasse. They settled happily in a house in what later proved to be prophetic, Carey Street, London; where Hannah apparently kept her husband well-filled and well-contented while they waited the birth of the first of their family of eight children.

The redoubtable Mrs. Hannah Glasse, whose *Art of Cookery* became an eighteenth-century best seller.

70

It was here that the new Mrs. Hannah Glasse (1708 to 1770) settled into the daily routine of running her own well furnished and provisioned home, catering for a husband now an attorney-at-law, and a growing family of ever-hungry young children. These long and sometimes lean years of housekeeping were the experience she drew on when she at last decided to commit her rules of domestic economy and the art of cooking into book form. When the last page was written and the hundreds of sheets sorted into order, she advertised that her volume of recipes would shortly be on sale ''in Mrs. Ashburn's China-Shop, the Corner of Fleet-Ditch; and at the *Bluecoat-Boy,* near the Royal-Exchange.''

The Art of Cookery made Plain and Easy, 1747, boasted on its title page that it was a work ''which far exceeds any Thing of the Kind ever yet published.'' This boast was well founded, for the clear and precise fashion in which its many recipes were set out, the clarity of the instructions given to inexperienced readers trying their hand at the more adventurous dishes, and the fact that there was a list of chapter headings at the front of the work and an alphabetical index at the back, set it well above any previous publication of this type. It became an immediate and enduring best seller (it was still being reprinted as late as 1824). Not until the appearance of Mrs. Beeton's classic well over a hundred years later was its success exceeded.

There were many who obstinately refused to believe that such a well-ordered work could possibly have been written by a mere woman. Guests, leaning back replete after a dinner where the mysterious Mrs. Glasse's recipes had been served, congratulated their host while probing the author's identity. One such conversation about *The Art of Cookery* has been preserved for us by the indefatigable James Boswell. He was in a party, dining at the house of publisher Charles Dilly, on April 15, 1778, when Samuel Johnson brought up the subject of cookery books and their shortcomings:

The subject of cookery having been very naturally introduced at a table where Johnson, who boasted of the niceness of his palate, owned that ''he always found a good dinner,'' he said, ''I could write a better book of cookery than has ever yet been written; it should be a book upon philosophical principles. Pharmacy is now made much more simple. Cookery may be made so to. A prescription which is now compounded of five ingredients, had formerly fifty in it. So in cookery, if the nature of the ingredients be well known, much fewer will do. Then, as you cannot make bad meat good, I would tell you what is the best butcher's meat, the best beef, the best pieces; how to choose young fowls; the proper season of different vegetables; and then how to roast and boil, and compound.''

Dilly: ''Mrs. Glasse's *Cookery,* which is the best, was written by Dr. Hill. Half the trade know this.''

Johnson: ''Well, sir. This shows how much better the subject of Cookery may be treated by a philosopher. I doubt if the book be written by Dr. Hill; for, in Mrs. Glasse's *Cookery,* which I have looked into, salt-petre and sal-prunella are spoken of as different substances, whereas sal-prunella is only salt-petre burnt on charcoal, and Hill could not be ignorant of this. However, as the greatest part of such a book is made by transcription, this mistake may have been carelessly adopted. But you shall see what a Book of Cookery I shall make! I shall agree with Mr. Dilly for the copy-right.''

Miss Seward: "That would be Hercules with the distaff indeed."
Johnson: "No, Madam. Women can spin very well; but they cannot make a good book of Cookery."

Unfortunately, no Johnsonian cookery book, written upon philosophical or any other principles ever made its appearance, so posterity has been denied the delight of sampling the fare of one who doubted if a whole synod of cooks could have produced better dinners than those of his old housekeeper. "For my part, I mind my belly very studiously, and very carefully; for I look upon it, that he who does not mind his belly will hardly mind any thing else."

These were sentiments the redoubtable Mrs. Glasse would have been pleased to echo, for she made it abundantly clear that she would have none of the frothy extravagances delighted in by Continental chefs. The filling of the round English belly with good wholesome fare was the principle she stood by, and she lamented that "so much is the blind folly of this Age, that they would rather be impos'd on by a French Booby, than give encouragement to a good English Cook!

"If I have not wrote in the high, polite Stile," she went on, "I hope I shall be forgiven; for my Intention is to instruct the lower sort, and therefore must treat them in their own Way. For example: when I should bid them lard a Fowl, if I should bid them lard with large Lardoons, they would not know what I meant! But when I say they must lard with little Pieces of Bacon, they know what I mean. So in many other things in Cookery, the great Cooks have such a high way of expressing themselves, that the poor Girls are at a Loss to know what they mean. In all Receipt Books yet printed, there are such an odd Jumble of things as would quite spoil *a good dish*."

There was no such nonsense in the pages of Mrs. Glasse's cookery book, and she did her best to live up to the title that this was indeed *The Art of Cookery made Plain and Easy*. "I have heard of a Cook that used six pounds of butter to fry twelve Eggs; when every Body knows (that understands Cooking) that Half a Pound is full enough—or more than need be used. But then it would not be French!" She added sarcastically.

To read through the list of her chapter headings immediately reveals how far in advance of her contemporaries, and those of all the cook books of past ages, Hannah stood in the field of culinary expertise and clarity of instruction. The book had been carefully planned by a first-class cook who was also a busy housewife. She knew well the frustrations of thumbing through endless pages of mixed and jumbled recipes while the wrong pans boiled and the expensive smell of burning victuals permeated her kitchen. It was thoughtfully divided into a total of twenty-two well laid out chapters, some of which listed well over three hundred and fifty related dishes and recipes. And the relevant page numbers were clearly printed alongside every recipe, making the book as simple a work of reference as any harassed housewife could desire.

As soon as an early edition of *The Art of Cookery* is met with and opened for the first time, one feels an immediate desire to confirm or deny the authorship of the famous phrase that is now linked forever with the name of Mrs. Glasse. Did she, or did she *not,* advise her naïve and artless readers to "First catch your Hare. . . ."? This self-evident admonition now has a firm place in the language of the English-speaking peoples and has ensured Hannah Glasse's immortality in the vocabulary of tens of thousands who have never opened a cookery book or even heard her name.

The legend that Mrs. Glasse was responsible for this useful admonition seems to have originated sometime in the middle of the nineteenth century, long after the good lady was dead and gone. No doubt she would have endorsed Andrew Kingsmill's thundering denunciation of human vice and folly that "Every man's skinne is the case of a sinner," which appeared

A political cartoon of 1789, which gives an interesting glimpse of the interior of a late-eighteenth-century kitchen.

THE HOUSEHOLD, or WHO RULES THE ROAST?

in his *Viewe of Man's Estate,* as long ago as 1574. Whether she permitted herself to read *The Costlie Whore,* 1633, is extremely unlikely, though it is there that the pertinent Aesopian warning occurs, telling the credulous to discover the deceits of a world in which "Hares and Asses weare the lion's case." Hannah was too busy preparing yet another appetizing repast for her family of hungry children to worry about who said what and when, and a skinned hare pudding, steaming with mouth-watering aroma, was the dish she set before her tableful of (one hopes!) appreciative children.

To those who know, or think they know, the attribution, it is an automatic reaction, on handling any of her early editions for the first time, to turn to chapter one, opening the leaves at the recipe which tells in plain and simple language how "To Roast a Hare." Despite the fact that the best and most reliable works of reference are unanimous in their verdict, acquitting Hannah of the charge of ever having said any such thing, it is difficult to resist a confirmatory glance at her recipe for hare, just in case a printer's error may have caught her out.

Scottifying the palate. Rowlandson's skit on Boswell attempting to make Johnson acquire a taste for Forth speldings during their tour of Scotland in 1773.

I have checked numerous editions, including the elusive first, only to find Hannah soberly instructing me to "Take your hare when it is cased . . ." (with the latter word printed "cas'd" in the earliest editions). The *Oxford English Dictionary* tells us that the word *case,* in the context used by Mrs. Glasse, means, quite simply, "the skin or hide of an animal," and they quote its use in this form from the mid-sixteenth century. No mention of having first to catch your hare in any edition consulted! Why, then, the attribution?

TO ROAST A HARE

Take your hare when it is cased, and make a pudding. Take a quarter of a pound of sewet, and as much crumbs of bread, a little parsley shredded fine, and about as much thyme as will ly on a sixpence, when shred. An anchovy shred small, a very little pepper and salt, some nutmeg, two eggs, and a little lemon-peel.

Mix all these together, and put it into the hare. Sew up the belly, spit it, and lay it to the fire, which must be a very good one.

Your dripping-pan must be very clean and nice. Put in two quarts of milk and a half a pound of butter into the pan. Keep basting it all the time it is roasting, with the butter and milk, till the whole is used, and your hare will be enough.

You may mix the liver in the pudding if you like it. You must first parboil it, and then chop it fine.

For a sauce for your hare: make a good gravy, thickened with a little piece of butter rolled in flour, and pour it into your dish. You may leave the butter out, if you don't like it, and have some currant jelly warmed in a cup, or red wine and sugar boiled to a syrup. Done thus: take half a pint of red wine, a quarter of a pound of sugar, and set over a slow fire to simmer for about a quarter of an hour. You may do half the quantity, and put it into your sauce-boat or bason.

"I do not pretend to teach professed cooks," Hannah Glasse told her readers, "but my design is to instruct the ignorant and unlearned (which will likewise be of great use in all private families), and in so plain and full a manner, that the most illiterate and ignorant person, who can but read, will know how to do every thing in cookery well." The contradictions of illiteracy and an ability to read passed her by, and she turned immediately to the task of describing her own concept of a well-ordered kitchen and the well-learned art of tending the vast and cavernous fireplace before which her culinary dramas were due to unfold.

"I shall first begin with roast and boiled of all sorts," she stated forthrightly, " and must desire the cook to order her fire according to what she is to dress. If any thing very little or thin, then a pretty little brisk fire, that it may be done quick and nice; if a very large joint, then be sure a good fire be laid to cake. Let it be clear at the bottom; and, when your meat is half-done, move the dripping-pan and spit a little from the fire, and stir up a good brisk fire; for, according to the goodness of your fire, your meat will be done sooner or later."

Her general directions for the treatment of various types of meat, and her descriptions of joints and cuts, were clear and concise, marking a refreshing departure from the convoluted sets of instructions of her predecessors. "If roasting beef, be sure to paper the top, and baste it well all the time it is roasting, and throw a handful of salt on the top," she advised, "but Pork must be well done, or it is apt to surfeit. When you roast a lion [loin],

A late-eighteenth-century kitchen preserved in its original form.

take a sharp pen-knife, and cut the skin across, to make the crackling eat the better. We never make any sauce to it but apple-sauce.''

Open *The Art of Cookery* at any chapter and some intriguing heading will immediately catch the eyes. The random selection of recipes culled from its pages and given below are a short list of favorites from the hundreds set out in Hannah's book. They could have been added to almost indefinitely from a vast store of original and carefully tried out dishes she committed to the press way back in the 1740s. Those used experimentally in the 1970s gained unstinted applause from modern-day gourmets, as they certainly did from their counterparts in Georgian days.

TO FRY EGGS AS ROUND AS BALLS

Having a deep frying-pan, and three pints of clarified butter, heat it as hot as for fritters, and stir it with a stick, till it runs like a whirlpool. Then break an egg into the middle, and turn it round with your stick, till it be as hard as a poached egg. The whirling round of the butter will make it as round as a ball. Then take it up with a slice and put it in a dish before the fire. They will keep hot half an hour, and yet be soft, so you may do as many as you please.

TO MAKE A WELCH RABBIT

Toast the bread on both Sides, then toast the Cheese on one side, lay it on the Toast, and with a hot Iron brown the other side. You may rub it over with Mustard.

TO MAKE A SCOTCH RABBIT

Toast a piece of Bread very nicely on both sides, then butter it. Cut a slice of Cheese about as big as the Bread, toast it on both Sides, and lay it on the Bread.

TO MAKE AN ENGLISH RABBIT

Toast a slice of Bread brown on both Sides, then lay it in a Plate before the Fire. Pour a Glass of Red Wine over it, and let it soak the Wine up. Then cut some cheese very thin, and lay it very thick over the Bread. Put it in a Tin Oven before the Fire, and it will be toasted and brown'd presently. Serve it away hot.

BREAD AND BUTTER PUDDING

Get a penny Loaf, and cut it into thin slices of Bread and Butter as you do for Tea. Butter your Dish as you cut them. Lay slices

The distaff side. Maids a-working in an English country house in the late eighteenth century.

all over the Dish, then strew a few Currants clean washed and picked, then a Row of Bread and Butter, then a few Currants, and so on till all your Bread and Butter is in. Then take a Pint of Milk, beat up four Eggs, a little Salt, half a Nutmeg grated: mix all together with Sugar to your Taste. Pour this over the Bread, and bake it for half an Hour. A Puff-paste under does best.

You may put in two spoonfuls of Rose-Water.

TO POT CHESHIRE CHEESE

Take three pounds of Cheshire Cheese, and put it into a mortar, with half a pound of the best fresh Butter you can get. Pound them together, and in the beating add a Gill of rich Canary Wine and half an ounce of Mace finely beat, then sifted fine like a fine powder.

When all is extremely well mixed, press it hard down in a Gallipot. Cover it with clarified Butter, and keep it cool.

A slice of this exceeds all the Cream-Cheese that can be made.

TO SAVE POTTED BIRDS THAT BEGIN TO BE BAD

I have seen potted Birds, which have come a great way, often smell so bad, that nobody could bear the Smell for the rankness of the Butter. By managing them in the following manner, I have made them as good as ever was eat.

Set a large Sauce-pan of clean Water on the Fire. When it boils, take off the Butter at the Top, then take the Fowls out one by one, throw them into the Sauce-pan of Water half a minute, whip them out, and dry them on a clean Cloth inside and out. So do all till they are quite done. Scald the pot clean. When the Birds are quite cold, season them with Mace, Pepper, and Salt to your mind. Put them close down in the Pot, and pour clarified Butter over them.

TO ICE A GREAT CAKE

Take the whites of twenty-four Eggs, and a pound of double refin'd Sugar beat and sifted fine. Mix both together in a deep earthen Pan, and with a Whisk whisk it well for two or three hours together till it looks white and thick. Then with a bunch of Feathers spread it all over the top and sides of the Cake. Set it at a proper distance before a good clear Fire, and keep turning it continually for fear of its changing colour; but a cool Oven is best, and an hour will harden it.

You may perfume the Icing with what perfume you please.

TO MAKE FAIRY BUTTER

Take the Yolks of two hard Eggs, and beat them in a Marble Mortar with a large Spoonful of Orange-flower water and two Tea Spoonfuls of fine Sugar beat to Powder.

Beat this all together till it is fine Paste, then mix it up with about as much fresh Butter out of the Churn and force it through a fine strainer full of little holes into a Plate. This is a pretty thing to set off a Table at Supper.

EVERLASTING SYLLABUBS

Take five half pints of thick Cream, half a pint of Rhenish wine, half a pint of Sack and the juice of two large Seville Oranges.

Grate in just the yellow rind of three Lemons, and a pound of double-refined Sugar well beat and sifted.

Mix all together with a spoonful of Orange-flower Water. Beat it well together with a whisk half an hour, then with a spoon fill your Glasses. These will keep above a Week, and are better made the day before.

The best way to whip Syllabub is, have a large Chocolate mill, which you must keep on purpose, and a large deep Bowl to mill them in. It is both quicker done and the Froth stronger.

TO MAKE MUFFINS

To a Bushel of Hertfordshire white flour, take a pint and a half of good Ale yeast, from pale Malt, if you can get it, because it is whitest.

Let the Yeast lye in water all night, the next Day pour off the water clear. Make two gallons of water just milk-warm, not to scald your Yeast, and two ounces of Salt. Mix your water, Yeast and Salt well together for about a quarter of an hour; then strain it and mix up your Dough as light as possible, and let it lye in your Trough an hour to rise.

Then with your hand roll it, and pull it into little pieces about as big as a large Walnut. Roll them with your hand like a Ball, lay them on your Table, and as fast as you do them lay a piece of Flannel over them, and be sure to keep your Dough covered with Flannel.

When you have rolled out all your Dough begin to bake the first, and by that time they will be spread out in the right form. Lay them on your Iron, as one side begins to change colour turn the other, and take great care they don't burn, or be too much discoloured, but that you will be a Judge of in two or three makings.

Take care the middle of the Iron is not too hot, as it will be, but then you may put a Brickbat or two in the middle of the Fire to slacken the heat.

When you eat your Muffins, toast them with a Fork crisp on both sides. Then with your Hand pull them open, and they will be like Honeycomb. Lay in as much Butter as you intend to use, then clap them together again and set them by the fire. When you think the Butter is melted turn them that both sides may be Buttered alike. But don't touch them with the Knife, either to spread or to cut them open. If you do they will be as heavy as Lead. Only when they are quite buttered and done, you may cut them cross with a Knife.

TO MAKE HYSTERICAL WATER

Take Betony, Roots of Lovage, Seeds of wild Parsnips, of each two ounces. Roots of single Peony four ounces; of Mystletoe of the Oak three ounces; Myrrh a quarter of an ounce; Castor half an ounce.

Beat all these together and add to them a quarter of a pound of dried Millepedes.

Pour on these three quarts of Mug-wort water, and two quarts of Brandy. Let them stand in a close Vessel eight days, then distil it in a cold Still posted up.

You may draw off nine pints of water and sweeten it to your Taste. Mix all together, and bottle up.

There still lingered the tradition that the cook was primarily responsible for the health and general hygiene of the home, and most cookery books of the period contained hints for the warding off and treatment of a variety of ills and diseases. Mrs. Glasse's monumental work was no exception, and she even went as far as giving directions "To prevent the Infection among horned Cattle." In her home hints she didn't mince words, and after recipes headed "A certain Cure for the Bite of a Mad Dog" and "Receipt against the Plague," she advised her readers:

HOW TO KEEP CLEAR FROM BUGGS

First take out of your Room all Silver and Gold Lace, then set the Chairs about the Room, shut up your Windows and Doors, tack a Blanket over each Window, and before the Chimney, and over the Doors of the Room, set open all Closets and Cupboard doors, all your Draws and Boxes.

Hang the rest of your Bedding on the Chair-backs, lay the Feather-bed on a Table, then set a large broad earthen Pan in the middle of the Room, and in that set a Chaffing-dish that stands on feet, full of Charcoal well lighted.

If your Room is very bad, a pound of rolled Brimstone; if you have only a few, half a pound.

Lay it on the Charcoal and get out of the Room as quick as you possibly can or it will take away your Breath.

Shut your door close, with the Blanket over it, and be sure to set it so as nothing can catch Fire. If you have any India pepper, throw it in with the Brimstone. You must take care to have the door open whilst you lay in the Brimstone, that you may get out as soon as possible. Don't open the Door under six hours, and then you must be very careful how you go in to open Windows; therefore let the Doors stand open an Hour before you open the Windows.

Then brush and sweep your Room very clean, wash it well with boiling Lee, or boiling Water, with a little unslaked Lime in it. Get a pint of Spirit of Turpentine, and an ounce of Camphire; shake all well together, and with a bunch of Feathers wash your bedstead very well, and sprinkle the rest over the Feather-bed and about the Wainscot of the Room.

If you find great swarms about the Room, and some not

dead, do this over again, and you will be quite clear.

Every Spring and Fall, wash your Bedstead with half a pint and you will never have a Bugg; but if you find any come in with new Goods, or Box, &c. only wash your Bedstead, and sprinkle all over your Bedding and Bed, and you will be clear; but be sure to do it as soon as you find one.

If your Room is very bad, it will be well to paint the Room after the Brimstone is burnt in it.

DIRECTIONS TO THE HOUSE-MAID

Always, when you sweep a Room, throw a little wet Sand all over it, and that will gather up all the Flew and Dust. It prevents it from rising, cleans the Boards, and saves the Bedding, Pictures, and all other Furniture from Dust and Dirt.

It appears certain that *The Art of Cookery made Plain and Easy* was a financial success for its author, for it very soon established itself at the head of the eighteenth century best-selling nonfiction charts. A dozen large editions had made their appearance by the time of Hannah's death in 1770, and fresh and newly set editions continued to make their appearance every few years until well into the nineteenth century. In addition, she wrote *The Complete Confectioner; or, The Whole Art of Confectionary made Plain and Easy* (issued undated in 1760); and that same year saw the publication of her *The Servant's Directory; or, House-Keeper's Companion*. Both these latter works passed through several editions within a few years, and all three titles now fetch large sums when early editions change hands. The present-day market value of a complete copy in good condition of the first edition of *The Art of Cookery,* 1747, would be well in excess of $4,000 if the volume was still clothed in a contemporary leather binding. But it is very seldom that this rare little folio is exhibited for sale.

Despite her literary and culinary successes, Mrs. Glasse eventually found herself cited in the list of bankrupts printed in the *London Gazette*. In May, 1754, she appeared as a Covent Garden warehouse keeper unable to meet her financial commitments. She had earlier set up as a dressmaker, with premises in Tavistock Street, Covent Garden, and in the fourth edition of *The Art of Cookery,* 1751, she displayed a large advertisement in which she styled herself "Habit Maker to Her Royal Highness, the Princess of Wales." Something must have gone drastically wrong, but the circumstances which ruined her have not been recorded in any contemporary account. It could well be that her husband, to whom, by law, every penny she earned must be handed over as soon as asked for, was the cause of her distress. We shall never know the truth, for by the mid-1760s she had totally disappeared from view. Only a brief notice in *The Newcastle Courant,* dated September 8, 1770, makes any mention of the woman who had brought the art of cookery within reach of every home. It stated merely that "Mrs. Glasse, sister of Sir Lancelot Allgood, died in London, last week." Her immortality stems from the cook book she left behind, a lasting monument to feminine ingenuity.

Cook's afternoon off. A caricature by G. M. Woodward (1760 to 1809) made for his *Specimens of Domestic Phrensy*, in which he depicts domestic bliss in a late-eighteenth-century kitchen.

D. Chodowiecki del.

A country market in the 1770s.

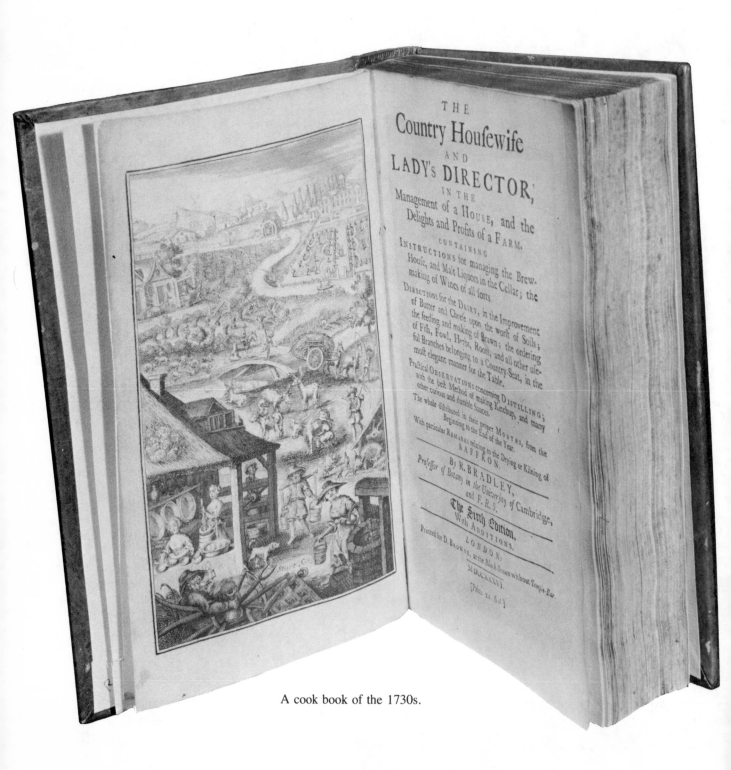

A cook book of the 1730s.

Chapter Six

FLUMMERIES AND SILLABUBS

In the eighteenth century, the name bookseller was synonymous with that of publisher, most of the leading booksellers commissioning and publishing their own titles. Even before the middle years of the century, business houses were being established that continued in existence far into Victoria's reign. Under amalgamated and variegated names, several still trade today.

It was a time of rapid expansion of business activities in many fields, British industry having benefited from the large-scale immigration of foreign artisans and craftsmen from the Continent from the late seventeenth century onward. Paper-making, glass-making, mechanical toy-making, and the establishment of light and heavy industry, due mainly to the remarkable scope of mechanical inventions and the development of ingenious new machinery, led to industrial expansion on a scale never before experienced. The printing and publishing trade benefited in equal degree. Far-seeing men of the caliber of John Newbery (1713 to 1767) soon realized the potential market the newly-created wealth had provided for literature and the arts. Newbery set out to exploit this potential in the specialist field of children's books, establishing himself as one of the first specialist booksellers to concentrate the majority of his resources into one particular aspect of literary production. In this he was eminently successful, and imitators were soon active amongst his rivals-in-trade. By the end of the eighteenth century, specialist territories in publishing expertise had been well defined, some houses catered almost exclusively for readers of religious and theological works, while others concentrated on travel and topography, colored-plate books, sporting books, or novels and romances and poetry and verse. Scientific books and educational works were another prov-

The maid found out. An illustration from *Elementarwerke für die Jugend,* 1774, by J. B. Basedow.

ince; but there was one type of sure-fire best seller which appeared almost without exception in every bookseller's list. Cookery books and works of domestic economy found a prominent place in the advertisements of every imprint. This field was hotly fought over by firms both big and small in much the same manner that the battle continues today.

Like the family Bible, almost every literate home could boast at least one cookery book, and with total sales figures being numbered in several hundred thousand copies every year there was enough profit to ensure every publishing house its share.

The original trickle of books devoted solely to cookery and the kindred arts started to increase rapidly in volume even before the end of the 1750s. Titles such as *The Complete Practical Cook,* 1730, by Charles Carter, who told his readers that his work had been "approved by divers of the Prime Nobility"; *The Modern Cook,* 1733, by Vincent la Chapelle, who, amongst many others, gave a recipe for "a strengthening broth" made up of the well-boiled plucked carcasses of two hundred freshly-caught sparrows; the instructional *House-Keeper's Pocket-Book*, 1733, by Mrs. Sarah Harrison; *The Young Lady's Companion in Cookery and Pastry*, 1734, "collected by a Gentlewoman who formerly kept a Boarding School"; *The Accomplish'd Housewife*, 1745, giving bills of fare for every month of the year, and issued under the imprint of John Newbery, at the Bible and Sun, St. Paul's Church-yard; *English Housewifery*, 1749, by Elizabeth Moxon; these and many others were readily available before the century was half way through.

Undoubtedly, one of the most interesting of the pre-1750 cook books was that issued about 1740 by Edward Kidder. He was a descendant of Richard Kidder (1633 to 1703), one-time bishop of Bath and Wells, but we know little else about this London pastry cook turned schoolmaster.

The frontispiece to his much-sought-after *Receipts of Pastry and Cookery*, depicts the author wearing a full-bottomed wig, the artist, Robert Sheppard, having styled him "Pastry-master." The engraved title page informed his readers that the book was "For the Use of his Scholars," and went on to say that Mr. E. Kidder "teaches at his School in Queen Street near St. Thomas Apostles. On Mondays, Tuesdays & Wednesdays, In the Afternoon. Also On Thursdays, Fridays & Saturdays, in the Afternoon, at

Published c.1740, Edward Kidder's cookery book was produced "regardless of expense," and was engraved throughout.

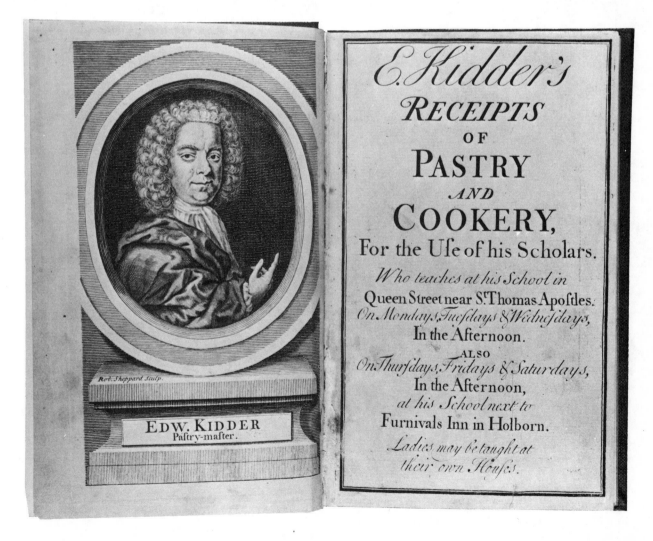

EDW. KIDDER
Pastry-master.

E. Kidder's
RECEIPTS
OF
PASTRY
AND
COOKERY,
For the Use of his Scholars.
Who teaches at his School in
Queen Street near St. Thomas Apostles.
On Mondays, Tuesdays & Wednesdays,
In the Afternoon.
ALSO
On Thursdays, Fridays & Saturdays,
In the Afternoon,
at his School next to
Furnivals Inn in Holborn.
*Ladies may be taught at
their own Houses.*

George Cruikshank

The royal toast. A scene after an eighteenth-century stag-party dinner depicted by George Cruikshank in *The Miser's Daughter*, 1842, by W. H. Ainsworth.

90

his School next to Furnivals Inn in Holborn. Ladies may be taught at their own Houses.'' It appears, therefore, that Kidder, having established himself as a master of pastry-making, was at that time spending every weekday afternoon teaching the ladies of London the art of cookery, with special emphasis on ''All sorts of Paste.'' How many more of these schools of cookery were in existence at that time we shall probably never know, but the fact that Kidder went to the expense and trouble of producing a specially prepared handbook for the use of his lady pupils points to a successful and well-attended business venture. His classes were an early example of adult education, though confined strictly to the culinary field. Fencing schools and dancing classes were other forms of self-education popular at that time, but Kidder's school of cookery is the first we know of.

His cookery book has another claim to fame: Its author had gone to the expense of having the entire work of over fifty octavo-sized leaves engraved throughout. Not only the folding plates of table plans, etc., but also the entire hand-written copperplate text had been carefully engraved before being printed off the plates, each leaf being used on one side only, the verso being left blank. (See illustration, page 89.) His claim to be the inventor of a superior quality of puff pastry is difficult to dispute as no earlier recipe for this useful and ever-popular form of pie and sausage-roll covering

Breakfast at Count Rumfords', by Daniel Chodowiecki, 1774.

Kidder's Receipts.

Blamangoes.

Make your jelly of $\frac{1}{2}$ of harts horn and 2 q.^{rts} of Spring water; run it thro' a napkin, put to it $\frac{1}{2}$ a pound of jordan almonds well beat, mix with it orange flower water, a pint of milk or cream the juice of 2 or 3 lemon^{s} and double refin'd Sugar, let it simmer over the fire and take care least it burn too run it thro' a Sive 2 or 3 times colour it if you please and put it in glasses.

A whipt Sillabub.

Take a pint of cream with a little orange flower water, 2 or 3 ounce^s of fine Sugar, the juice of a lemon, the white of 3 eggs: whisk these up light together and having in your glasses rhennish wine and Sugar and clarret & Sugar, lay on the froth w.th a Spoon heap'd up as high as you can.

A Sack Posset.

Take 14 eggs, leave out half of the whites & beat them with a quarter of a pound of white sugar oringoe roots slic'd very then with a quarter of a pint of Sack, mix it well together, Set it on the fire and keep Stirring it all one way: when it is scalding hott let another whilst you stirr it, pour into it q.^{rt} of cream boiling hot with a grated nutmeg boil'd in it: Then take it off the fire, clap a hot pye plate on it and let it Stand a quarter of an hour.

Orange Butter

Take ye yolks of 5 hard eggs, a pound of butter, a little fine Sugar & a spoonfull of orange flower water & work it thro' a Sive Almond & Pistachia butter is made ye same way only blanch & pound them.

L.1.

Recipes in *Receipts of Pastry and Cookery*, c.1740, by Edward Kidder.

has yet been discovered, although the name itself was in use as early as the first quarter of the seventeenth century. He is also associated with puff-paste mince pies, though these bear no resemblance to the Christmastime temptations we find a place for today.

PUFF PASTE

Lay down a pound of flower; break into it 2 ounces of butter & 2 eggs: then make it into Paste with cold water; then work the other part of the pound of butter to the stiffness of your paste; then roul out your paste into a Square Sheet. Stick it all over with bitts of butter; flower it, and roul it up like a collar, double it up at both ends that they may meet in ye middle. Roul it out again as aforesaid, till all the pound of butter is in.

MINC'D PYES

Shred a pound of neat's tongue parboil'd with two pound of beef Suet, 5 Pippins & a green Lemon Peel: Season it with an Ounce of Sweet Spice, a pound of Sugar, 2 pound of Currants, ½ a pint of Sack, a little Orange flower water, the juice of 3 Lemons, a quarter of a pound of Citron Lemon and Orange peel.

Mix these together and fill your pyes.

Sweet Spice is Cloves, Mace, Nutmeg, Cinnamon, Sugar & Salt.

TO BOYLE A CODS-HEAD

Set a kettle on the fire with water, vinegar & Salt, a faggot of Sweetherbs & an Onion or two.

When the liquor boyls, put in the head on a fish bottom, and in the boyling put in cold water & vinegar.

When it is boyl'd take it up & put it in a dish that fits your fish bottom.

For the Sauce take gravy & clarret boyl'd up with a faggot of Sweet-herbs & an Onion; 2 or 3 anchovys drawn up with 2 pound of butter, a pint of Shrimps, oysters, ye meat of a Lobster shred fine.

Then put the Sauce in Silver or China Basons. Stick small toast on the head, lay on and about it the Spaune, milt & liver, garnish it with fry'd Parsley, Sliced Lemon, Barberries & horse-radish, and fryed fish.

By the time this latter dish was prepared for the table the original cod's head seems to have disappeared completely from view, but, nothing daunted, Kidder hurries his student readers into the art of sweet and pudding making, the lessons they had learned in his school of cookery apparently supplying the many deficiencies of his text:

Baker.

Kneading dough for a wood-fired oven. An illustration from *The Book of English Trades*, 1824.

BLAMANGOES

Make your jelly of ½ of harts horn and 2 quarts of Spring water. Run it through a napkin. Put to it ½ a pound of jordan almonds well beat. Mix it with orange flower water, a pint of milk or cream, the juice of 2 or 3 lemons, and double refin'd sugar.

Let it simmer over the fire and take care lest it burn. Run it thro' a Sive 2 or 3 times.

Colour it as you please and put it in glasses.

A WHIPT SILLABUB

Take a pint of cream with a little orange flower water, 2 or 3 ounces of fine Sugar, the juice of a lemon, the white of 3 eggs.

Whisk these up light together, and having in your glasses Rhennish wine and Sugar, and clarret and Sugar, lay on the froth with a Spoon heaped up as high as you can.

There we must leave Mr. Edward Kidder as he hovers helpfully over his class of long-sleeved and hoop-petticoated maids and housewives back in the days of George II. As the lessons in his school of cookery in St. Martin's le Grand finished for the day, the blancmanges and sillabubs in a rainbow of contrasting colors having been judged and tasted and praised and tutted over, one sees him clamping his tricorn hat firmly on his powdered wig before locking the doors and departing for home. Whether the little pastry master minced off to bachelor lodgings, or strode purposefully to a well-found home and the appetizing smell of dinner cooked by his ever-loving wife, is a matter for hopeful speculation.

Meanwhile, publishers were now exploring the highways and by-ways of other feminine interests, and *A Present for a Servant-Maid; or, The Sure Means of Gaining Love and Esteem,* 1743, was priced at only "one Shilling, or 25 for a Guinea to those who give them away." The title headings conjure up a fascinating picture of the dramas and intimacies enacted below stairs, the whole book being "calculated for making both Mistress and the Maid happy." They deserve to be listed in full:

Observance	Washing Victuals
Avoiding sloth	Quarrels with Fellow Servants
Sluttishness	Behaviour to the Sick
Staying on Errands	Hearing things against a Master or Mistress
Telling Family Affairs	Being too free with Men-Servants
Secrets among Fellow-Servants	Conduct towards Apprentices
Entering into their Quarrels	Mispending Time
Tale-bearing	Publick Shows
Being an Eye-Servant	Vails
Carelessness of Children	Giving Advice too freely
Of Fire, Candle, Thieves	Giving Saucy Answers
New Acquaintances	Liquorishness
Fortune-Tellers	Apeing the Fashion
Bringing in Chair-women	Dishonesty

This little booklet was one of the first to exploit the potential market for cheaply produced literature aimed at satisfying the romantic needs, in strictly didactic fashion, of the hundreds of thousands of "damp souls of housemaids sprouting despondently at area gates." Female servants not so well endowed and languishing on the shelf, could at least hopefully sigh over the carnal temptations likely to be professionally offered by a married master while wistfully rehearsing the techniques needed to ward off the embraces of employers who remained single. Then on to the next chapter, where the master's son and a queue of gentleman lodgers were patiently

Britain's first successful restaurateur who made a fortune by employing only big-busted pretty waitresses in her chain of London coffee houses and chop houses. Three of her most famous were in Queen's-head Passage, Paternoster Row, and Newgate Street, London, in the mid-1750s.

DOLLY OF THE CHOP HOUSE.

waiting their turn to offer the joys of backstairs ruin to those with imagination enough to let them in.

Adam's Luxury, and Eve's Cookery; or, The Kitchen-Garden Display'd, 1744, was advertised as being "designed for the Use of all who would live Cheap, and preserve their Health to old Age." It came near to being one of the first strictly vegetarian cook books, but the fact that meat gravies were used in some of the recipes makes it obvious that the unknown author's intention was to cheapen his recipes by keeping the use of the more expensive meat, fish, and fowl to the minimum. "Cheap, healthful, and palatable Dishes" were given in profusion, with footnotes extolling the physical virtues of every herb and root.

Most cookery books of the period contained at least one or two "palatable dishes" which, if the directions were carefully followed, would allow a sitting of at least half a dozen hungry eaters to be well and adequately filled for less than an old-fashioned penny apiece. Mrs. Glasse's *Art of Cookery* contained several, of which "lights and loaves" pudding is one of the best:

A kitchen in the 1770s, depicted by the Polish painter and engraver Daniel Chodowiecki (1726 to 1801).

ENGLISH JEWS PUDDING

Take a calf's lights, boil them, chop them fine, and the crumb of a twopenny loaf softened in the liquor the lights were boiled in.

Mix them well together in a pan; take about half a pound of kidney fat of a lion of veal or mutton that is roasted, or beef. If you have none, take suet. If you can get none, melt a little butter, and mix in.

Fry four or five onions, cut small, and fried in dripping, not brown, only soft, with a very little winter savoury and thyme, a little lemon-peel shred fine. Season with all-spice, pepper and salt to your palate. Break in two eggs; mix all well together, and have ready some sheep's guts nicely cleaned, and fill them, and fry them in dripping.

This is a very good dish, and a fine thing for poor people, because all sorts of lights are good, and will do—as hogs, sheep's, and bullock's; but calf's are best. A handful of parsley

Eighteenth- and early-nine-teenth-century cook books in the author's collection.

Engraved frontispiece to *The Compleat Housewife*, by Elizabeth Smith, a work first published in 1727.

boiled, and chopped fine, is very good, mixed with the meat. Poor people may, instead of the fat above, mix the fat the onions were fried in, and they will be very good.

This "excellent dish," as Mrs. Glasse dscribed it, "feeds six or seven people for the expense of sixpence"; but despite its name, its Gentile origin is immediately betrayed by the advice that "hog's lights" might well be substituted if calf's lights cannot be procured.

In complete contrast, Elizabeth Smith's *The Complete Housewife; or, Accomplish'd Gentlewoman's Companion,* 1727, was still passing through new and enlarged editions. This was the work which gave the following "economical" recipe for:

ASPARAGUS SOOP

Take twelve pounds of lean beef, cut in slices; then put a quarter of a pound of butter in a stew pan over the fire, and put your beef in.

Let it boil up quick till it begins to brown; then put in a pint of brown ale, and a gallon of water, and cover it close. Let it stew gently for an hour and a half. Put in what spice you like in the stewing, and strain off the liquor, and scum off all the fat. Then put in some vermicelly, and some sallery Wash'd and cut small, half a hundred of Asparagus cut small, and palates boiled tender and cut. Put all these in and let them boil gently till tender.

Just as 'tis going up, fry a handful of spinage in butter, and throw in a French roll.

Exactly how many this "economical" recipe, with its "twelve pounds of lean beef," and its "half a hundred of Asparagus" was supposed to feed is not made clear by the author. There must have been a brisk demand for the work, for the eighth edition, "with very large Additions; not in any of the former Impressions," made its appearance in 1737 (see illustration, page 99), and the eighteenth edition in 1773.

Elizabeth Smith's cook book maintained a large sale, but Hannah Glasse's nearest rival in contemporary popularity was probably Elizabeth Raffald (1733 to 1781), although the book by which she is remembered did not make its appearance until the year before Hannah's death *The Experienced English House-Keeper, for the Use and Ease of Ladies, House-Keepers, Cooks, &c. Wrote Purely from Practice,* 1769, is a remarkable book in many ways, not least in that the London publisher Robert Baldwin, of Paternoster Row, is reputed to have paid her £1,400 for the copyright in 1773, some four years after the book's first appearance under its original Manchester imprint.

Like Mrs. Glasse, Elizabeth's obituary occupies just over a column in *The Dictionary of National Biography* (neither Mrs. Isabella Beeton nor her husband were included in these august pages), and we are indebted to C. W. Sutton for much that we know of her.

M^{RS} RAFFALD.

Hampton Prince & Cattles, York.

Mrs. Elizabeth Raffald; an engraving used as a portrait-frontispiece to the 1805 edition of *The Experienced English House-Keeper*.

Elizabeth's father was Joshua Whittaker, and she was born in Doncaster, Yorkshire, in 1733, being baptized there on July 8 of that year. At the age of fifteen she entered into service, and for the next fifteen years—from 1748 to 1763—she acted first as kitchen maid, then parlor maid, and finally housekeeper to a number of local families. Her most rewarding and important post was as housekeeper to Lady Elizabeth Warburton, at Arley Hall, Cheshire. A few years after taking up her post, she married the head

THE
Experienced Englifh Houfe-Keeper.

Elizh CHAP. I. *Raffald*

Obfervations on SOUPS.

WHEN you make any Kind of Soups, particularly Portable, Vermicelli, or brown Gravy Soup, or any other that have Roots or Herbs in, always obferve to lay your Meat in the Bottom of your Pan, with a good lump of Butter; cut the Herbs and Roots fmall, lay them over your Meat, cover it clofe, fet it over a very flow Fire, it will draw all the Virtue out of the Roots or Herbs, and turns it to a good Gravy, and gives the Soup a very different flavour from putting Water in at the firft: When your Gravy is almoft dried up fill your Pan with Water, when it begins to boil take off the Fat, and follow the Directions of your Receipt for what Sort of Soup you are making: When you make old Peafe Soup, take foft Water, for green Peafe, hard is the beft, it keeps the Peafe a better Colour: When you make any white Soup, don't put in Cream 'till you

A

To prevent pirated editions, Mrs. Elizabeth Raffald signed every copy of the first edition of her cook book on the first page of text.

gardener of Arley Hall, John Raffald, by whom, over a period of eighteen years, she gave birth to no less than sixteen daughters. How many of these children survived to womanhood is not known: nothing further is heard of them in any of her books or papers.

Soon after their marriage in 1763, the couple moved to Manchester, where Raffald attempted to set up business as a florist and market gardener. But his fondness for "ardent spirits" and his convivial good nature meant that business was neglected for the pleasures of the gin shop and ale house.

Mrs. Raffald was, however, made of much sterner stuff, and despite her almost constant pregnancies, she set about making her mark in the business world of Manchester. She conceived the idea of setting up a registry office for domestic servants, the first the town had known, and ran this side by side with her own cooked meat and confectioner's shop in Fennel Street. Within twelve months of moving to Manchester she was advertising in the local papers to announce her expansion of business:

Just arrived, and now selling wholesale and retail, at Mrs. Raffald's, in Fennel Street, fine Canterbury and Derbyshire Brawn whole. Half a quarter collars of the Canterbury-grown at 16d the pound, and those of Derbyshire, 14d the pound.

As several of Mrs. Raffald's friends in the country have mistook her Terms and Designs of her Register Office, she begs leave to inform them, that she supplies Families with Servants, for any place, at ONE shilling each.

Masters and servants, therefore, at any Distance, may be supplied on the shortest notice, by directing (Post Paid) to Mrs. Raffald at the REGIS-TER OFFICE in Fennel Street, Manchester.

She also continues to supply Families with made dishes, cold suppers, &c., as usual.

A year later Mrs. Raffald's shop in Fennel Street had expanded its scope considerably, and her 1765 advertisements advised potential customers that she could now offer them: "Yorkshire Hams, Tongues, Newcastle salmon, Potted Meats, portable soup, Sweetmeats, pickles and all kinds of made dishes. Likewise a large quantity of Lemon Preserve, Mushrooms and Mushroom Ketchup, is now ready for sale." Another advertisement informed the public at large that "the Register Office continues as usual. Masters and Mistresses may be provided with Servants, and servants who want places can apply. N.B. No servant need apply without they can have a character from the Persons they have served."

Business was so good that, in 1766, she outgrew her Fennel Street premises and moved to a larger shop in Exchange Alley, near the Bull's Head, in the Market Place, Manchester. "Here can be seen a large assortment of fresh Confectionery goods, as good and as cheap as in London. There may be had Creams, Possets, Jellies, Flummery, Lemon Cheese Cakes, best boiled Tripe, and pickled Walnuts. Also Yorkshire Hams, Tongues, Brawn, Newcastle salmon, Sturgeons, all sorts of pickles, and Ketchups of many kinds. Coffee, Tea and Chocolate of the finest sorts, and the best portable soup for Travellers. Mrs. Raffald returns thanks for the great Encouragement she meets with in making Bride and Christening Cakes, and those who are pleased to favour her with their commands, may depend on being served with such cakes as shall not be exceeded."

Her enterprise paid her large dividends, and she invested some of the money (that by rights her husband could instantly have claimed) in starting *Prescott's Manchester Journal*, which commenced publication on March 23, 1771. But it was in *The Manchester Mercury and Harrap's General Advertiser*, that the first preliminary announcement of the book which was eventually to make her nationally famous made its appearance on April 4, 1769:

Ready for the Press, and speedily will be published, an entirely new work, wrote for the use and care of Ladies, Housekeepers, Cooks, &c., entitled *The Experienced English House-Keeper*, by Elizabeth Raffald, wrote purely from practice and dedicated to the Lady Elizabeth Warburton whom the Author lately served, consisting of nearly 800 Original Receipts, most of which never before appeared in print. . . .

To prevent pirated editions being too readily accepted as genuine, she stated that each and every copy of the first edition would be signed across the top of the first page of text; and all copies which have survived the rigors of tens of thousands of kitchen consultations display to this day Elizabeth Raffald's signature.

Despite this precaution, the immense popularity her cookery book achieved tempted unscrupulous publishing houses into issuing pirated editions. From 1769 to 1810 a total of fifteen authorized editions were issued, but during this same period no less than twenty-five pirated editions also appeared. For these unauthorized printings neither the author nor her descendants received a cent in royalties.

In the preface to her work, Elizabeth Raffald made clear that she was by no means certain that her collection of recipes would be well received:

> When I reflect upon the Number of Books already in print upon this Subject, and with what Contempt they are read, I cannot but be apprehensive that this may meet the same Fate, from some who will censure it before they either see it or try its Value. . . . As I can faithfully assure my Friends, that they are truly wrote from my own Experience, and not borrowed from any other Author, nor glossed over with hard Names or Words of high Stile, but wrote in my own plain Language . . . and every Sheet carefully perused as it came from the Press, having an Opportunity of having it printed by a Neighbour, whom I can rely on doing it the strictest Justice, without the least Alteration.

She went on to assure her readers that "it has been my chiefest Care to write in as plain a Style as possible, so as to be understood by the weakest Capacity." This was no idle boast for her many recipes are couched in language that almost any cook or kitchen maid could readily understand, and are a refreshing change from the turgidity of many of her earlier rivals in the same field. She was unable to resist puffing the cakes and confectionary offered for sale in her shop near the Exchange, Manchester, and then went on to detail her own credentials:

> I am not afraid of being called extravagant, if my Reader does not think I have erred on the frugal Hand.
>
> I have made it my Study to please both the Eye and the Palate, without using pernicious Things for the sake of Beauty.
>
> And though I have given some of my Dishes French Names, as they are only known by those Names, yet they will not be found very Expensive, nor add Compositions but as plain as the Nature of the Dish will admit of.
>
> The Receipts for the Confectionary, are such as I daily sell in my own Shop, which any Lady may examine at pleasure, as I still continue my best Endeavours to give Satisfaction to all who are pleased to favour me with their Custom.
>
> It may be necessary to inform my Readers, that I have spent fifteen Years in great and worthy Families, in the Capacity of a House-keeper, and had the Opportunity of travelling with them; but finding the common Servants generally so ignorant in dressing Meat, and a good Cook so hard to be met with, put me upon studying the Art of Cookery more than perhaps I otherwise should have done; always endeavouring to join economy with Neatness and Elegance, being sensible that valuable Qualities these are in a House-keeper or Cook; for of what use is their Skill, if they put their Master or Lady to an immoderate Expense in dressing a Dinner for a small Company, when at the same Time a prudent Manager would have dressed twice the Number of Dishes, for a much greater Company, at half the Cost.

I have given no Directions for Cullis, as I have found by Experience, that Lemon Pickle and Browning answers both for Beauty and Taste (at a trifling Expense) better than Cullis, which is extravagant. . . .

As a businesswoman she hated waste or extravagance of any kind, and later editions of *The Experienced English House-Keeper* carried a folding copperplate engraving of a triple-fired series of stoves made to her own design. Its legend told her readers that "The plate is the design of three stove-fires for the kitchen, that will burn coals or embers instead of charcoal, (which I have always found expensive, as well as pernicious to the cooks). . . ."

Most of her recipes sound positively mouth-watering, but her sweets and confectionary were obviously her delight, as were her numerous carefully contrived meat dishes. Many of these, when cold, were displayed for sale in her shop. The one secret she did *not* reveal was the recipe for her famous brawn, a delicacy she sold sliced by the pound, and which had customers throughout the length and breadth of Lancashire.

À LA-MODE BEEF

Take the bone out of Rump of Beef, lard the top with Bacon, then make a Force-meat of four Ounces of Marrow, two Heads of Garlick, the Crumbs of a Penny Loaf, a few sweet Herbs chopped small, Nutmeg, Pepper and Salt to your Taste, and the Yolks of four Eggs well beat.

Mix it up, and stuff your Beef where the Bone came out, and in several Places in the lean part.

Skewer it round and bind it about with a Fillet.

Put it in a Pot with a Pint of Red Wine, and tie it down with strong Paper; bake it in the Oven for three Hours. When it comes out, if you want to eat it hot, skim the Fat off the Gravy, and add half an Ounce of Morels, a Spoonful of pickled Mushrooms, thicken it with Flour and Butter.

Dish up your Beef and pour on the Gravy. Lay round it Force-meat Balls, and send it up.

CALF'S-FOOT PUDDING

Boil a Gang of Calf's-Feet, take the Meat from the Bones, and chop it exceeding fine. Put to it the Crumbs of a Penny Loaf [*a whole Penny Loaf crumbled*], a Pound of Beef Suet shred very small, half a Pint of Cream, eight Eggs, a Pound of Currants well cleaned, four Ounces of Citron cut small, two Ounces of candied Orange cut like Straws, a large Nutmeg grated, and a large Glass of Brandy.

Mix them very well together. Butter your Cloth, and dust it with Flour. Tie it close up, boil it three Hours.

When you take the Pudding up, it is best to put it in a

Bowl that will just hold it, and let it stand a quarter of an Hour before you turn it out. Lay your Dish upon the Top of the Bason, and turn it out upside down.

TO MAKE FLUMMERY

Put one Ounce of bitter, and one of sweet Almonds into a Bason. Pour over them some boiling Water to make the Skins come off, which is called Blanching. Strip off the Skins, and throw the Kernels into cold Water. Then take them out and beat them in a Marble Mortar, with a little Rose Water to keep them from Oiling. When they are beat, put them into a Pint of Calf's Foot Stock; set it over the Fire, and sweeten it to your Taste with Loaf Sugar.

As soon as it boils strain it thro' a Piece of Muslin or Gawz. When a little cold put it into a Pint of thick Cream, and keep stirring it often 'till it grows thick and cold. Wet your Moulds with cold Water, and pour in the Flummery. Let it stand five to six Hours at least before you turn them out. If you make the Flummery stiff, and wet the Moulds, it will turn out without putting it into warm Water, for the Water takes off the Figures of the Mould, and makes the Flummery look dull.

TO MAKE A SYLLABUB UNDER THE COW

Put a bottle of strong Beer, and a Pint of Cyder into a Punch Bowl, and grate in a small Nutmeg. Sweeten it to your Taste, then milk as much Milk from the Cow as will make a strong Froth, and the Ale look clear.

Let it stand an Hour, then strew over it a few Currants, well washed, picked, and plumped before the Fire. Then send it to Table.

TO MAKE A DRUNKEN LOAF

Take a French Roll hot out of the Oven, rasp it, and pour a Pint of Red Wine upon it. Cover it close up for half an Hour.

Boil one Ounce of Mackarony in Water, 'till it is soft, and lay it upon a Sieve to drain. Then put the size of a Walnut of Butter into it, and as much thick Cream as it will take. Then scrape in six Ounces of Pumasant Cheese [Parmesan cheese], shake it about in your Tossing Pan, with the Mackarony 'till it be like a fine Custard. Then pour it hot upon your Loaf; brown it with a Salamander,* and serve it up.

It is a pretty Dish for Supper.

*"Brown it with a Salamander" would not have puzzled any of her contemporary readers, the expression being derived from the superstition that the large lizard of that name was able to endure and

During the period when her cookery book was being constantly consulted in the kitchens of Britain, Mrs. Raffald's enterprise and hard work not only increased the circulation of her local chain of newspapers but also vastly multiplied the turnover of her cooked-meat shops in the Manchester district. How she achieved all this during an almost constant series of pregnancies is difficult to comprehend. Almost every year she dutifully bore her well-oiled husband yet another offspring, and with monotonous regularity the squawking child held up for inspection turned out to be another daughter. The sixteenth of these little girls proved to be the last, for within a few days of its birth the hard-working and, one imagines, well nigh worn out Elizabeth Raffald relapsed into a coma and died.

The cause of death was almost certainly child-bed fever, puerperal fever as we know it on the rare occasions when a case occurs today. Paradoxically, with a wealth of experience behind her, Elizabeth had just completed a book on the arts of midwifery, a discipline where antiseptic precautions are all important. Rudimentary cleanliness on the part of those

Domestic bliss in a well-stocked kitchen of the 1770s. An engraving by Daniel Chodowiecki (1726 to 1801), for *Elementarwerke für die Jugend,* by J. B. Basedow.

positively enjoy scampering about in the embers of a charcoal fire and sucking in the flame from brightly burning kindling wood. Later, the term came to be applied to any article, such as asbestos, capable of withstanding great heat. But to the housewife, it meant a circular iron plate, heated to redness, that was then placed over a pie or pudding to brown the crust. The electric or gas grill is our modern counterpart.

delivering her sixteenth child might well have saved her; instead the disease took its inevitable course. Mrs. Raffald died on April 9, 1781, at the age of forty-eight. She was buried at Stockport parish church, where her headstone can still be seen today. Her husband, supported no doubt in convivial fashion by a team of obedient daughters, lived on until 1809. What happened to the shops and newspapers and other financial interests so painstakingly built up by his indefatigable spouse is a matter for conjecture. The spirit Elizabeth Raffald displayed in overcoming the manifold injustices suffered by any woman seeking a degree of emancipation in the masculine environment of the eighteenth century, and the energy and character she showed in every enterprise she fostered, deserve a greater recognition than she has so far been accorded. Her only lasting monument has been her cookery book; she still awaits her biographer.

What else happened in the culinary field in 1769, the year that saw the first appearance of *The Experienced English House-Keeper?* It was certainly a vintage year for cookery books, several important titles jostling for recognition. *The Art of Cookery and Pastry Made Easy and Familiar,* 1769, by John Skeat, was described by the author as having been written by one who was "a professional cook, in much demand for banquets, feasts, and routs, in Norwich and King's Lynn"; while *The Lady's, Housewife's, and Cook-Maid's Assistant,* 1769, by E(lizabeth) Taylor, of Berwick-upon-Tweed, noted, in passing, that her husband ran a bookselling business. Probably the most important title to appear in England that year, other than Mrs. Raffald's classical work, was *The Professed Cook; or, The Modern Art of Cookery, Pastry, and Confectionary,* 1769, a work which admitted that it was "translated from *Les Soupers de la Cour,*" with what it called "the Addition of the best Receipts which have ever appear'd in the French Language." It had been adapted "to the London Markets by the Editor, who has been many years Clerk of the Kitchen in some of the first Families of the Kingdom." In fact, the book had been taken from the original French edition of 1755, written by Menon, the author of many Continental cookery books. Later editions of the English version of this work gave the translator's name as B. Clermont.

The rest of the eighteenth century was a reiteration, with many intriguing and expensive and most elusive titles, of much that had appeared before in various guises. *The Court and Country Confectioner; or, The House-Keeper's Guide,* 1770, by a Spanish gentleman we know only as "Borella" (and that not until much later editions); and *The New London and Country Cook; or, The Whole Art of Cookery Displayed in the Newest and Most Fashionable Taste,* 1770, by Caroline Butler, who told her readers that she had "practised Cookery in all its various Branches, and in the best Families, upwards of Thirty Years":

> Her plain Directions you may see,
> To roast, boil, fry, or fricassee:
> To make, with Nicety and Ease,
> What will the daintiest Palate please:
> That when each sav'ry Dish is dress'd,
> You'll be allow'd a Cook Profess'd.

These are only two examples that could be multiplied at will if the scope of this work allowed space for a comprehensive bibliography of titles.

The following text appears within the illustration:

GROCERY SWEETMEATS HAMS
TONGUES STARCH PLUMBS FIGS
VERMICELLI TRIPE BARLEY PICKLES
MUSTARD SOAP HOGS PUDDINGS &
SOLD HERE BY PETER FIGG

SUGAR LOAF

Cattle Life
Insurance
Cow Lane
Smithfield

A Terrible
Scene that
the Grocers Wife
at Norwich
or M.rs Figgs bottom
exposed owing to
the bottom of
M.r Figgs Whiskey
breaking through

Ann Peckham's *The Complete English Cook; or, Prudent Housewife,* which first appeared under a Leeds imprint in 1767, was still making its bow in the bookshops, seemingly secure in its boast that:

> In cooking Fowl, or Flesh, or Fish,
> Or any nice, or dainty Dish,
> With Care peruse this useful Book,
> 'Twill make you soon a perfect Cook.

The London Cook, 1762, by William Gelleroy, was the first book of cookery, as Arnold Oxford remarks in his *English Cookery Books,* 1913, to contain only "a modest preface." *The British Housewife,* 1770, by Martha Bradley "late of Bath," contained a chapter of specific cures, in which powdered earthworms are strongly recommended to combat the ague; while Mrs. Maciver, of Edinborough, brought out her *Cookery and Pastry,* 1773, a work still in print as late as 1800.

The grocer's wife's bottom exposed. A scene from the caricaturist G. M. Woodward's *Specimens of Domestic Phrensy* depicting a Norwich grocer's shop in the late eighteenth century.

Printed for & sold by Carington Bowles.

Nº 69 in St Pauls Church Yard London.

The Hoſt and his Gueſts.

Shopping in the 1780s.

The last few years of the eighteenth century saw new cookery book titles being issued every few months. *The London Art of Cookery,* 1783, by John Farley, ''principal cook at the London Tavern,'' made its first appearance, with the ninth edition being published before the turn of the century. Farley contributed much to the popularity of the London Tavern as an eating house, an inn whose generous helpings attracted customers from far and wide. A glance at his recipe for a Christmas Pie reveals why those with trencherman appetites sometimes had the greatest difficulty in heaving themselves upright at the end of a Farley, a seven-course dinner washed down with a gallon or two of his equally famous London Malt Beer.

YORKSHIRE CHRISTMAS PIE

Having made a good standing crust, with the wall and bottom very thick, take and bone a turkey, a goose, a fowl, a partridge, and a pigeon. Season them well, and take half an ounce of mace, the same quantity of nutmegs, a quarter of an ounce of cloves, and half an ounce of black pepper, all beat fine together.

Then add two large spoonfuls of salt; mix all well together.

Open the fowls all down the back, and bone, first the pigeon, then the partridge, and cover them. Then proceed in the same manner with the fowl, goose, turkey, which must be large.

Season them all well, and then lay them in the crust, so that it may look only like a whole turkey.

Then have a hare ready cased, and wiped with a clean cloth. Disjoint the hare in pieces, season it, and lay it as close as you can on one side; and on the other side put woodcocks, moor-game, and whatsoever sort of wild fowl you can get. Season them well and lay them close. Put at least four pounds of butter into the pie, and then lay on your lid, which must be very thick. Let it be well baked, in a very hot oven. It will take four hours of baking at the least.

This crust will take a bushel of flour.

Flour by the bushel to encase a copse full of game! Who could possibly demolish such a mountain of calories?

A picture is conjured of the candle-lit scene in one of the smoke-filled private rooms in the upper floors of the London Tavern in its heyday in the 1790s. The annual pre-Christmas supper party of a club of tried and trusted friends clamors with genial goodwill and assured expectancy as the massive pie makes its entrance. It is carried to the crowded table, hot from the oven and streaming with mouth-watering aromas, on a double-handled trencher board by two burly London potmen, before being set reverently in front of the elected chairman. Red-faced and beaming with the pleasures to come, he heads the table at a Pickwickian-style repast that all know will continue well into the December night. The log fire crackles in the moment's comparative quiet as the inch-thick crust is ceremoniously pierced and steam billows high to the ceiling of the inn. Then the cheers and laughter and volume of appreciative hubbub as the pewter plates are piled high, the jugs of gravy circulate, and the clinked tankards swill the board with the froth of this long-awaited evening.

For the rapidly mellowing guests, there is the added comfort of the thought of the many courses yet to come. A welcome starter of the dimensions of John Farley's famous Christmas pie, consumed with relish and washed down with London ale, served only to line and prepare the stomach for the sterner tasks ahead.

OYSTER SOUP

Take what quantity may be wanted of fish-stock, which must be made in this manner:

Take a pound of skate, four or five flounders, and two big eels. Cut them into pieces and put to them as much water as will cover them. Season with mace, an onion stuck with cloves, a head of celery, two parsley roots sliced, some pepper and salt, and a bunch of sweet herbs.

Cover them down close, and let them simmer an hour and a half, and then strain off the liquor for use.

Being thus provided with your fish-stock, take what quantity of it you want.

Then take two quarts of oysters bearded, and beat them in a mortar with the yolks of ten eggs boiled hard. Put them to the fish-stock, and set it over the fire. Season it with pepper and salt, and grated nutmeg, and when it boils, put in the eggs and oysters. Let it boil till it be of a good thickness, and like fine cream.

Oysters were one of the cheapest dishes it was possible to procure in the latter half of the eighteenth century, and as late as 1837 Charles Dickens was able to say that "poverty and oysters always seem to go together." And Mrs. Maria Rundell told her readers in 1808 that one had only to procure a peck or two and they could be fattened in your own kitchen or backyard:

TO FEED OYSTERS

Put them into water, and wash them with a birch besom until quite clean. Then lay them downwards into a pan, sprinkle them with flour or oatmeal and salt, and cover with water. Do the same every day and they will soon fatten. The water should be pretty salt.

N.B. A peck of the best native oysters may be purchased out of the boats at Billingsgate for nine shillings; there are about 436 in a peck, about four a penny. The common oysters are from two shillings to half a crown a peck.

Fattening oysters became a pastime, though how many housewives had a few score plumping themselves in the baby's bath ready for a special

Drawn & Etch.d by Theodore Lane.   Pub.d by Geo Hunt, 16. Tavistock Street, Covent Garden.   Eng.d by Geo Hunt.

NEW YEARS MORNING,
The OLD ONE OUT and The NEW ONE COMEING IN

dinner-party, or as the main ingredient in a nourishing soup in the style of John Farley's recipe, is a matter for surmise. The number of late-eighteenth-century and early-nineteenth-century engravings and lithographs depicting London street scenes in which colorful itinerant oyster-sellers played a prominent role is an indication of the popularity of this modern luxury. They were readily available at prices most families could then afford, until the gradual pollution of the oyster beds and the well-publicized cases of food poisoning that became increasingly frequent blighted the market and finally put an almost complete stop to the trade. Their import into London from clear and unsullied beds far distant from the capital increased their price to an extent that placed them far beyond the reach of the vast mass of the population. This remains true today.

Farley's work passed through nine editions before the turn of the century. It was a century whose final decade saw the publication of a

The night before the morning after. A Dickensian New Year's celebration in the 1830s. Hot punch and broiled bones, with ladles and toothpicks provided.

diversity of titles embracing almost every aspect of culinary practice and domestic cookery.

Such was the ever increasing popularity of the cookery book that every conceivable aspect of the pleasures of the table and domestic and household management was explored by writers and nonwriters of both sexes anxious to cash in on the public demand. The eccentric Dr. John Trusler (1735 to 1820), ordained priest turned medico and lately publisher as well, produced one of the earliest good food guides and rules of table manners to appear on the juvenile market. *The Honours of the Table; or, Rules for Behavior During Meals; with the Whole Art of Carving, Illustrated with a Variety of Cuts,* 1788 (the last part of the title apparently being an unconcious pun), informed the public that the book was for "the use of young people." The author undertook to instruct them in "directions for going to Market, and the method of distinguishing good Provisions from bad. . . . To do the honours of the table gracefully, is one of the outlines of a well-bred man; and to carve well, little as it may seem, is useful twice a day. . . ." Later, in the text, he confidentially informs his young readers that "present habit has made a pint of wine after dinner almost a necessity to a man who eats freely."

Amongst other important titles making their first appearance in the remaining years of the eighteenth century was *The Lady's Complete Guide; or, Cookery and Confectionary in all Their Branches,* 1789, by Mrs. Mary Cole. She boasted later that the first edition of several thousand copies had been "quite sold out in less than six weeks." Three years later saw the publication of *The Universal Cook, and City and Country Housekeeper,* 1792, by Francis Collingwood and John Woollams, "principal Cooks at the Crown & Anchor Tavern in the Strand," a work successful enough to be translated into French for an 1810 edition. The reverse was true of *The French Family Cook,* 1793, which was translated from the original French into English for the London edition. The work was issued as being "a complete System of French Cookery. Adapted to the Tables not only of the Opulent, but of Persons of moderate Fortune and Condition." Amongst a host of exotic recipes were nearly forty dishes with eggs as their main ingredient, and the preamble to this section of the work is worth reprinting:

WAYS TO DRESS EGGS

Excepting meat, nothing furnishes a greater variety in the kitchen than eggs; but before I proceed to the various ways of dressing them, I shall speak of their utility. The yolks of new-laid eggs beat up in warm water, is called hen's milk, and, taken going to bed, is good for a cold. The fine skin within the shell, beat and mixed with the white, is excellent for chapped lips.

The shell, burnt and pounded, will whiten the teeth: taken in wine, it is good for stopping a spitting of blood.

Chapter Seven

COOKERY MADE EASY

The nineteenth century opened with a plethora of cook books, each competing for popular favor with eye-catching titles as varied as the domestic and culinary advice they contained. Almost every month a new work made its appearance, and these took their place in the bookshops alongside the reprints and new editions of tried and trusted titles from the past.

The new titles included: *The Housekeepers' Valuable Present; or, Lady's Closet Companion,* 1800, a little book of some hundred pages, advertised as being available at 2s. sewed, or 2s.6d. neatly bound; and *The Complete British Cook,* 1800, by Mary Holland, described by her publishers as being a "professional cook." This popular title later appeared as *The Complete Economical Cook,* passing through nine editions before 1840.

The Ladies Best Companion; or, A Golden Treasury for the Fair Sex, 1800, not only gave its readers scores of recipes, but promises methods that, if faithfully adhered to, would "delay the Ravages of Time on the Features of the Fair Sex." The author was Mrs. Amelia Chambers, poet turned cook, whose pages exhibited several little jingles in her own manufacture:

> *Here Cooks may learn with wond'rous Ease*
> *The longing Appetite to please;*
> *The Art of Beauty how to reach,*
> *By skilful Methods too we teach;*
> *The Fair who with our Rules comply,*
> *May catch the Heart, and charm the Eye.*

Once back in the kitchen, the industrious housewife was advised how to charm and content her husband, as well as the rules of polite behavior at table in "the most modern taste."

Fat and Lean.

An eighteenth-century caricature of the perils of marrying a wife whose cookery fills the place of sexual frolics.

Choice Viands and a skilful Cook invite
The Puny and Capacious Appetite,
Then let Politeness, join'd to hunger, haste
And learn the Method how to Dine in Taste.

Several more books on polite behavior, and deportment for servants and the lower orders were available for purchase by the mistress of the household for communicating to those lucky enough to be in her employ. Amongst these, *Domestic Management; or, the Art of Conducting a Family; with Instructions for Servants in General,* 1800, emanated from the "Literary Press" of H. D. Symonds, 62, Wardour Street, Soho. It was issued without an author's name on the title page, and may well have been from the proprietor himself. Some of the strictures deserve to be quoted at length.

The title page made it clear that this was "the best of presents to Servants of all Denominations," and especially addressed itself to "young housekeepers setting up home for the first time." They were to read out to illiterate servants the points they most wished driven home, especially from the Do's and Don't's section. This, among many other useful hints, contained much sound advice to the footman as: "If he is ordered at dinner to break the claw of a lobster, he is not under any circumstances to crack it between the hinges of the dining-room door. He must take it at once into the kitchen, where force can be applied out of earshot of the master and mistress . . ." Furthermore, when dispatched on a rainy day for a hackney coach, he must trot beside it on the way back to the house, and *not* ride inside it. To do so "will render it uncomfortably damp for those members of the household or their guests for whose use the coach has been summoned."

The instructions and rules for maids of all classes are many and detailed. They commence soon after dawn (hours before this in the winter months), and continue long after the underpaid and under-privileged girls have thankfully retired to their draughty attic rooms in search of well-earned rest. A typical example gives instructions on how to deport oneself when suddenly wakened from slumber by the ringing of the bedroom bell:

Should a chamber maid be rung for in the night, she must fly immediately to the room where help is required, making all speed, as soon as she hears the bell. She must not forget to take her tinder-box with her. She may not be aware of the consequences of a moment's delay. Many a life has been lost by the night-mare, for want of momentary assistance; and a person who has just rung the bell may be suffocated, whilst the maid stays to rub her eyes, light her candle, or adjust her cap . . .

One can imagine the comments of any spirited but downtrodden chambermaid reading this passage as the picture of her tyrannical mistress suffocating for "want of momentary assistance" is conjured before her eyes. Not, surely, for her the perilous dash down unlighted stairs, tinder-box in hand and with the comforting candle left behind! Make haste more slowly, while the mistress struggles to breathe, and hope she arrives too late!

> The footman rode, sopping,
> Back home in the coach;
> While Anna, the maid,
> Made her tardy approach
> To the lady who dined
> On a large lobster's claw,
> That her servant had cracked
> In the dining-room door:
> Her nightmare had summoned
> The maid from her bed;
> But long before morning
> The mistress was dead!

It was by such dreams of fortune that life below stairs was rendered bearable for those unfortunates who were sometimes forced to labor fourteen

Mrs. Maria Rundell (1745 to 1828); a silhouette taken by John Field in 1804, just before the publication of *A New System of Domestic Cookery*.

or more hours a day for a scanty keep and a yearly pittance. Others were more fortunate in the lowly stations to which Providence had called them.

It was the appearance of *A New System of Domestic Cookery; Formed upon Principles of Economy, and Adapted to the Use of Private Families*, 1806, ''By a Lady,'' that really opened up the new and up-to-date era of nineteenth-century cook books. The credit goes to the anonymous lady concerned, Mrs. Maria Eliza Rundell (1745 to 1828), the only child of Abel Ketelby of Ludlow, Shropshire. Early in life she married a wealthy London businessman, Thomas Rundell, a partner in the well-known firm of jewelers and silversmiths Rundell & Bridges, Ludgate Hill. What little we know of Maria's life in the capital indicates that she enjoyed a happy marriage there, rearing a family of several daughters. After the death of her husband, she retired to live in Bath, frequently visiting and staying with one or other of her now-married daughters.

It was at Swansea, at the home of one of these, that she finally settled to the task of editing and putting into order the hundreds of handwritten recipes and remedies she had compiled and collected during more than four decades. For years her daughters had tried to persuade her to let them have a permanent record of the hundreds of dishes she had invented during their lifetime, and which they had enjoyed at countless meals throughout their childhood and early life. So, in 1804, in her sixtieth year, while relaxing and letting others order the housework and superintend the cooking, she started to sift and examine her manuscript sheets, rewriting some and discarding others, until the whole voluminous collection of a lifetime's culinary trials and errors had been sorted and indexed.

It was at this stage that she had intended to have them copied in the laborious copperplate script that would make them plainly legible to any harassed cook, before having sufficient identical copies bound up to enable all her daughters to be presented with one apiece, while their widowed mother retained the master copy for herself. Had it not been for the family's friendship with the London publisher John Murray, this might well have been the end of the affair as far as the reading public was concerned. As matters turned out, their next meeting resulted in Murray's eventual rescue from possible financial disaster and the reluctant author's name being perpetuated in the annals of culinary fame.

John Murray (1778 to 1843) had inherited his publishing business from his late father, John MacMurray, a Scot who had dropped the prefix "Mac" from the family name soon after setting up business in London. He had retired on half-pay from the Marines, fulfilling an ambition by purchasing the old-established publishing business of William Sandby, Fleet Street, in 1768. On his death in 1793, his son was only sixteen years of age, and the business fell into the hands of the late John Murray's chief assistant, Samuel Highley, as regards its day to day management, with the Murray family retaining sufficient financial interest to enable young John to take his place thereupon coming of age. By the time he was twenty-five, John Murray, Jr., was in sole command, his ambitions leading him to expand the firm at a rate which ultimately led to a serious shortage of liquid capital.

Despite an impressive list of steadily selling titles, including the London rights of many of the early works of Walter Scott, he desperately needed a sure-fire best seller that he could run through several editions in a matter of months and still have an eager public asking for more. His business was dangerously extended, the purchase of copyrights and half-shares in established titles having left him extremely short of cash.

It was at this critical juncture in the expanding firm's affairs that a chance visit to his old friends the Rundells in the summer of 1805 led to his hearing about Maria's newly completed manuscript of cookery recipes. Both families had been friends for many years, John Murray, senior, and Mrs. Rundell's late husband, being frequent visitors to each other's homes and the dinner parties that so often accompanied the hospitality extended. No doubt young John already knew the quality of Maria's cookery, for he had no hesitation in immediately offering to publish her manuscript.

Flattered by the offer, she allowed herself to be persuaded to have the work printed under the Murray imprint, and by December 1805, *A New System of Domestic Cookery* was on sale in bookshops throughout the country. Murray had dated the title page forward to 1806 (though the engraved frontispiece bore the legend "Nov. 1st. 1805"), and, despite a large original printing, the first edition was sold out within a few months of publication. Within weeks he was pressing Maria for revisions to allow an expanded and corrected second edition to be published. On July 4, 1806, the authoress replied: "I am sorry I am so slow with the second edition, and much vexed that ill-health delays it, as several of my young friends are just setting out on household concerns and wish the book as a companion. I am indeed flattered that it is deemed useful in its present defective state and hope it will have more merit when it is reproduced."

So far, Mrs. Rundell had not received a penny in payment or by way of royalties, and, in her preface to the early editions, she stated quite clearly that the author "will receive from it no emolument, so she trusts it will escape without censure." Nor had she allowed her name to appear on the title page of the work. To be connected with any work of commerce, paid or not, was beneath the dignity of a lady of social standing. The words "By a Lady," were the only clue she allowed to her identity, and so it remained throughout her lifetime.

When the second edition, dated 1807, finally appeared (it was completed at Ambleside where Mrs. Rundell was staying for a time with another of her married daughters), she wrote to Murray telling him that: ". . . the proofs have been miserably prepared for the press. Pray employ some proper person to correct it after me. . . . As to receiving remuneration for such trifles, I beg you will not think of it."

Issued in a binding of paper-covered boards, with the title printed on a paper label on its spine, the fat little book sold at 7/6d a copy (70 cents). There were ten full-page copperplate engravings supplied as illustrations, and the leaf edges were left uncut. Yet despite its drab and uninteresting format, within a few months sales started to multiply to a degree that had the second edition oversold. John Harding, St. James's Street, London, had a share in the risk of the early editions, as did Archibald Constable, Edinburgh, and all three publishers reaped a rich benefit from the book's growing popularity. In September, 1808, having so far paid her not a penny, Murray enclosed a draft for £150 in a letter to Mrs. Rundell. She was delighted, and replied:

> Your very handsome and most unexpected present I have just received; I can truly say I never had the smallest idea of any return for what I considered, and which really was, a free gift to one whom I had long regarded as my friend . . . I will not affront your noble sentiment by returning it . . .

The work's immediate and continuing popularity was largely due to the fact that it covered almost every aspect of household management. It was an ideal wedding present for any new bride, and Maria sighed over the fact that no such compendium of all the most useful day-to-day recipes and tips for the successful running of a well-ordered home had been available when she herself first entered married life. "This little work would have been a treasure to [me] when [I] first set out in life . . ." she told her readers. A glance at the book's list of contents gives an idea of its usefulness to any apprehensive young housekeeper-to-be, and this drastically abridged list of hints (which were given along with its many recipes) reveals the wide scope of interest for a housewife:

To make wash-balls
Paste for chapped hands
Paste for chapped lips
Lavender water
Black paper for drawing patterns
To preserve furs and furniture from moths
To clean plate
To clean looking-glasses

To give a gloss to fine oak wainscot
To blacken the fronts of stone chimney-pieces
Fine blacking for shoes
Floor cloths—How to clean them
Black ink, two ways of making
To cement broken china
To take stains, Iron-moulds, and mildew out of linen

To make flannels keep their colour, and not shrink
To dye gloves to look like York tan or Limerick.
To dye white gloves a beautiful purple
To give a fine colour to mahogany
To clean the back of the grate
To prevent the creaking of a door
To take the black off the bright bars of polished stoves in a few minutes

And so on! These household hints (and there were scores of others), were subsidiary to well over a thousand recipes for every conceivable type of dish likely to be needed to feed a family or tempt the appetite of the most fastidious gourmet. Some of her own favorites are given here; amongst them the first printed recipe for Bubble and Squeak:

BUBBLE AND SQUEAK

Boil, chop, and fry it, with a little butter, pepper, and salt, some cabbage, and lay it on slices of underdone beef, lightly fried.

This old English dish had been a favorite fry-up during the eighteenth century, the earliest printed use of the term so far discovered being in Thomas Bridges's *A Burlesque Translation of Homer*, 2 vols., 1767. This young man, disinherited by his furious father for the manner in which he sent Homer up the creek, wrote how Neptune, sated with fish, craved meat for supper:

We therefore cook'd him up a dish
Of lean bull-beef with cabbage fried,
And a full pot of beer beside:
Bubble they call this dish, and squeak;
Our taylors dine on't thrice a week.

This recipe was the shortest in the whole of Mrs. Rundell's cook book, and is given merely as an early example of the use of the term. She was far more eloquent when she turned her attention to her pies and fricassees:

DUCK PIE

Bone a full-grown young duck and a fowl. Wash them, and season them with pepper and salt, and a small proportion of mace and allspice in the finest powder.

Put the fowl within the duck, and in the former a calf's tongue pickled red, boiled very tender and peeled.

Press the whole close; the skins of the legs should be drawn inwards, that the body of the fowls may be quite smooth.

If approved, the space between the sides of the crust may be filled with fine forcemeat, made according to the second recipe given for making forcemeat.

Bake it in a slow oven, either in a raised crust, or pie-dish with a thick crust, ornamented.

The large pies in Staffordshire are made as above; but with a goose outwards, then a turkey, a duck next, then a fowl; and either a tongue, small birds, or forcemeat, in the middle.

And so *ad infinitum!* One is reminded of those plump gaily painted wooden dolls which unscrew around the circumference of their bulging tummies, to reveal a slightly smaller but identical doll nestling inside, which itself unscrews to reveal a yet smaller doll, and so on and so on, until the final tiny embryo is discovered in the very center of the mass of discarded shells. The ultimate lark's tongue stuffing the wren!

GIBLET PIE

After very nicely cleaning goose and duck giblets, stew them with a small quantity of water, onion, black pepper, and a bunch of sweet herbs, till nearly done.

Let them grow cold. If not enough to fill the pie, lay beef, veal, or two or three mutton steaks at the bottom.

Put the liquor of the stew to bake with the above; and when the pie is baked, pour into it a large tea-cupful of cream.

Sliced potatoes added to it eat extremely well.

APPLE CHARLOTTE

Cut as many thin slices of white bread as will cover the bottom and line the sides of a baking dish, but first rub the dish thick with butter. Put apples, in thin slices, into the dish in layers, till full, strewing sugar between each layer and bits of butter.

In the mean time, soak as many thin slices of bread as will cover the whole, in warm milk, over which lay a plate, and a weight to keep the bread close on the apples.

Bake slowly for three hours.

To a middling-sized dish use half a pound of butter in the whole.

CHEAP AND EXCELLENT CUSTARDS

Boil three pints of new milk, and a bit of lemon-peel, a bit of cinnamon, two or three bay-leaves, and sweeten the mixture. Meanwhile rub down smooth a large spoonful of rice-flour into a cup of cold milk, and mix with it two yolks of eggs well beaten.

Take a basin of the boiling milk, and mix with the cold,

and then pour that to the boiling; stirring it one way until it begins to thicken, and is just going to boil up.

Then pour it into a pan, stir it some time, add a large spoonful of peach-water, two tea-spoonfuls of brandy, or a little ratafia.

Marbles, boiled in custard, or anything likely to burn, will, by shaking them in the sauce-pan, prevent it from catching.

A VERY FINE CAKE

Wash two pounds and a half of fresh butter in water first, and then in rose-water.

Beat the butter to a cream. Then beat twenty eggs, yolks and whites separately, half an hour each. Have ready two pounds and a half of the finest flour, well dried, and kept hot; likewise a pound and a half of sugar pounded and sifted, one ounce of spice reduced to the finest powder, three pounds of currants nicely cleaned and dry, half a pound of almonds blanched, and three quarters of a pound of sweetmeats cut not too thin.*

Let all be kept by the fire; mix all the dry ingredients. Pour the eggs, strained, to the butter. Mix half a pint of sweet wine with a large glass of brandy, then pour it in the butter and eggs mixture. Mix well, then have all the dry things put in by degrees.

Beat them all very thoroughly; you can hardly do this too much.

Having half a pound of stoned jar-raisins chopped as fine as possible, mix them carefully so that there shall be no lumps, and add a tea-cupful of orange flower-water. Beat the ingredients together a full hour at least. Have a hoop** well buttered, or, if you have none, a tin or copper cake-pan. Take a white paper, doubled and buttered, and put in the pan around the edge. The cake batter must not fill it more than three parts, for space must be left for rising.

Bake in a quick oven. It will require three hours.

ASSES' MILK

Far surpasses any imitation of it that can be made. It should be milked into a glass that is kept warm by being in a basin of hot water.

The fixed air that asses' milk contains gives some people a pain in the stomach. To relieve this wind a tea-spoonful of rum may be taken with it, but this must not be added to the milk until the moment that it is to be swallowed.

*Sweetmeats would today equate with candied-peel or glacé fruits, chopped.
**A hoop was a tin with a loose bottom that could be pressed upward to remove the cake when baked.

The whole of Part XII was devoted to ''Cookery for the sick, and for the poor''; the early pages giving dozens of recipes which Maria Rundell recommended for the sick room. Not all would be welcomed by patients today:

TOAST AND WATER

Toast slowly a thin piece of bread till extremely brown and hard, but not the least black.

Then plunge it into a jug of cold water, and cover it over an hour before use.

This is of particular use in weak bowels. It should be of a fine brown colour before drinking it.

A GREAT RESTORATIVE

Simmer six sheep's trotters, two blades of mace, a little cinnamon, lemon-peel, a few hartshorn shavings, and a little isinglass, in two quarts of water. When the amount of water has been reduced to one quart, leave to go cold. Take off the fat.

Give near half a pint twice a day, warming with a little new milk.

Mrs. Rundell's final exhortation was to middle- and upper-class housewives to salve their consciences, as they prepared their seven- and eight-course dinners, by instructing their cooks to set aside scraps for the relief of the destitute and semi-starved poor who thronged the streets of the towns and cities and were ever-present in villages and hamlets throughout the land.

I promised a few hints [she told her readers] to enable every family to assist the poor of their neighbourhood at a very trivial expense; and these may be varied or amended at the discretion of the mistress.

Where cows are kept, a jug of skimmed milk is a valuable present, and a very common one. When the oven is hot, a large pudding may be baked, and given to the sick or a young family. Thus made, the trouble is little: Into a deep coarse pan put a pound of rice, four ounces of coarse sugar or treacle, two quarts of milk, and two ounces of dripping. Set this mixture cold in the oven. It will take a good while to cook, but will be an excellent solid food.

The cook should be charged to save every discarded scrap of boiled meat, ham, tongue, &c., however salt. It is easy to use only a part of that, and the rest of fresh water, and, by the addition of more vegetables, the bones of meat used by the family, the pieces of meat that come from the table and are left on the plates after eating, and rice, Scotch barley, or oatmeal, there will be some gallons of nutritious soup for the poor two or three times every week.

The bits of meat should only be warmed in the soup, and remain whole; the bones, &c., boiled till they yield their nourishment.

If the things are ready to put in the boiler as soon as the meat is served to the family, it will save lighting the fire and a second cooking.

Should the soup be poor of meat, the long boiling of the bones, and different vegetables, will afford better nourishment than the laborious poor can obtain; especially as they are rarely tolerable cooks, and have not fuel to do justice to what they buy.

But in every family there is some superfluity; and if it be prepared with cleanliness and care, the benefit will be very great to the receiver, and the satisfaction no less to the giver.

I found, in the time of scarcity, ten or fifteen gallons of soup could be dealt out weekly, at an expense not worth mentioning, though the vegetables were bought.

If in the villages about London, abounding with opulent families, the quantity of ten gallons were made in ten gentlemen's houses, there would be a hundred gallons of wholesome agreeable food given weekly for the supply of forty poor families, at the rate of two gallons and a half each.

It very rarely happens that servants object to seconding the kindness of their superiors to the poor; but should the cook of any family think the adoption of this plan too troublesome, a gratuity at the end of the winter might repay her, if the love of her fellow-creatures failed of doing it a hundred fold. Did she readily enter into it, she would never wash away, as useless, the peas or grits of which soup or gruel had been made; broken potatoes, the green heads of celery, the necks and feet of fowls, and particularly the shanks of mutton, and various other articles which in preparing dinner for the family are thrown aside. What a relief to the labouring husband, instead of bread and cheese, to have a warm comfortable meal! To the sick and infant branches, and the aged, how important an advantage! Nor less to the industrious mother, whose forbearance from the necessary quantity of food, that others may have a larger share, frequently reduces the strength upon which the welfare of her family essentially depends.

This was the first manual of household management and domestic economy which could claim any pretension to completeness, as *The Dictionary of National Biography* has already pointed out. As such, Mrs. Rundell's cookery book deserved the success which attended each new edition. It was the totally unexpected extent of the book's financial success that ultimately caused strained relations between the author and her publisher, who meanwhile was reaping benefits amounting to thousands of pounds from the sale of the work. No doubt prodded into action by her daughters and other members of her family, Mrs. Rundell finally issued writs against Murray, seeking to restrain him from issuing further editions until a satisfactory financial settlement was made between them. In 1821, she placed an improved and extended version in the hands of Longman & Company for immediate publication, but Murray retaliated by obtaining an injunction from the Lord Chancellor's office restraining publication under any other imprint but his own. After months of litigation and threatened litigation a compromise was reached. John Murray agreed to pay Maria the sum of £1,000 for the outright purchase of her copyright, plus a further sum of £1,000 to defray the costs of her legal action against him and his firm.

Five years later, with her health failing, Mrs. Rundell retired to live in Lausanne, Switzerland. It was here that she died, aged eighty-three, on December 16, 1828, leaving a numerous progeny of grandchildren and great-grandchildren to relate mouth-watering tales told by their mothers and grandmothers of the birthday and Christmas feasts enjoyed when old Maria was so happily in charge of the well-stocked kitchens of earlier years.

Several other titles have been laid at Mrs. Rundell's door, notably *The New Family Receipt-Book*, 1810, also issued under the John Murray imprint (second edition "augmented, corrected, and considerably improved," 1811). This title, issued as a companion volume to *A New System of Domestic Cookery*, is quite definitely *not* by Mrs. Rundell. In fact, the preface makes it quite clear that the author was a man "possessed of a farm of near three hundred pounds a year," and one who was more interested in disseminating the latest and most novel methods of mixing "compost dunghills" and of "preventing the Smut in Wheat" than in recipes for Christmas pudding or Staffordshire beef steaks. The work was in no way in competition with Maria's best seller, and Murray made it clear in his advertisements that it was a companion work, of farm remedies and practical household hints, to the cookery book lately issued "By a Lady."

First editions of *A New System of Domestic Cookery*, 1806, if in the original publisher's binding and in tolerably good condition, are now catalogued at well over $600 on the few occasions when a copy comes on the market. Any edition dated before 1830 in a contemporary binding would now command a sum well into double figures, the earlier issues selling for $150 to $300 a piece or more. Collectors must be careful to collate the text and plates: early cook books are notorious in bibliographical circles for the frequency in which they are found to be incomplete when carefully examined. Many a leaf of text has apparently been pressed into service as a spill to light a kitchen fire or gas stove when harassed cook was late in preparing dinner for an impatient family upstairs. Even lettuce leaves and bacon rashers were used, allegedly, as bookmarks!

There were many attempts to cash in on the financial success of Mrs. Rundell's *New System of Domestic Cookery*. One of the earliest occurred in 1810 with the first appearance of *Domestic Management; or, The Healthful Cookery-Book*, published anonymously but known to have been written by Annabella Plumptre. Annabella was a minor novelist and sister of the well-known Miss Anne Plumptre (1760 to 1818), whose fervent adulation of Napoleon Bonaparte and statement that she would welcome him with open arms if he invaded Britain did little to endear her to most of the rest of her fellow countrymen. Annabella was in some ways as forthright as her sister, denouncing indulgent vices in a diversity of fields including, as she put it, "pernicious modes of cookery." Her remarks on our national beverages are typical of her method of attack:

TEA

The frequent drinking of a quantity of tea, as is the general practice, relaxes and weakens the tone of the stomach, whence proceeds nausea and indigestion, with a weakness of the nerves, and flabbiness of the flesh, and very often a pale wan complexion.

Milk, when mixed with it in some quantity, lessens its bad qualities, by rendering it softer, and nutritious; and, with a moderate quantity of sugar, it may then be a proper breakfast, as a diluent, to those who are strong, and live freely, in order to

cleanse the alimentary passages, and wash off the salts from the kidneys and bladder.

But persons of weak nerves ought to abstain from it as carefully as from drams and cordial drops; as it causes the same kind of irritation on the tender delicate fibres of the stomach, which ends in lowness, trembling, and vapours. It should never be drank hot by any body.

Green tea is less wholesome than black or bohea.

COFFEE

Coffee affords very little nourishment, and is apt to occasion heat, dryness, stimulation and tremours of the nerves, and for these reasons is thought to occasion palsies, watchfulness, and leanness. Hence it is very plain that it must be pernicious to hot, dry, and bilious constitutions. If moderately used, it may be beneficial to phlegmatic persons, but, if drank very strong, or in great quantities it will prove injurious even to them.

"Never forget," she warned her readers, "that the throat has destroyed more than the sword!" Attention to diet was all important: "Bad air, want of cleanliness, want of exercise, excessive bodily fatigue, mental uneasiness, and, amongst females, absurdities in dress, are all unfavourable to health, but have not so immediate an influence upon it as our food." Her "wholesome vegetable dishes" included one of her favorites:

CARROT PUDDING

Scrape a raw carrot very clean, and grate it. To half a pound of this grated carrot, put half a pound of grated bread, half a pound of fresh butter melted, half a pint of cream, half a pint of sack, some orange-flavor water, sugar to the taste, a little nutmeg grated, and eight eggs. Before adding the eggs, leave out half the whites. The whole must then be well beaten with a little salt.

The mixture must be of a moderate thickness: if it is too stiff put in a little more cream.

This dish will either bake or boil. If it is to be baked, pour it into a dish with a puff paste under it, and bake it an hour. Sift powdered sugar over it when it comes from the oven.

If it is to be boiled, pour it into a well buttered basin, and boil it an hour and a half.

Serve it up with white wine sauce.

In complete contrast to Miss Plumptre's austere treatise was *The Imperial and Royal Cook; Consisting of the Most Sumptuous Made Dishes, Ragouts, Fricassees, Soups, Gravies,* &c., 1809, by Frederick Nutt, an author whose *The Complete Confectioner; or, the Whole Art of Confectionary: Forming a Ready Assistant to All Genteel Families,* had made its first

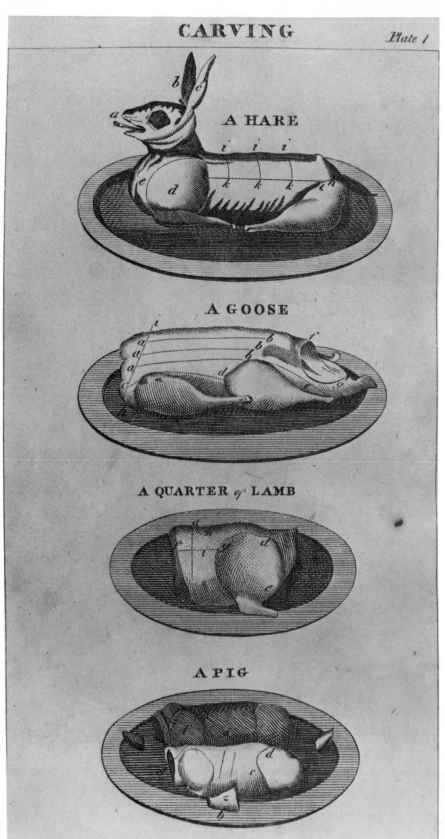

A full-page plate from *The Young Woman's Companion; or, Frugal Housewife,* 1811, showing the most economical way to carve.

appearance as early as 1789. Nutt, who was once an apprentice confectionary at the well-known cake and pie shop of Negri & Witten, Berkeley Square, appears to have been a culinary snob. His "genteel families" of his earlier title, were replaced in the blurb to his gaily extravagant *Imperial and Royal Cook* by the "opulent families" for whom he said the book had been specially written. In fact, the work was only for those in a position "to give handsome and occasional entertainments to their select friends," and other housekeepers need not apply! Reading some of his recipes, with blithe instructions to the chef of aristocratic households to "take the yolks of four dozen eggs," or prepare for cake-making by sending the underchef for several pounds of best butter and buckets of candied peel, one smells the odor of well-heeled opulence oozing from its pages. Frederick Nutt moved as confectioner in only the best society whose select friends were apparently endowed with elephantine appetites and stomachs capable of infinite extension. No doubt he knew his place.

The *Imperial and Royal Cook* was a bloated exception to the modern trend in cook books. The vast majority of new titles were aimed at the middle-class market rather than the select band of vastly-landed gentry to whom expense in the kitchen on other than servants' wages was a matter of no concern. More to the public taste in the first quarter of the nineteenth century were such titles as *The Female Economist; or, A Plain System of Cookery,* 1810 (fifth edition, 1817), by an unknown Mrs. Smith; or, *The Young Woman's Companion; or, Frugal Housewife,* 1811, published anonymously under a Manchester imprint. These were the class of works popular with housewives of the period, to whom the very supervision of servants, especially temperamental cooks, was a fatigue to be avoided. In much the same way that their modern counterparts select labor-saving dishes and convenience foods so that leisure time is augmented and kitchen chores are sidestepped. *The Frugal Housekeeper's Companion: Being a Complete System of Cookery, the Result of Thirty-Six Years' Actual Experience in Some of the Most Respectable Families in the Kingdom,* 1812, by Elizabeth Alcock; and *Modern Domestic Cookery, and Useful Receipt Book,* 1817, by Elizabeth Hammond; were other fashionable works current during and just after the end of the Napoleonic Wars. It was in the latter title, after a series of recipes couched in terms that, in those fruitful days, qualified as being pared down to "the strictest economy," that a section devoted to medical recipes was printed. Amongst these is one notable for advocating "cataplasms of fresh cow-dung" as a specific for bruises. Readers were advised *not* to apply this remedy "immediately before retiring or offence might possibly be given to others in the household." A sentiment no doubt heartily endorsed by the spouse of the bruisee!

The basic trend, emphasized by the titles issued by London and provincial publishing houes, was now toward "cookery made easy." The vast majority of those who purchased new cook books were middle-class housewives. Often these were newly-wed, smart young women of the day who demanded the latest and most up-to-date work filled with economical labor-saving recipes. Even in a well-staffed home, they considered themselves far too busy to cope with dishes needing days of careful preparation. They were occupied with the problems of raising a family and keeping a husband in a reasonably contented frame of mind and body, as well as with social and charitable affairs.

Some of the recipes for special gravy to pour over joints of meat before and after serving that were given in eighteenth-century cook books needed days of preparation and the use of up to a dozen different kinds of expensive ingredients. These now old-fashioned books, called this essence of choice cuts of meat and well-hung game: "cullis." At the end of all this rendering down of juices, all one had to show for many hours of skilled endeavor would be a moderately-sized sauceboatful of rich and aromatic liquid. The change in social circumstances at home marked by the end of the Napoleonic Wars and the rise of the second generation *nouveau riche* resulting from the aftermath of the Industrial Revolution put an end to much of this type of culinary extravagance. Cullis, and similar luxurious embellishments, often used to pour on a single meat dish at dinner, were fast becoming merely aromatic nostalgias in the dinner-party stories of elderly pre-war hostesses. The young housewives of the day were far more concerned with keeping domestic harmony within the home than in taxing the ingenuity of their own hard-pressed cooks and kitchen staff with orders for exotic and time-consuming dishes.

Good cooks, as always, were difficult to find, and for the mistress of the house to be able to keep her staff below-stairs in an equitable frame of mind was an achievement to feel proud of. Finding a replacement for an honest, reliable, sober, and perhaps industrious cook was a task no housewife relished. A homespun gravy, culled from the pages of past experience by her domestic treasure, augmented by the hints and recipes to be found in the latest "economical" cookery book, was infinitely to be preferred to any extravagant dish larded with the mysteries of the past, or a cullis prepared after days of care and poured with the reverence usually lavished on a fine old crusty port.

Chapter Eight

AMERICAN COOK BOOKS

Although many of the housewives that victualed and fed the early pioneering families must have relied upon their own trusted collections of handwritten recipes, printed cookery books were almost unknown in North America during the first 150 years of her colonial history. The handful of published copies in circulation had all been brought over from Europe by the hopeful young wives of emigrant settlers in New England, and it was as late as 1742, almost two and a half centuries after the first printing of a cookery book in England, that the earliest cook book to carry an American imprint made its appearance.

Even this modest forerunner of the tens of thousands of similar works that were to follow owed little or nothing to the American heritage. The book had been compiled in England, and various reprints and new editions had been circulating there for the past fifteen years. But this printed edition of *The Compleat Housewife,* 1742, by Eliza Smith, not only had the distinction of being first in the field, but could claim to have been published by that early American craftsman-printer William Parks (c. 1698 to 1750). Parks had learned his trade in Shropshire, England, before setting sail for the New World. He set up his press in Williamsburg, Virginia, the old colonial capital of the state. It was here that he founded the *Maryland Gazette* in 1727, and the *Virginia Gazette* in 1736, two of the earliest American newspapers, before settling down to publishing books he believed to be of literary and historical importance. Few could have been as useful and as appreciated as *The Compleat Housewife,* even though no mention occurred in its pages of the often strange but abundant fare so easily available to its readers in the expanding American homeland.

Within a few months it had reached the top of the American bestseller list, and the work was still in brisk demand some fifty years later. Few copies have survived the rigors of a cook book's existence to the present

A butcher's shop in Boston, Massachusetts, U.S.A., in the late 1830s.

day. Those we know of include a 1752 edition that was printed and sold at Williamsburg by William Hunter. He was the one-time apprentice of William Parks, and succeeded to the business when his master was drowned at sea. Hugh Gaine (1726 to 1807), famous as the founder of the *New York Mercury* in 1752, published an edition of the same work under his New York imprint in 1761, followed by a 1764 reprint.

By this time there were several other rivals in the field. Chief among these were *The Servants' Directory; or, Housekeeper's Companion*, 1760, by the redoubtable Mrs. Hannah Glasse. Two years later, copies of *The Cyder-Maker's Instructor, Sweet-maker's Assistant, and Victualler's and Housekeeper's Director*, by Thomas Chapman, were finding a ready sale. Issued under both Boston and Philadelphia imprints, the work sold freely in several states at only a shilling a copy.

Two other welcome additions to the American kitchen were *The Frugal Housewife; or, Complete Woman Cook*, 1772, by Susannah Carter, the London edition of which had originally appeared under the famous imprint of the firm started by John Newbery; and *The New Art of Cookery, According to the Present Practice*, 1792, by Richard Briggs. This author proudly described himself on the title page as having been "for many years

132

cook at the Globe Tavern, Fleet Street, the White Hart Tavern, Holborn, and now at the Temple Coffee-House, London.''

But still no cookery book compiled by an American had made its appearance. In fact it was nearly the turn of the century before the name of an American author appeared on the title page of a cookery book printed in the United States. When this happy event did in fact occur the impact was immediate and lasting, even though the compiler of the work was forced to have it printed at her own expense. About Mrs. Amelia Simmons, who described herself as ''an American orphan,'' we know very little. But it was thanks to her efforts that in June, 1796, priced at ''2/3d,'' *American Cookery; or, The Art of Dressing Viands, Fish, Poultry and Vegetables, and the Best Modes of Making Pastes, Puffs, Pies, Tarts, Puddings, Custards and Preserves, and all Kinds of Cakes, from the Imperial Plumb to Plain Cake,* made its welcome if belated appearance under the imprint of Hudson & Goodwin, Hartford, Connecticut.

In the preface to her work, the author made it quite clear to her readers that she had specially adapted the book to meet the needs of the American housewife. She admitted borrowing a few recipes from English works, but the rest was an original compilation, thoroughly American in spirit and couched in the language her compatriots could understand. In its pages appeared the first recipes using corn meal as the basic ingredient, and there were earthy and vernacular directions for brewing spruce beer and soft American gingerbread. Molasses took the place of the European treacle, and slapjacks had ousted the Scottish griddlecakes. Foreign collections of European recipes contained no mention of the dozens of appetizing dishes made with the meats and vegetables freely available in Amelia's native land, and she delighted in redressing the balance with descriptions of mouth-watering buffalo steaks, wild turkey roasts, pumpkins, and paw-paws, New England election cakes, and the famous Southern mint juleps. It was a homespun work of her own, specially written for the use of American wives ''in all grades of life.''

It was the first cook book to challenge the imported collections of recipes that were often quite alien to the needs and culinary aspirations of the housewives of the New World. Within some months the original edition was heavily oversubscribed, the work quickly attaining a popularity which kept it continuously in print through dozens of improved and extended editions until well into the 1830s. Here, for the first time, one encountered recipes for pumpkin pies and cranberry sauce, watermelon-rind chutney, and the dark and wholesome bread affectionately known as ''Rye 'n' Injun.''

Typical of her original American recipes printed in the first edition of 1796 were the following:

A NICE INDIAN PUDDING

Take 3 pints scalded milk and add 7 spoons of fine Indian meal. Stir well together while hot, then let the mixture stand until cooled.

Add 7 whole eggs, well beaten, half pound raisins, 4 ounces butter, spice and sugar to taste.

Bake for 1½ hours.

INDIAN SLAPJACK

To one quart of milk, add 1 pint of Indian meal, stirring well. Add 4 whole eggs, well beaten, 4 spoons of flour, a little salt. Beat all together. Bake on griddles, or fry in a dry pan. May also be baked in a pan which has been rubbed with suet, lard or butter.

Thanksgiving Dinner – basting the turkey ; a photograph taken in 1885, showing a Boston, Mass., housewife at work in her New England kitchen. Freshly-baked bread is on her black-leaded cast-iron all-purpose stove.

FOR BREWING SPRUCE BEER

Take 4 ounces hops, let them boil half an hour in one gallon of water. Strain the hop water then add 16 gallons of warm water, two gallons of molasses, eight ounces of essence of spruce, which has been dissolved in one quart of water.

Put all in a clean cask, then shake it well together. Add half a pint of emptins [*yeast*] then let it stand and work for one

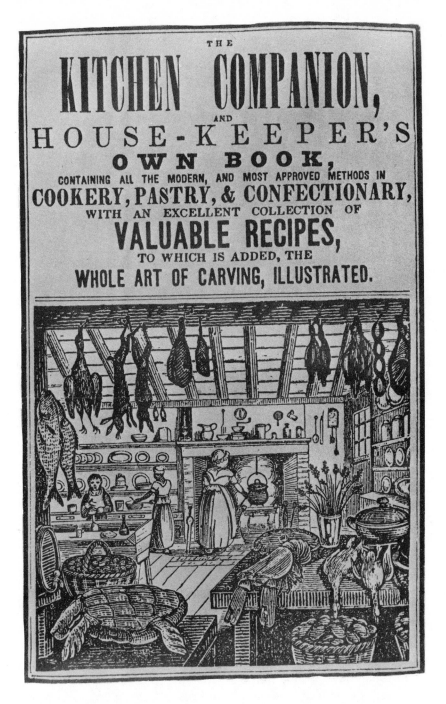

Title page of an 1844 Philadelphia, U.S.A., cook book.

week. If very warm weather less time will do. When it is drawn off to bottle, add one spoonful of molasses to every bottle.

THE AMERICAN CITRON

Take the rind of a large watermelon, not too ripe. Cut it into small pieces.

Take two pound of loaf sugar, one pint of water. Put all together in a large kettle. Let it boil gently for four hours; then put it in pots for use.

Dyeing Easter eggs in New England, U.S.A., in the 1870s. Corncob husks were dried and saved as fuel for kitchen stoves.

This was the type of recipe in use in the towns and cities of the Eastern States. Out on the plains and deep in the backwoods of the newly-emerging America things were very different. The trail-blazers still found the going tough, and subsisted almost entirely on the game, fish, and the wild fruit and vegetables the land provided.

Buffalo meat still formed the source of most of the easily-procurable protein available to the frontiersmen and their families; but the scarcity of salt for preserving the huge numbers of animals killed meant that thousands of carcasses were left to rot where they fell. In times of plenty, only the much-prized tongue was extracted, whole herds being ruthlessly slaughtered in order to procure this delicacy. The American buffalo (correctly *bison*) had served the American Indians as food from time immemorial; but the coming of the white man, complete with his quick-firing rifle, decimated and finally almost exterminated the vast herds that once extended over hundreds of square miles of prairie.

During the time buffalo meat was still plentiful, its preparation was the concern of many of the hand-written recipes of the period, although methods of carving cuts of the meat and its subsequent cooking were often crude in the extreme. Many recipes for cooking and preserving buffalo tongue exist, and for that of the "fleece" (the flesh between the spine and the massive ribs). The marrow bones were another delicacy, for these were the source of the "hunter's butter" in which slices of the tongue were fried. "Carefully push out the marrow with a round stick," says one contemporary account, "when it may be stored in a small barrel to use to season and flavor biscuits and to act as butter when spread on them."

As the main ingredient in that invaluable traveler's standby, pemmican, buffalo meat was indispensable. Pemmican was possibly the most valuable portable food ever devised, without which much of the exploration of the late eighteenth and early nineteenth century in America and Canada would have been impossible. Cut into strips about an inch thick, the buffalo meat was shredded and pounded to a fine paste before being mixed with several types of animal fat. To this was added pulverized berries and dried fruits, the finished product being tightly packed in skin bags. It would keep fresh and edible for months, enabling trappers engaged in the prosperous fur trade to extend their field of operation to the most distant beaver streams in the West.

So complete was the dependence of the early pioneer travelers on the buffalo as they pushed farther and farther westward that at times use was even made of it to assuage the burning extremities of thirst. More than one dust-stained and sun-burnt emigrant on his way to the Far West was reduced to drinking the green and slimy contents of a freshly-killed buffalo's paunch. "At the time it seemed like an invigorating draught, although it was procured from the distended stomach of a buffalo we killed." A survivor of an overland trek wrote in the 1820s. And there were many stories that never entered the cookery books about trappers and hunters who were finally reduced to lopping off and eating the ears of their pack horses before urging the unfortunate animals to one last effort to reach help.

Salt was of the utmost importance in these early days. It assumed a priority unequaled by any other commodity except food itself. Not only was it vital for preserving meat in times of scarcity, but the location of salt licks for the domestic animals the settlers brought with them was mandatory. Without them cattle and sheep would quickly die. The legendary frontiersman Daniel Boone (1734 to 1820), added much to his reputation as scout and explorer amongst the pioneers by his seemingly uncanny knack of locating cattle licks. His last land grant, on the Missouri River, is still known as Boone's Lick, sometimes spelled Booneslick. It was here that cattle and sheep could thrive, making use of the salt and other trace elements contained in the licks natural to the area, before the placing of the man-made varieties in common use today.

These were the days of the fried corn meal mush, immortalized in Joel Barlow's epic poem "The Hasty Pudding" which now gives it its name:

> . . . *how I blush*
> *To hear the Pennsylvanians call thee* Mush!

complained Mr. Barlow way back in 1796; and a verse in the famous marching song "Yankee Doodle" tells us how:

> *Father and I went down to camp*
> *Along with Captain Goodin,*
> *And there we saw the men and boys*
> *As thick as hasty puddin'.*

The recipe itself is as simple as the ingredients it contains, yet has the reputation of being one of the most filling and satisfying concoctions to place before a hungry man.

HASTY PUDDING

5 cups boiling water	2 egg yolks
2 cups yellow corn meal	2 tablespoons milk
1 teaspoon salt	Bread or cracker crumbs
2 cups cold water	Bacon fat or butter

Use top of a double boiler to heat water. Mix corn meal and salt then stir in 2 cups cold water. Tip into boiling water a little at a time, stirring constantly. Cook over high heat for about four minutes. Cover mixture and cook over boiling water for 15 minutes. Pour into a greased pan and cool. When firm, cut into slices about ½-inch thick. Beat egg yolks with milk, dip slices into the mixture, then coat with the dry bread crumbs or cracker crumbs. Fry in hot bacon or butter fat until crisp and golden. Serve hot with warm maple syrup.

Next on the list of home productions was *The Universal Receipt Book; or, Complete Family Directory; Being a Repository of Useful Knowledge in the Several Branches of Domestic Economy; Containing Scarce, Curious, and Valuable Receipts, and Choice Secrets,* 1814, which, according to its title page, had been compiled by "a society of gentlemen in New York." The same work, with the added bonus of "some advice to farmers," appeared under a Philadelphia imprint in 1818 as the "second edition," this time purporting to have been written by "Priscilla Homespun." Meantime, dozens of English cookery books continued to be imported, almost every title being pirated under American imprints within a few months of their first appearance in the U.S.A. Mrs. Maria Rundell's *A New System of Domestic Cookery* was a particular favorite with American readers, and New York and Boston publishers dressed it up in a variety of different disguises. *American Domestic Cookery, Formed on Principles of Economy,* 1823; and, *The Experienced American Housekeeper, or Domestic Cookery,* 1823; were two titles invented by rival New York publishing houses, both of which were culled from the latest London edition of Maria Rundell's work.

The following year saw the first appearance of *The Virginia Housewife,* 1824, published anonymously, but known to have been written by Mrs. Mary Randolph. "Method is the soul of management," she told her readers, presaging Mrs. Beeton's admonition to "cleanliness, neatness, order, regularity, and celerity of action . . . in the business of the kitchen."

It was the late 1820s that saw the final ousting of foreign cookery books in favor of the indigenous American variety, although reprints of the most popular European models continued to appear for another decade. Cook books, Yankee-style, now started to grace the bookshelves from New York to New Orleans, and the Southern States contributed their own quota of culinary aids with new additions each passing year. *The Cook Not Mad; or, Rational Cookery; Being a Collection of Receipts . . . Prevalent with the American Public,* 1830, produced by an unknown hand, commenced a new era; with *The Practice of Cookery, Adapted to the Business of Every-*

day Life, 1830, by Mrs. Dalgairns, running it a close second in popular esteem. Some of the time-honored American receipts were now being printed for the first time, and the secret formulae of the Philadelphia Pepper Pot, Pumpkin Soup, Codfish Chowder, and Boston Brown Bread were soon common knowledge amongst American housewives from Portland to Sacramento. "Brown bread and the Gospel is good and holy fare," goes an old Puritan proverb, and, one might add, especially when served with Boston Baked Beans.

BOSTON BROWN BREAD

1 cup rye flour	1 teaspoon salt
1 cup of self-rising flour	¾ cup molasses
1 cup of corn meal	2 cups buttermilk
½ teaspoon baking soda	1 cup of chopped raisins.

All the dry ingredients should be sifted together, then add buttermilk, molasses, and raisins. If available, the batter should be placed in three well-buttered 1 pound coffee cans (two buttered 1 quart pudding basins will do instead), filling them about ¾ full. These molds must be tightly covered, buttered lids being tied in place and taped so the bread will not force off the cover when it rises. Steam for about 2½ hours, by placing in a pan of boiling water which covers molds up to halfway. Turn out and serve hot with butter and Boston Baked Beans.*

BOSTON BAKED BEANS

5 cups of butter beans	1 teaspoon pepper
1 pound of salt pork	1 cup molasses
1 tablespoon dry mustard	1 small onion
1 tablespoon salt	

Cover beans with cold water, and leave to soak, preferably overnight. Drain, cover with fresh water, then simmer over a slow heat until the skins burst. Drain. Scald the pork by letting it stand in boiling water for 10 minutes. Cut off two thin slices, one to line bottom of pan, the other to be cut into small pieces. Mix dry mustard, salt, pepper, and molasses. Put alternate layers of beans and this mixture spinkled with pieces of pork into pot. Bury the onion in middle layer. When full, push the remaining piece of pork into the beans, with the rind, if any, outward. Cover with boiling water, place lid on pan, and bake all day (a minimum of 6 hours) in an oven of not less than 250 degrees. Add boiling water if needed from time to time. Tip into a deep earthenware casserole that has been previously heated, and serve to table with lid in place. Recipe serves ten people.*

*This is a modern version of the recipe.

Mrs. Lydia Maria (Frances) Child (1802 to 1880), prefaced her cook book with the admonition that "a fat kitchen maketh a lean will," adding that "economy is a poor man's revenue; extravagance a rich man's ruin." Nevertheless, her *The Frugal Housewife*, 1829, which she dedicated "to those who are not ashamed of economy," ran through seven editions in less than three years, its title then being changed to *The American Frugal Housewife*, probably to avoid confusion with an English book of the same name. In the meantime, *Modern American Cookery*, 1831, by Miss Prudence Smith, had made its appearance; being closely followed by *The Cook's Own Book*, 1832, which boasted of being "a complete culinary encyclopedia—compiled by a Boston housekeeper." Who this lady was has never been discovered.

From that time the flood gates were opened, newly written cookery books and reprints of old favorites crowding the bookstalls throughout America. Many achieved the distinction of becoming standard works, in particular *The Good Housekeeper; or, The Way to Live Well and to Be Well While We Live*, 1839, by Mrs. Sarah Josepha Buell Hale (1788 to 1879). She was the editor of *The Ladies' Magazine*, the first significant publication of its kind in America. In 1837 she was appointed literary editor of the famous *Lady's Book*, which she helped to make the best known of any women's periodical of its day. And she achieved immortality as the author of possibly the most often quoted nursery rhyme in the world:

> *Mary had a little lamb,*
> *Its fleece was white as snow;*
> *And everywhere that Mary went*
> *The lamb was sure to go.*

And so on, through three more verses. This she wrote in Boston in 1830, the words first appearing in print in *The Juvenile Miscellany*, and then in her volume of verse *Poems for Our Children*, 1830.

In her day, some of her recipes given in *The Good Housekeeper* seemed almost as well known. In 1844, Nathaniel Hawthorne, forced to do his own cooking while his wife was away, wrote to her jubilantly of his success at the stove:

> The corned beef is exquisitely done, and as tender as a young lady's heart, all owing to my skilful cookery; for I consulted Sarah Hale's cookbook at every step, and precisely followed her directions. To say the truth, I look upon it as such a masterpiece in its way, that it seems irreverential to eat it.

Within a few months of Hawthorne tucking his napkin under his chin to do full justice to his exquisite corned beef, *A Treatise on Domestic Economy for the Use of Young Ladies at Home and at School* had been published. It came from the pen of the woman writer on whom could be bestowed the sobriquet of "The American Mrs. Beeton." Catharine Esther Beecher (1800 to 1878), daughter of the eminent Presbyterian clergyman, the Reverend Lyman Beecher, was the eldest of a large family which included the famous Harriet Beecher Stowe, author of *Uncle Tom's Cabin*. In the 1820s Catharine Beecher started a girls' school at Hartford, later moving to a larger establishment in Cincinnati where she promoted Harriet to the post of assistant headmistress.

It was as a result of her experiences in instructing her young women pupils in the techniques of homemaking and in domestic science, that she gained the ideas that led her to write her *Treatise on Domestic Economy*, followed in 1846 by *Miss Beecher's Domestic Receipt Book*. She was unequivocal in her condemnation of the vast majority of the cook books then available to the American housewife. Many still had an English background, and these dishes, she told her readers, might well be acceptable to those struggling to cook and bake in wet and foggy England, but "in America, owing to our brighter skies and more fervid climate" lighter and more delicately blended recipes bearing a Mediterranean flavor were called for. "Half of the recipes in our cook-books," she stridently complained, "are mere murder to such constitutions and stomachs as we grow here." This was a sentiment to which Mrs. Sara Payson Willis Parton (1811 to 1872) heartily applauded. Mrs. Parton, better known to her readers as "Fanny Fern," dressed up the phrase that still brings comfort to plain but hopeful girls: "The way to a man's heart is through his stomach."

Catharine Beecher's *Domestic Receipt Book,* was only one of her many works aimed at the domestic emancipation of the American housewife. *The American Woman's Home; or, Principles of Domestic Science,* 1869; *The New Housekeeper's Manual,* 1873; and *Housekeeper and Healthkeeper,* 1873, were some of the many aids to domestic efficiency that issued from her pen. "The housewife is the sovereign of an empire, and should regard her duties as dignified, important and difficult," she declared in one of her many best sellers. In any history of the cook book Catharine Beecher must be accorded an honored place as one of the earliest pioneers in the homemaking movement of nineteenth-century America.

Early American Recipes

HUSH PUPPIES

An old Southern recipe, Hush Puppies takes its name from the practice of quieting hunting dogs yelping for scraps from their master's table when he and his family dined *al fresco*. To silence the hounds, the cook had ready small pieces of corn meal which he had dropped into heated batter used for frying fish. These morsels were tossed to the dogs by members of the family, with the gentle plea of "Hush, puppy! Hush, puppy!"

1½ cups corn meal	1 egg, well beaten
½ cup flour	¾ cup milk
2 level teaspoons baking powder	1 small onion, grated fine
½ level teaspoon salt	Fat for deep frying

Sift together flour, corn meal, baking powder, and salt. Beat egg, milk, and onion together in a bowl. Combine with the dry ingredients and mix well. Drop small spoonfuls into hot fat. When the Hush Puppies are crisp and golden (about 1 minute) lift from fat in wire basket and drain in heated colander. Serve hot with fried fish. Recipe makes about 20.

A NUN'S SIGH

This American soufflé has been described as being as light as a nun's sigh. It is still a favorite dessert in the more exclusive and expensive restaurants in New York and other East Coast cities.

Castor sugar	¼ cup of butter
1 cup of flour	4 eggs
Pinch of salt	1 level teaspoon vanilla
1 cup of water	Fat for deep frying

Sift together sugar, flour, and salt. Heat water containing ¼ cup of butter until butter is melted. Add dry ingredients and stir quickly with wooden spoon until dough leaves sides of pan and forms lump. Remove from heat and beat in eggs singly, whisking hard after each addition. Stir in vanilla. Drop dough by heaping teaspoonfuls into preheated fat (375 degrees). When the soufflé is puffed with pride and golden brown, drain and sprinkle with castor sugar. Serve hot. Recipe is enough to make several dozen Nun's Sighs.

PEACH COBBLER

(1)	(2)
¾ cup sugar	1½ cups flour
1 tablespoon flour (self-rising)	1 tablespoon baking powder
3 cups fresh peach slices	Pinch of salt
½ teaspoonful cinnamon	3 tablespoonsfuls butter
4 tablespoons butter	½ cup milk

(1) Mix sugar and all flour in saucepan, then add peaches and cook over low heat, stirring constantly. When fruit is tender (about 5 minutes) pour into pan about 9 inches square, dot with butter and sprinkle with cinnamon.

(2) Sift together flour, baking powder, and salt. Rub in butter, then, with a fork, stir in milk until a soft dough is made. Place on lightly-floured wooden board, and knead for about 1 minute. Roll into a 10-inch square of pastry (about ½ inch thick), and place on top of peaches, molding and pinching dough to form a rim to the pie. Bake in preheated oven at about 425 degrees for 25 to 30 minutes until browned. Serve warm with thick cream.*

*This is a modern version of the recipe.

HAYMAKER'S SWITCHEL

Down in the Eastern States it was said that the hay was in the barn in half the usual time if jugs of Switchel were sent out to the fields at haymaking time. Spiked with rough-cut cider or homemade brandy, it not only had the wains loaded at record speed but most of the farmworkers as well. Shotgun marriages were often the result a few months later.

Mix ½ cup molasses with ¾ cup vinegar. Combine mixture with 1 cup brown sugar, ½ teaspoonful powdered ginger, stirred into 2 quarts of cold water. Lace generously with rough-cut cider (or brandy), add crushed ice, then leave to chill.

FISH HOUSE PUNCH

There's a little place just out of town,
Where, if you go to lunch,
They'll make you forget your mother-in-law
With a drink called Fish-House Punch.

This Philadelphia speciality dates back to the early eighteenth century, and is supposed to have originated at the exclusive State Country Club, Schuylkill. Bowls of punch large enough to have "swimm'd half a dozen young geese" were prepared there in the early days.

The cooking class. A photograph of 1888, showing the daughters of prominent citizens of Detroit, Michigan, frozen in carefully posed attitudes of domesticity.

143

Dissolve 1 pound sugar in the minimum possible amount of cold water, then stir in 1 quart of unsweetened lemon juice. When mixed, pour slowly over a large lump of ice, before adding 2 quarts Jamaica rum, 1 quart French cognac, and ¾ cup peach brandy. Stir well and serve in chilled glasses.

SHAKER SPINACH WITH ROSEMARY

No religious group in America was more industrious than the devout and celibate Shakers on their communal farms in New York, Kentucky, and Ohio.

Founded about 1747 in England by James and Jane Wardley, they were strong believers in the Second Coming of Christ. In 1774, the sect moved to America, there forming the first communistic settlements in the U.S.A. They were the first to sell packaged garden seeds, and medicinal and culinary herbs and spices. Their preserved fruits and vegetables soon became famous for their purity and high quality. The sect has long since passed into history, but Shaker recipes, revived in dozens of contemporary cook books, are eaten and appreciated throughout the U.S.A.

A corn supplier's sack label of the 1850s, used by retailers in the U.S.A. The name of the supplier was written in by hand.

2 pounds spinach leaves
1 medium-sized onion, sliced
    and chopped
2 tablespoonfuls butter

½ teaspoonful fresh rosemary
    (or same amount dried)
4 sprigs parsley, well chopped
Salt and pepper to taste.

Wash spinach in cold water, chop larger leaves and place in large saucepan with all other ingredients. Cook in covered pan (in its own juices) for about 6 minutes, and serve when limp but still bright green in color. Serves 4.

SISTER ABIGAIL'S BLUE FLOWER OMELET

This old Shaker recipes uses chive flowers when in season. Flowers of wild garlic, or crushed nasturtium seeds, may be substituted if chive flowers are unobtainable.

Break and whip lightly 4 eggs in bowl to which 4 tablespoonfuls of milk have been added. Add dash of pepper, 1 tablespoonful finely chopped parsley, 1 tablespoonful chopped chives, ½ teaspoonful salt, and 12 chive blossoms (or garlic flowers or nasturtium seeds). Blend ingredients together. Lightly grease hot omelet pan with butter, then stir in mixture when pan is smoking. Stir gently with silver fork until eggs begin to set, then cook a little more, to lightly brown underside of omelet. Roll up omelet so it's tube-shaped and tip out onto heated plate. Serves 2.

BUCKWHEAT CAKES

James McNeill Whistler (1834 to 1903), the American artist, introduced buckwheat cakes to sophisticated London society. He had brought the recipe from his hometown, Lowell, Massachusetts. Buckwheat cakes are still one of the most popular breakfast staples in America.

Small packet active dry yeast
¼ cup warm water
2 cups milk
2 cups buckwheat flour

½ teaspoonful salt
1 tablespoonful molasses
Large pinch baking soda

Dissolve yeast in warm water. Boil milk, then cool to lukewarm. Blend together yeast, milk, buckwheat, and salt, beating hard for 3 minutes. Cover with clean cloth and let stand in warm room overnight. Next day, mix in the molasses and baking soda. Pour onto a hot well greased griddle (which should be hot enough to sizzle water dropped on it). Brown the cakes on both sides. Serve immediately with lashings of butter and warm maple syrup.*

*This is a modern version of the recipe.

MARYLAND CRAB CAKES

6 slices white bread	1½ pounds crabmeat
¾ cup olive oil	Paprika
2 teaspoonsful Worcestershire Sauce	3 eggs, separated
	¼ teaspoon dry mustard
3 tablespoons butter	½ teaspoon salt

Trim all crusts from bread and lay the slices on a shallow metal dish. Pour oil over them and let soak well in. Combine egg yolks with mustard, Worcestershire Sauce, and salt. Beat lightly, then stir in bread and crabmeat. Beat egg whites until stiff, then gently fold into the mixture. Shape into small servings. Sprinkle with paprika and sauté in heated butter until golden brown on both sides. Serves 6.

NEW ENGLAND POACHED SALMON WITH EGG SAUCE

From the time of the digging of the first new potatoes and early peas, it has been traditional in New England to serve Poached Salmon with Egg Sauce on the Fourth of July. Throughout the nineteenth century, cook books emphasize that housewives should take advantage of the low price of the plentiful eastern salmon which is in full "run" at this time and while succulent new vegetables are filling the baskets in the marketplace for all to have. The price of fresh salmon in the 1970s will make this recipe a luxury dish to the majority of wives who budget the family income; but as an appetizer from the good old days it is here for the mind's eye to devour.

Purchase a whole fresh salmon, or obtain a 5-pound to 6-pound cut from the center of a prime fish.

Clean and wash the salmon, then wrap securely in a long piece of clean muslin. Leave long ends over in order to make removal of the salmon easy from the broth when it is cooked. Bring 3 quarts of salted water to the boil, having first added a bay leaf, four peppercorns, and several thin slices of lemon. Boil for 15 minutes. Reduce heat to simmering, add the wrapped salmon, then turn up heat until water boils. Reduce once again to a low simmer and leave until salmon is cooked through. (Average about 7 to 8 minutes per pound weight.)

When salmon is tender and flakes easily, lift from broth and unwrap muslin. Place on a large heated plate and carefully skin the fish. Garnish and decorate, using lemon slices and sprigs of parsley. While the salmon is cooking, prepare the Egg Sauce:

1 cup milk	1 cup single cream
1 bay leaf	3 tablespoons flour
2 small onions, thinly sliced	3 tablespoons butter
1 whole clove	2 hard-boiled eggs
1 teaspoon salt	Shake of pepper

Heat milk and cream with the onion slices, bay leaf, and the clove, until skin forms. Skim the pan. Melt butter in saucepan, stir in flour, keeping a smooth texture, and cook over a low heat for a few minutes. Pour in milk mixture and cook over low heat, stirring continuously until mixture boils. Remove from heat, season with salt and pepper, and strain into saucepan. Add eggs, coarsely chopped, and heat through. Do not boil. If sauce is too thick, add a little more single cream. Serve salmon with Egg Sauce to cover fish.

RED FLANNEL HASH

According to legend, this recipe was created in the Green Mountains of Vermont, where it was a favorite dish of the Revolutionary soldier Ethan Allen (1738 to 1789), and his stalwart band of Green Mountain Boys.

4 medium-sized beetroots, well cooked	¾ cup butter
2 large potatoes, well cooked	1 large onion, chopped
1½ pounds minced cooked steak	1 tablespoon thick cream
	Salt and pepper to taste

Mash the beetroots and potatoes, then mix with the minced steak. Add salt and pepper. Add half the butter to a separate pan, together with the chopped onion, and cook until onion is tender but not brown. Stir in the meat and vegetable mixture and cook over a low heat for about 12 minutes. Spoon out mixture into a flat baking dish. Melt remaining butter and mix with the cream to make a smooth sauce. Pour this over the partly cooked hash. Brown for 5 minutes under grill until a golden crust has formed. Delicious with poached eggs atop. Serves 6.

THE MYSTERIE AND TRADE OF BAKING

All services that to the Baker's Trade
Or mysterie belong, be here displaid,

Which my rude Arts in order shall recount,
And those in number to thirteen amount,
Being (how ere such Tradesmen used to coozen
In their scale measure) just a Baker's dozen.

First [1]Boulting, [2]Seasoning, [3]Casting up, and [4]Braking,
[5]Breaking out dowe, next [6]Weighing, or weight making
(Which last is rarely seene), then some doe [7]Mould;
This [8]Cuts, that [9]Seales and Sets up, yet behold
The seasoner [10]Heating, or with Barin fires
Preparing the oven as the case requires;

One carrying up, the Heeter peeleth on
And playes the [11]Setter, who's no sooner gone
But the hot mouth is [12]Stopt, so to remaine
Untill the setter [13]drawes all forth againe.

Thus bakers make and to perfection bring,
No less to serve the Beggar than the King,
All sorts of Bread, which being handled well,
All other food and Cates doth farre excell.
Let Butchers, Poultrers, Fishmongers contend
Each in his own trade, in what he can Defend,
Though Flesh, Fish, Whitemeat, all in fitting season,
Nourish the body, being used with reason,
Yet no man can deny (to end the strife)
Bread is worth all, being the staff of life.

A series of pictures and rhymes taken from an early-nineteenth-century *Book of Trades* produced for a juvenile audience.

Chapter Nine

JOHN BULL'S PUDDINGS

No sooner had the Battle of Waterloo been brought to a satisfactory conclusion than the field of culinary endeavor back in Britain witnessed a spate of outlandish publications. Some had made their appearance long before this. Odd and whimsical tracts devoted to domestic economy and cuisine, apparently inspired by the need to say something entirely new and catch the public's eye, had been on the counters of bookshops for several years. *The Return to Nature; or, A Defence of the Vegetable Regimen*, 1811, by John Frank Newton, ranked high amongst these, with its dogmatic assertions that the lower orders had been carefully programmed by an ''All-Seeing God'' specially for the menial stations he had allotted them.

> Considering what are the disgusting offices which ill-health entails upon servants, the attendants of the sick, it seems a merciful dispensation in their behalf that the sense of smelling should be universally deficient in them.

These sentiments would have been applauded by that equally strange character Dr. William Kitchiner (1775 to 1827), who, not long afterward, made his own dramatic appearance on the stage of culinary and scientific affairs.

Born the son of a London coal merchant who had succeeded in business far beyond his own wildest expectations, young William was found a place in the exclusive confines of Eton College. His stay there was apparently rambustious in the extreme, and not only on the playing fields. During one particularly hectic game of darts, Kitchiner was so wounded in the eyes as to become permanently blind in one of them. After making a speedy recovery from his injury, he was back at school, this time sporting a monocle, thus earning for himself the nickname ''quiz-fish'' from his fellow students. What happened in the intervening years is none too clear, but he is

Charming well again

A political cartoon of October 1816 showing the Prince Regent (later George IV) partaking of the lightest of meals during his convalescence.

next heard of at Glasgow University, where he eventually obtained a degree in medicine. Professional jealousies south of the border ensured that Scottish degrees were not recognized in England, so Kitchiner was not able to practice in London. This setback was the least of his worries, as he was now totally independent financially. On the death of his father, when William was still at University, he had inherited an income of several thousands of pounds per year. He was not long in putting the money to what he considered very good use.

By his mid-twenties he was already displaying many eccentric traits of character; but he delighted his many friends and acquaintances by his open-handed hospitality. His sumptuously furnished residence, 43 Warren Street, Fitzroy Square, London, was soon famous for the banquets he devised and largely organized. It was here that he gave his controversial luncheons and dinners, at any of which, to arrive only a few minutes late was to be denied an entrance. These rivaled the equally well-known breakfasts of several hours duration provided by Kitchiner's banker friend Samuel Rogers (1763 to 1855). Rogers, a poet of no mean standing, whose *An Ode to Superstition*, 1786, was often quoted in literary circles, may well have prompted Dr. William to give some of his scientific discoveries the permanence of publication. Kitchiner's monocular vision seemingly lent weight to his discourses in such titles as *A Companion to the Telescope*, 1811, and other works of a similar nature on which he lavished much time and a considerable amount of money.

A few years later he issued the work which ensured him a place in any history of cook books: *Apicius Redevivus, or The Cook's Oracle*, 1817. In this interesting and unwittingly amusing work, he revealed to his readers many of the delicacies which he had himself invented in the well-stocked kitchens of Warren Street. The work was issued anonymously, but he could not resist informing his readers that his dishes were "the Result of Actual Experiments Instituted in the Kitchen of a Physician, for the Purpose of Composing a Culinary Code for the Rational Epicure, and for Augmenting the Alimentary Enjoyments of Private Families." His dishes "were so composed, as to be as agreeable and useful to the stomach, as they are inviting to the appetite; nourishing without being inflammatory, and savoury without surfeiting."

His choice of words brought a new spice to cookery books, as his "alimentary enjoyments" brought pleasure or dismay to those bold enough to try them. "I have taken as much pains in describing, in the fullest manner, how to make, in the easiest, most agreeable, and most economical way, those Dishes which daily contribute to the comforts of the middle rank of Society, as I have in directing the preparation of those piquante and elaborate relishes, the most ingenious and accomplished 'Officers of the Mouth' have invented for the amusement of Grand Gourmands."

An after-dinner treat. Grandville's (J. I. I. Gérard) satire on master and servant in his *Les Métamorphoses du Jour*, 1828.

XXXVI.

Ma femme est sortie, ma petite chatte..... Hi!..... hi!... hi!.....

His use of the title gourmand, instead of the more usual gourmet, was unfortunate in its modern sense of a gluttonous, that is, greedy, feeder, rather than that of a connoisseur of the delights of the table; but it is doubtful if Dr. Kitchiner was the least concerned with nuances of expression on his title pages or elsewhere. A guest at many of his meals, William Jerdon (1789 to 1869), the well-known journalist, described in *Men I Have Known,* 1866, his memories of one such encounter with the strange dishes his host set before his often apprehensive diners:

A stag party. A caricature by "Grandville" (J. I. I. Gérard) of the Georgian equivalent of a present-day Rotary Club dinner. It appeared in his *Les Métamorphoses du Jour,* 1828.

His medical and gastronomic practices were wonderfully combined as Peptic Precepts, insomuch that it was not always easy to tell, in partaking of what was before you, whether you might be swallowing a meal or a prescription at his hospital, or as the case might be, his hospitable board . . . However, the dinners at which he entertained his friends were by no means as bizarre as rumour gave them out. If the oddities were there, there was always a fair

counterbalance of the relishable and genuine. But a tureen of soup was not liked any the better for having its ingredients minutely explained, and the price—perhaps only sixpence or sevenpence—recorded for all to hear. To give him his due, this economical fare might well be followed by a costly cut of fresh Severn Salmon, and there was generally a liberal joint of meat, to save you experimenting on the made dishes, which, I must own, seemed often of dark and dubious quality, and the wines partook of the same mixed and strange variety.

Within a few months of its first appearance Dr. Kitchiner's cook book was universally known simply as *The Cook's Oracle,* and when the second edition made its appearance, dated 1818, the first part of the title had already disappeared from the printed page. New editions continued to be issued almost every twelve months, with about twenty different versions circulating before 1840. Each carried the doctor's now famous maxim, which today sounds rather like the latest TV jingle:

Masticate, Denticate, Chump, Grind, and Swallow!

Kitchiner started his book, not with a recipe for the table, but with a sure-fire prescription for easing constipation: "We must evacuate before we can accommodate!" He told his uneasy readers, and then went on to detail his prescription that would clear the lower decks for action:

TO MAKE FORTY PERISAULTIC PERSUADERS

Take of Turkey Rhubarb, finely pulverized—2 drachms
Syrup (by weight)—1 drachm
Oil of Carraway—10 drops
Make into convenient Pills, each of which will now contain 3
         grains of Rhubarb.

The dose of the persuaders must be adapted to the constitutional peculiarity of the Patient. Those stubborn cases who wish to accelerate or greatly augment the Alvine exoneration must take two, three, or more than the usual dose, depending on the effect they wish to produce. Only Two Pills will do as much for one person as five or six for another. But they will generally very regularly perform their good offices as to what you wish today—without interfering with what you hope will happen tomorrow. They are as convenient an argument against Constipation as any we are acquainted with, and as many as two or four Persuaders may be taken at any time by the most delicate of Females.

As soon as the final rumbles had died away it was time to try one of the good doctor's experimental dishes "so composed as to be as agreeable and useful to the stomach, as they are inviting to the appetite."
A burst of introductory rhetoric set the scene for the culinary dramas that followed:

The following Receipts are not a mere marrowless collection of shreds and patches, of cuttings and pastings—but a *bona fide* register of Practical facts, accumulated by a perseverance not to be subdued or evaporated by the igniferous terrors of a Roasting Fire in the Dog-days. Moreover, the Author has submitted to a labour no preceeding Cookery-Book-maker, perhaps, ever attempted to encounter—having *eaten* each Receipt before he set it down in his book.

Each and every one of them have been heartily welcomed by a sufficiently well-educated Palate, and a rather fastidious Stomach. The Stomach is the Grand Organ of the human system, upon the state of which all the powers and feelings of the individual depend. The faculty the Stomach has of communicating the impressions made by the various substances that are put into it, is such, that it seems more like a nervous expansion from the Brain than a mere receptacle for Food . . .

I am perfectly aware of the extreme difficulty of teaching those who are entirely unacquainted with the subject, and of explaining my ideas effectually by mere Receipts, to those who never shook hands with a Stewpan. Our neighbours in France are so justly famous for their skill in the affairs of the Kitchen, that the adage says, *"As many Frenchmen, as many Cooks."* Surrounded as they are by a profusion of the most delicious Wines, and seducing *Liqueurs* offering every temptation to render drunkenness delightful, yet a tippling Frenchman is a *rara avis*. They know how, so easily, to keep Life in sufficient repair by good eating, that they require little or no screwing up with liquid Stimuli. Their elastic Stomachs, unimpaired by Spirituous Liquors, digest vigorously the food they sagaciously prepare—wisely contriving to get half the work of the Stomach done by Fire and Water, till

> *The tender morsels on the palate melt,*
> *And all the force of Cookery is felt.*

Worthy William Shakespeare declared he never found a philosopher who could endure the Toothache patiently; the Editor protests that he has not yet overtaken one who did not love a Feast.

Every individual who is not a perfect imbecile and void of understanding is an Epicure in his own way—the Epicures in boiling of Potatoes are innumerable. The perfection of all enjoyment depends on the perfection of the faculties of the Mind and Body; therefore the *Temperate Man* is the greatest Epicure, and the only true Voluptuary . . . The Stomach is the mainspring of the System—if it is not sufficiently wound up to warm the Heart and support the circulation the whole business of Life will, in proportion, be ineffectually performed. We can neither *Think* with precision; *Walk* with vigour; *Sit down* with comfort; nor *Sleep* with tranquility . . .

A good Dinner is one of the greatest enjoyments of human life; and, as the practice of Cookery is attended with so many discouraging difficulties, so many disgusting and disagreeable circumstances, and even dangers, we ought to have some regard for those who encounter them to procure us pleasure . . .

And so on! It was in such a style that Dr. Kitchiner continued his lecture for over thirty closely printed pages, leaving his readers more than a little breathless when they finally came to his recipes. Even these were liberally strewn with pungent homilies. "In the affairs of the Mouth," he told them on the opening page, "the strictest punctuality is indispensable. The Gastronomer ought to be as accurate an observer of Time as the Astronomer. *The least delay produces fatal and irreparable Misfortunes.*" With this stern warning ringing in their ears they were at last permitted to sample his wares:

ROAST SUCKING-PIG

A sucking-pig is in prime order for the spit when about three weeks old. It loses part of its goodness every hour after it is killed: if not quite fresh, no art can make the *Crackling* crisp.

To be in perfection, *it should be killed in the morning to be eaten at dinner*. It requires very careful roasting. A sucking-pig, like a young Child, must not be left for an instant.

The ends of the pig must have more fire than the middle; for this purpose is contrived an Iron to hang before the middle part, called a *Pig Iron*. If you do not have this, use a common flat Iron, or keep the fire fiercest at the two ends.

For the stuffing, take of the crumb of a stale loaf about five ounces; rub it through a colander; mince fine a handful of sage (i.e., about two ounces), and a large onion (about an ounce and a half). Mix these together with an egg, some pepper and salt, and a bit of butter as big as an egg. Fill the belly of the pig with this, and sew it up. Lay it to the fire, and baste it with Salad oil till it is quite done. Do not leave it a moment; it requires the most vigorous attendance.

Roast it at a clear fire at some distance. To gain the praise of the Epicurean Pig-Eaters, the Crackling must be *nicely crisped* and delicately *lightly browned,* without being either blistered or burnt.

A small three-weeks' old Pig will be done enough in about an hour and a half.

Before you take it from the Fire, cut off the head, and part that and the body down the middle. Chop the Brains very fine with some boiled Sage leaves, and mix with a good veal gravy, or Beef gravy, or what runs from the Pig when you cut its head off. Send up a tureenful of this Gravy when the Pig is served. Currant Sauce is still a favourite with some of the old school.

Lay your Pig back to back in the dish, with one half of the head on each side, and the Ears one at each end, which you must take care to make nice and *crisp,* or you will get scolded, and deservedly, as the silly fellow was who bought his wife a pig with only one ear.

N.B. A Pig is a very troublesome subject to roast. Most persons have them *Baked;* send a quarter of a pound of butter, and beg the baker to baste it well.

GREEN PEASE

Young Green Pease well dressed are one of the most delicious of the vegetable kingdom. They must be young; it is equally indispensable that they be *fresh gathered, and cooked as soon as they are shelled,* for they soon lose both their colour and sweetness. If you wish to feast upon pease *in perfection,* you must have them gathered the same day they are dressed, and put on to boil within half an hour after they are shelled.

Pass them through a riddle, i.e., a coarse sieve, which is made for the purpose of separating them. This precaution is necessary, for the large and small pease cannot be boiled together, as the former will take more time than the latter.

For a peck of pease, set on a sauce-pan with a gallon of water in it. When it boils, put in your pease, with a table-spoonful of salt. Skim it well; keep them boiling quick from twenty to thirty minutes, according to their age and size. The best way to judge of their being done enough, and indeed the only way to make sure of cooking them to, and not beyond, the point of perfection, or, as Pea-eaters say, of *"boiling them to a bubble,"* is to take them out with a spoon, and taste them.

When they are done enough, drain them on a hair-sieve. If you like them buttered, put them into a pie-dish, divide some butter into small bits, and lay them on the pease. Put another dish over them, and turn them over and over: this will melt the butter through them: but as all people do not like buttered pease, you had better send them to table plain, as they come out of the sauce-pan, with melted butter in a sauce-tureen.

N.B. A peck of young Pease will not yield more than enough for a couple of hearty Pea-eaters. When the Pods are full, it may serve for three.

According to Dr. Harte, in his *Essay on Diet,* 1633, "A Red Herring doth nourish little, and is hard of concoction, but very good to make a cup of good drink relish well, and may well be called 'The Drunkard's Delight.'"

RED HERRINGS

They should be cooked in the same manner as now practised by the Poor in Scotland. They soak them in water until they become pretty fresh; then they hang them up in the Sun and Wind on a stick through their eyes, to dry; and they are then boiled or broiled. In this way they eat almost as well as if they were new caught. The larger fish should be steeped about twelve hours, the smaller about two. To Herring, and to all sorts of boiled Salt Fish, sweet oil is the best basting.

A GOOD SCOTCH HAGGIS

Make the haggis-bag perfectly clean; parboil the draught*; boil the liver very well, so as it will grate; dry the oatmeal before the fire; mince the draught and a pretty large piece of beef very small; grate about half of the liver; mince plenty of the suet and some onions small; mix all of these materials very well together with a

*Draught: the entrails, or pluck, of a sheep or cow.

handful or two of the dried meal. Spread them on the table, and season them properly with salt and mixed spices. Take any of the scraps of beef that are left from mincing, and some of the water that boiled the draught, and make about a choppin [a quart] of good stock of it. Then put all the haggis meat into the bag, and that broth in it. Sew up the bag, but be sure to put out all the wind contained in it before you sew it quite close.

If you think the bag is thin, you may put it in a cloth.

If it is a large haggis, it will take at least two hours' boiling.

With this recipe, as with others, Kitchiner acknowledged his source, attributing it to Mrs. MacIver, of Edinburgh, who published a book of cookery there in 1787. For those Sassenachs, like myself, to whom a haggis will always remain a steaming mystery, I quote a present-day interpretation of this famous Burns supper dish: "A haggis consists of the heart, lungs, and liver of a sheep, calf, etc., or sometimes of the tripe and chitterlings. This is minced with suet and oatmeal, seasoned with salt, pepper, onions, etc., and boiled like a large sausage in the stomach (or maw) of the animal."

The main kitchen of Brighton Pavilion, built by the Prince Regent in 1784.

A kitchen of the 1780s (at Brighton Pavilion), which has been preserved in original form to the present day.

The "bag," mentioned in the recipe for "A Good Scotch Haggis" is, of course, the stomach of whatever animal the draught is removed from.

The next recipe Kitchiner printed acknowledged no source but his own experimental kitchen, and he headed it simply:

MY PUDDING

Beat up the yolks and whites of three Eggs; strain them through a sieve (to keep out the treadles*), and gradually add to them about a quarter of a pint of Milk. Stir these well together.

Rub together in a mortar two ounces of moist Sugar, and as much grated Nutmeg as will lie on a sixpence. Stir these into the Eggs and Milk; then put in four ounces of Flour, and beat it into a smooth Batter. By degrees stir into it seven ounces of Suet *(minced as fine as possible),* and three ounces of Bread-crumbs.

Treadles: chicken embryos.

158

Mix all thoroughly together at least half an hour before you put the pudding into the pot.

Put it into an earthenware pudding-mould that you have well buttered; tie a pudding-cloth over it very tight; put it into boiling water, and boil it for three hours.

Put one good *Plum* into it. You may then tell the *Economist* that you have made a good *Plum Pudding* without Plums! This would be what Schoolboys call *"Mile-Stone Pudding,"* i.e., "a Mile between one Plum and another."

Before retiring for the night it was the good Doctor's invariable practice to imbibe a glass or two of his favorite beverage. It was, he said, "A right Gossip's Cup, that far exceeds all the Ale that ever Mother Bunch made in her life-time!" For reasons of his own he had named it:

TEWAHDIDDLE

A pint of Table Beer (or Ale, if you intend it for a supplement to your "Night-Cap"), a table-spoonful of Brandy, and a tea-spoonful of brown Sugar. A little grated Nutmeg or Ginger may be added, and a roll of very thin-cut Lemon-Peel.

Now before our readers make any remarks on this Composition, we beg them to taste it. If the materials are good, and their palate vibrates in unison with our own, they will find it one of the pleasantest beverages that they ever put to their lips.

Finally, there was his patented appetizer which could be bought ready-bottled at his home address, or at "Butler's Herb Shop, opposite Henrietta Street, Covent Garden; where may also be had *The Cook's Oracle*." With an eye for the snap title which would do credit to any modern public relations firm, he named his product:

ZEST
*Will add life to your
chops, sauces and made dishes!*

This piquant quintessence of *Ragoût* imparts to whatever it touches the most delicious Relish ever imagined! It awakens the Palate with Delight, refreshes the Appetite, and instantly excites the good humour of *every Man's master*—the Stomach.

ZEST has a hundred uses. With two Drachms of ZEST in half a pint of melted butter you have a quick-made Savoury Sauce! Let it boil up and strain it through a sieve before serving. Or, each guest may add it, at table, like Salt, and so adjust the vibrations of his Palate to suit his own fancy.

The ebullient Dr. Kitchiner well deserved any financial success which accrued from his enterprise, if only for his audacity in being at least

A London butcher's boy of 1821, pictured by Richard Dighton.

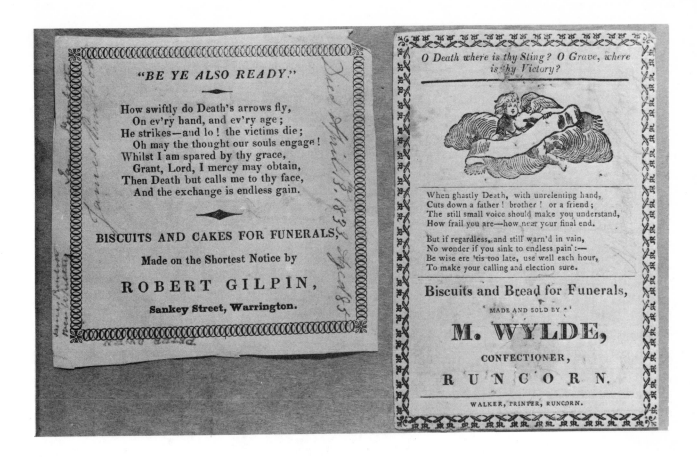

"BE YE ALSO READY."

How swiftly do Death's arrows fly,
   On ev'ry hand, and ev'ry age;
He strikes—and lo! the victims die;
   Oh may the thought our souls engage!
Whilst I am spared by thy grace,
   Grant, Lord, I mercy may obtain,
Then Death but calls me to thy face,
   And the exchange is endless gain.

BISCUITS AND CAKES FOR FUNERALS,

Made on the Shortest Notice by

ROBERT GILPIN,

Sankey Street, Warrington.

O Death where is thy Sting? O Grave, where is thy Victory?

When ghastly Death, with unrelenting hand,
Cuts down a father! brother! or a friend;
The still small voice should make you understand,
How frail you are—how near your final end.

But if regardless, and still warn'd in vain,
No wonder if you sink to endless pain:—
Be wise ere 'tis too late, use well each hour,
To make your calling and election sure.

Biscuits and Bread for Funerals,

· MADE AND SOLD BY · '

M. WYLDE,

CONFECTIONER,

R U N C O R N.

WALKER, PRINTER, RUNCORN.

Bakers' advertisements for funeral bread and cakes from the early 1830s.

forty years before his time. This was the period which elapsed before the rest of the market had awakened to the fact that convenience foods and savories would be almost instantly snapped up by thousands of heavily-burdened females oppressed with household chores. Canning of food was invented by a M. Appert of Paris as early as 1810, but the bottling of sauces and other piquants branded with household names seems certainly to have started with our own Dr. Kitchiner.

His own domestic life appears not always to have been happy. In August 1799, at the age of twenty-four, he married a Miss Cripps of York. She was able to stand his eccentricities for only a few months, after which the pair parted for good. Miss Cripps returned thankfully to the bosom of her family, and Dr. William found solace in the arms of another, an episode which resulted in the birth of a son out of wedlock. He adopted the boy as his heir, but the lad caused his father growing concern and increasing anxiety as he grew to manhood. In one of his letters, Kitchiner complained bitterly that he was in "the utmost distress on account of the sad conduct of my son at Cambridge—which breaks down all my philosophy."

Overeating and too free indulgence in the grosser pleasures of life finally began to take their toll of the doctor when only in his late forties. His end, at the age of fifty-two, was probably as he would have wished it, and his epigraph could well have been simply: "Found dead—after a good dinner!"

His friend, William Jerdon, mentioned above, was with him at the last dinner party the doctor attended. It was held on February 20, 1827, an evening "redolent with charming music, (and) was concluded by the usual *petit souper,* which means a rather luxurious supper . . . He [Dr. Kitchiner] forgot all about his rule of retiring at eleven, and was above all delighted with a pet macaw. But this was a mere screen to conceal a cloud of carking care . . . We learned afterwards that, owing to domestic circumstances, he had prepared a settlement which would inflict contingencies or restrictions on the inheritance of his son, and that the following day was fixed for his signature. At nine in the morning he was dead . . .''

As the new will remained unsigned, Kitchiner's son inherited his father's entire estate. One wonders what a modern inquest might have revealed, for a faint odour of mystery surrounds Dr. William Kitchiner's very convenient death.

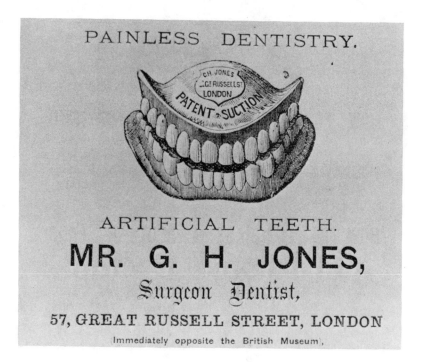

Mastication made easy. An advertisement of 1877 that would have delighted Dr. Kitchiner's heart.

During the last few months of his life, Kitchiner had been working hard to finish a companion work, entitled *The Traveller's Oracle; or Maxims for Locomotion,* 2 volumes, 1827, which finally made its appearance in September of that year, some six months after his death. Needless to say, there are any number of puffs for Kitchiner's own works, and his pills and "persuaders." "Let a Traveller carry with him a Copy of *The Cook's Oracle,* of which there is just published, by Cadell and Co. Edinburgh, and Geo. B. Whittaker, Ave Maria Lane, a New Edition, in 12mo. price 7s.6d. boards." And, a little later in the text, "*The Cook's Oracle* we consider as the *ne plus ultra* of the science of Eating, and the very acme of excellence in Culinary literature. So much good sense, combined with such exquisite *Gourmanderie*—so much plain *Pot-information,* conveyed in so truly humorous and original a style, place this Work on the very eminence of the ample Dome of Cookery." Who could say more! The public must have liked it, for a second edition of *The Traveller's Oracle* was called for and made its appearance that same year, all the profits going to Dr. William's son and heir.

Contemporary accounts vary as to what happened next; some glee-
fully detailing the way the young man is alleged to have squandered the
fortune unwittingly left him by his father. The last we hear of him is a report
from the poet Thomas Hood that W. Brown Kitchiner, "son of the doctor,"
and his wife were present at a reception given at that most respectable of
venues, the home of the Speaker of the House of Commons. Which hardly
equates with the stories of dissipation and social ruin.

It was Hood who, shortly after William Kitchiner's death, penned an
ode to his memory:

> *Immortal Kitchener! thy fame*
> *Shall keep itself when Time makes game*
> *Of other men's—yea, it shall keep, all weathers,*
> *And thou shalt be upheld by thy pen feathers.*
> *Yea, by the sauce of Michael Kelly!*
> *Thy name shall perish never,*
> *But be magnified for ever—*
> *By those whose eyes are bigger than their belly.*

One wonders which would have incensed the worthy doctor the
most: the fact that Hood misspelled his name, or the disparaging reference to
his famous Zest sauce by linking it with the name of the Irish actor Michael
Kelly.

The year 1818 saw the publication of *The Family Receipt Book* by
Mrs. Westcott, "late housekeeper to the Right Hon. The Earl of Morley,"

"The Cook's Oracle."

A cartoon by Thomas Hood in
his *Whims and Oddities*, 1826,
depicting his friend the well-
known Dr. Kitchiner.

with its chapters of medical recipes containing such intriguing names as ''Oil of Charity,'' and ''Live-long; an excellent Stomachic.'' Her ''Restorative Jelly'' called for several handfuls of ''well-crushed garden snails.'' *The Alphabetical Receipt Book, and Domestic Adviser,* 1826, by Robert Huish, sprang what must have been a disconcerting surprise upon its readers before they had finished perusing the letter ''A,'' by inserting amongst recipes for apple pie and artichokes, a ''certain remedy for Ruptures in the Navel, the Thigh, and the Scrotum.'' The colored frontispiece to this startling octavo of some 822 pages showed a well-proportioned lady of the day. The caption beneath read: ''Adjustment of Dress.''

The Females Best Friend; or, The Young Woman's Guide to Virtue, Economy, and Happiness: Containing a Complete Modern System of Cookery, 1826, edited and compiled by Watkin Poole, Esq., appeared the following year. It was Mr. Poole who wrote the verse beneath the frontispiece of a doting matron intent on furthering his own domestic well-being:

> *Who gilds my childrens infant day*
> *With cultivation's dawning ray*
> *And points to heaven and leads the way?*
> *My wife!*

The editor promised his readers that the book contained ''memoirs of illustrious females, eminent for their piety, virtue, and accomplishments,'' and that the work would form a pleasing companion for any ''respectable mother.''

The 1830s saw the continuing stream of new cook books rising to a flood, with provincial printers and publishers each adding their quota to the dozens of titles issued by the London publishing houses.

The price of many of the smaller works intended to tempt the cheaper end of a vastly extended market was now often as low as a shilling a copy, with the woodcut illustrations thrown in free of charge. *A Collection of Upwards of 220 Recipes,* 1830, was published under a Canterbury imprint at only a shilling; as was *The Housewife's Guide; or, An Economical and Domestic Art of Cookery, Adapted to Trademen's Families,* 1830, by Deborah Irwin. She boasted that she had been ''twenty-three years cook to a tradesman with a large family.''

Going one step upward in the social scale was *The Housewife's Guide; or, A Complete System of Modern Cookery,* 1838, ''by a Lady.'' This anonymous gentlewoman told her readers that her shilling booklet was ''particularly adapted for the middle class of society.'' But it was left to Captain Benson E. Hill to climb the topmost rung. *The Epicure's Almanac; or, Diary of Good Living; Containing a Choice and Original Receipt or a Valuable Hint for Every Day of the Year,* 1841, by ''the author of 'Recollections of an Artillery Officer,' 'A Pinch of Snuff,' &c. &c.,'' haughtily informed its readers that the hints and recipes Captain Hill had deigned to lay before them were ''the result of actual experience, applicable to the enjoyment of the good things of life, consistent with the views of those whose stations require them to practice only the most genteel economy.'' To practice any economy which was not genteel was to put oneself outside the pale of the gallant captain's circle of readership, a fact he made very clear in his text.

His views were doubtless applauded by the novelist daughter of the Duke of Argyll, Lady Charlotte Bury (née Campbell) (1775 to 1861), whose fastidious romances were causing a flutter in the upper-class boudoirs of the day. Her titles speak for themselves, with *Self Indulgence*, 2 volumes, 1812; *Flirtation*, 3 volumes, 1827; *A Marriage in High Life*, 1828; *The Disinherited and the Ensnared*, 3 volumes, 1834; and *The History of a*

An early nineteenth-century picnic, pictured by H. Heath in 1829.

Flirt, 3 volumes, 1840; being typical of her canon of work. She was one of the leading exponents of what came to be known as the Silver Fork School, those dainty novels of fashionable high-life that preceded the publication of Thackeray's *Vanity Fair* in 1848.

It was in 1840 that her publisher, Henry Colburn, issued the anonymous cloth-bound volume *The Lady's Own Cookery Book, and New Dinner-Table Directory*. According to its title page, the cookery book was "adapted to the use of Persons Living in the Highest Style, as well as those of Moderate Fortune." Had Colburn, when he published the third edition, dated 1844, not blazoned Lady Bury's name in letters of gold on the spine of the volume (though still with no acknowledgment on the title page), it is doubtful if any certain attribution could be given. Although, with hindsight, there are plenty of clues as to the author's identity contained in the preface to the work:

> The Receipts composing the Volume here submitted to the Public have been collected under peculiarly favourable circumstances by a Lady of distinction, whose productions in the lighter department of literature entitle her to a place amongst the most successful writers of the present day. Moving in the first circles of rank and fashion, her associations have qualified her to furnish directions adapted to the manners and taste of the most refined Luxury . . .

It seems that Charlotte Bury's manuscript notes and recipes were put into order by one of Colburn's editors, a fatiguing task she left to lesser mortals. But she read and corrected the proofs, and laid down strict instructions as to the book's format and general design, as well as supplying a set of rules that any good cook would be required to follow:

GENERAL RULES FOR A GOOD DINNER

There should always be two soups, white and brown; two fish, dressed and undressed; a bouilli and petits-patés; and on the sideboard a plain roast joint, besides many savoury articles, such as a hung beef, Bologna sausages, pickles, cold ham, cold pie, &c., some or all of these according to the number of guests, the names of which the head-servant ought to whisper about to the company, occasionally offering them. He should likewise carry about all the side-dishes or *entrées,* after the soups are taken away in rotation. A silver lamp should be kept burning, to put any dish upon that may grow cold.

It is indispensable to have candles, or plateau, or epergne, in the middle of the table.

Beware of letting the table appear loaded; neither should it be too bare.

The soups and fish should be despatched before the rest of the dinner is set on; but, lest any of the guests eat of neither, two small dishes of patés should be on the table. Of course, the meats and vegetables and fruits which compose these dinners must be varied according to the season, the number of guests, and the tastes of the host and hostess. It is also needless to add that without iced champagne and Roman punch, a dinner is not called a dinner.

These observations and the following directions for dinners are suitable for those who choose to live *fashionably;* but the receipts contained in this book will suit any mode of living, and the persons consulting it will find matter for all tastes and all establishments. There is many an excellent dish not considered adapted to a fashionable table, which, nevertheless, is given in these pages.

"Beef, mutton, and veal, are in season all the year," she told her readers, "house lamb in January, February, March, April, October, November, and December. Grass lamb comes in at Easter and lasts till April or May; pork from September till April or May; roasting pigs all the year; buck venison in

June, July, August, and September; doe and heifer venison in October, November, December, and January."

The very first recipe she printed set the tone for the whole book;

ALMOND SOUP

Take lean beef or veal, about eight or nine pounds, and a scrag of mutton.

Boil them gently in water that will cover them, till the gravy be very strong and the meat very tender; then strain off the gravy and set it on the fire with two ounces of vermicelli, eight blades of mace, twelve cloves, to a gallon.

Let it boil till it has the flavour of the spices.

Have ready one pound of the best almonds, blanched and pounded very fine. Pound them with the yolks of twelve eggs, boiled hard, mixing as you pound them with a little of the soup, lest the almonds should grow oily. Pound them until they are a mere pulp.

Add a little soup by degrees to the almonds and eggs until mixed together. Let the soup be cool when you mix it, and do it perfectly smooth.

Strain it through a sieve; set it on the fire; stir it frequently; and serve it hot.

Just before you take it up add a gill of thick cream.

In complete contrast was her:

PORTABLE SOUP FOR TRAVELLERS

Strip all the skin and fat off a leg of veal; then cut all the fleshy parts from the bone, and add a shin of beef, which treat in the same way.

Boil it slowly in three gallons of water or more according to the quantity of meat. Let the pot be closely covered. When you find it, in a spoon, very strong and clammy, like a rich jelly, take it off and strain it through a hair sieve into an earthen pan.

After it is thoroughly cold, take off any fat that may remain, and divide your jelly clear of the bottom into small flat-tish cakes in chinaware cups covered. Then place these cups in a large deep stewpan of boiling water over a stove fire, where let it boil gently till the jelly becomes a perfect glue; but take care the water does not get into the cups, for that will spoil it all.

These cups of glue must be taken out, and, when cold, turn out the glue into a new piece of coarse flannel, and in about six hours turn it upon more fresh flannel, and keep doing this until it is perfectly dry. If you then lay it in a warm dry place, it will presently become like a dry piece of glue.

When you use it in travelling, take a piece the size of a

large walnut, seasoning it with fresh herbs, and if you have an old fowl, or a very little bit of fresh meat, it will be excellent.

Before the days of tinned or packet soup such leathery concoctions were much prized by travelers abroad, and expecially those engaged in exploration or military campaigns. Dropped into a can of boiling water, and supplemented with whatever game or meat was available, it gave body to an otherwise watery meal. One of its original proponents was Elizabeth Raffald, who told her readers that "by pouring a pint of boiling water on one cake of my portable soup an excellent bason of broth can be quickly made. Also, it will make gravy for a turkey or fowl; the longer it is kept the better . . ."

Charlotte Bury's book contained well over 1,500 recipes. Many were as simple to prepare as others were complex, and the difficulty has been to select a representative sample:

LOBSTER FRICASSEE

Cut the meat of a lobster into dice; then put it in a stewpan with a little veal gravy. Let it stew for ten minutes.

A little before you send it to the table beat up the yolk of an egg in cream: put it to your lobster, stirring it till it simmers. Add pepper and salt to your taste.

Dish it up very hot, and garnish with lemon.

MACKAREL PIE

Cut the fish into four pieces; season them to your taste with pepper, salt, and a little mace, mixed with a quarter of a pound of beef suet, chopped fine. Put at the bottom and top, and between the layers of fish, a good deal of young parsley, and instead of water a little new milk in the dish for gravy. If you like it rich, warm about a quarter of a pint of cream, which pour into the pie when it is baked. If not, have boiled a little gravy with the fish heads. It will take the same time to bake as a veal pie.

PIKE—GERMAN WAY

Take a pike of moderate size. When well washed, gutted and cleaned, split it down the back, close to the bone, in two flat pieces. Set it over the fire in a stewpan with salt and water; half boil it.

Take it out; scale it; put in some mushrooms, truffles, and morels, an equal quantity, cut small; add a bunch of sweet herbs.

Let it stew very gently, closely covered, over a very slow fire, or the fish will break. When it is almost done, take out the herbs, put in a cupful of capers, chopped small, three anchovies split and shred fine, a piece of butter rolled in flour, and a tablespoonful of grated Parmesan cheese. Pour in a pint of white wine, and cover the stewpan quite close.

When the ingredients are mixed, and the fish quite done, lay it on a warm dish, and pour the sauce already in the pan over it.

BOAR'S HEAD WHOLE

When the head is cut off, the neck must be boned, and the tongue taken out. The brains must also be taken out on the inside, so as not to break the bone and skin on the outside.

When boned, singe the hair off, and clean it; then put it for four or five days into a red pickle made of saltpetre, bay salt, common salt, and coarse brown sugar, rubbing the pickle in every day.

When taken out of the pickle, lay the tongue in the centre of the neck or collar; close the meat together as close as you can, and bind it with strong tape up to the ears, the same as you would do brawn.

Then put it into a pot or kettle, the neck downward, and fill the pot with good broth and Rhenish wine, in the proportion of one bottle of wine to three pints of broth, till it is covered a little above the ears. Season the wine and broth with small bunches of sweet-herbs, such as basil, winter savory, and marjoram, bay leaves, shallots, celery, carrots, turnips, parsley-roots, with different kinds of spices.

Set it over the fire to boil; when it boils, put it on one side to boil gently till the head is tender.

Take it out of the liquor, and put it into an earthen pan. Skim all the fat off the liquor; strain it through a sieve into the head. Put the boar's head by until it is quite cold, and then it will be fit for use.

CURRY POWDER

This receipt was given me by a Resident in India. Half a pound of coriander seed, two ounces of black pepper, two ounces of cummin seed, one ounce of turmeric, one ounce and a half of ground rice. All the above must be finely pounded; add cayenne to your taste.

Mix well together; put it into a dish close to the fire; roast it well for three or four hours. When quite cold, put it into a bottle for use.

Take a ham of young pork; sprinkle it with salt, and let it lie twenty-four hours.

Having wiped it very dry, rub it well with a pound of coarse brown sugar, a pound of juniper berries, a quarter of a pound of saltpetre, half a pound of bay salt, and three pints of common salt, mixed together and dried in an iron pot over the fire, stirring them the whole time.

After this, take it off the fire when boiled, and let it lie in an earthen glazed pan three weeks, but it must be often turned in the time, and basted with the brine in which it lies.

Then hang it up until it has done dripping, and dry it in a chimney with deal saw-dust and juniper berries.

HAM—TO CURE ANOTHER WAY

Wash the ham clean. Soak it in pump water for an hour; dry it well, and rub into it the following composition: Saltpetre two ounces, bay salt nine ounces, common salt four ounces, lump sugar three ounces; but first beat them separately into a fine powder. Mix them together, dry them before the fire, and then rub them into the ham, as hot as the hand can bear it.

Then lay the ham on a sloping table; put on it a board with forty or fifty pounds weight; let it remain thus for five days; then turn it, and, if any of the salt is about, rub it in, and let it remain with the board and weight on it for five days more. This done rub off the salt, &c.

When you intend to smoke it, hang the ham in a sugar hogshead, over a chafing-dish of wood embers. Throw on the fire a handful of juniper-berries, and over that some horse-dung, and cover the cask with a blanket.

This may be repeated two or three times the same day, and the ham may be taken out of the hogshead the next morning.

The quantity of salt here specified is for a middle-sized ham.

There should not be a hole cut in the leg, as is customary, to hang it up by, nor should it be soaked in brine.

Hams thus cured will keep for three months without another smoking, so that the whole quantity for the year may be smoked at the same time.

The ham need not be soaked in water before it is used, but only washed clean.

If you have no chafing-dish, make a hole for the fire in the ground, and therein put your fire. It must not be fierce.

Be sure to keep the mouth of the hogshead covered with a blanket to retain the smoke.

MUTTON CUTLETS

Cut a neck of mutton into cutlets; beat it till it is very tender; wash it with thick melted butter, and strew over the side which is buttered some sweet herbs, chopped small, with grated bread, a little salt, and nutmeg.

Lay the cutlets on a gridiron over a charcoal fire, and turning them, do the same to the other sides as before.

Make a sauce of gravy, anchovies, shallots, thick butter, a little nutmeg, and lemon.

Pour over the cutlets and serve hot.

TONGUES–TO CURE

Take two fine bullock's tongues; wash them well in spring water; dry them thoroughly with a cloth, and salt them with common salt, a quarter of a pound of saltpetre, a quarter of a pound of treacle, and a quarter of a pound of gunpowder.

Let them lie in this pickle a month. Turn and rub them every day; then take them out and dry them with a cloth.

Rub a little gunpowder over them, and hang them for a month, when they will be fit to eat, previously soaking a few hours as customary.

PLUM CAKE

Take eight pounds and three quarters of fine flour well dried and sifted, one ounce of beaten mace, one pound and a half of sugar.

Mix them together, and take one quart of cream and six pounds of butter, put together, and set them over the fire till the butter is melted.

Then take thirty-three eggs, one quart of yeast, and twelve spoonfuls of sack. Put it into the flour, stir it well together, and when well mixed set it before the fire to rise for an hour.

Then take ten pounds of currants washed and dried, and set them to dry before the fire; also one pound of citron minced, one pound of orange and lemon-peel together, sliced.

When your oven is ready, stir your cake thoroughly; put in your sweetmeats and currants; mix them well in, and put into tin hoops.

The quantity here given will make two large cakes, which will take two hours' baking.

WINTER CREAM CHEESE

Take twenty quarts of new milk warm from the cow; strain it into a tub. Have ready four quarts of good cream boiled to put to it, and about a quart of spring water, boiling hot. Stir all together. Put in your earning [*rennet*], and stir it well in; keep it by the fire till it is well done.

Then take it gently into a sieve to whey it, and after that put it into a vat, either square or round, with a cheese-board upon it, of two pounds weight at first, which is to be increased by degrees to six pounds. Turn it into dry cloths two or three times a day for a week or ten days, and salt it with dry salt the third day.

When you take it out of the vat, lay it upon a board, and turn and wipe it every other day till it is quite dry.

It is best to be made as soon as the cows go into fog.*

The cheeses are fit to eat in Lent, sometimes at Christmas, according to the state of the ground.

CHARLOTTE PUDDING

Cut as many thin slices of white bread as will cover the bottom and line the sides of a baking-dish, having first rubbed it thick with butter.

Put apples in thin slices into the dish in layers till full, strewing sugar and bits of butter between. In the mean time, soak as many thin slices of bread in warm milk as will cover the whole dish, over which lay a plate and a weight to keep the bread close to the apples.

Bake slowly for three hours.

To a middling-sized dish put half a pound of butter in the whole.

This last is one of the first recipes for what became famous as Apple Charlotte in the households of Britain, though on the Continent Marie Antoine Careme's "Charlotte de Pommes" had been baked and devoured since the early 1820s. In England, the unknown compiler of *The Lady's Own Cookery Book* took the credit of having invented the dish, and her recipe was copied by Eliza Acton and dozens of other writers who followed.

Two recipes Lady Bury was proud to have invented, and by which her health was anonymously drunk on many later occasions, are both contained in the final chapter of her book. This chapter was solely devoted to recipes for "Wines, Cordials, and Liqueurs."

VERY RARE ALE

When your ordinary good quality ale has been turned into a vessel that will hold eight or nine gallons and has done working and is ready to be stopped up, take a pound and a half of raisins of the best quality, stoned and cut into pieces, and two large oranges. Pulp and pare the oranges, then slice them thin. Add the

Fog: the aftermath of long rank grass left standing through the winter.

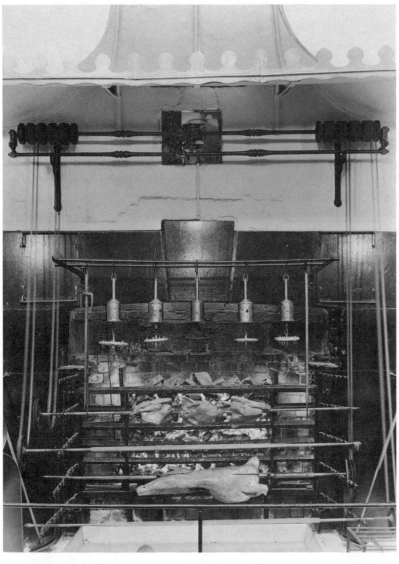

A late - eighteenth - century kitchen hearth, the clockwork and semi-automatic spits still in place. At Brighton Pavilion.

rind of one lemon, a dozen cloves, and one ounce of coriander seeds well bruised.

Put all these into a cloth bag and hang them in the vessel, then stop it up close.

Fill the bottles but a little above the neck to leave room for the liquor to play. Put into every one a large lump of fine sugar.

Stop the bottles close, and let the ale stand a month before you drink it.

MILK PUNCH

To twenty quarts of the best rum or brandy put the peels of thirty Seville oranges and thirty lemons, pared as thin as possible. Let them steep twelve hours. Strain the spirit from the rinds, and put to it thirty quarts of water previously boiled and let to stand till cold.

Take fifteen pounds of double-refined sugar, and boil it in a proper proportion of the water to a fine clear syrup.

As soon as it boils up, have ready to beat to a froth the whites of six or eight eggs, and the shells crumbled fine. Mix them with the syrup. Let them boil together, and, when a cap of scum rises to the top, take off the pot and skim it perfectly clear. Then put it on again with some more of the beaten egg, and skim it again as before. Do the same with the remainder of the egg until it is quite free from dirt. Then let it stand to be cool. Strain it into the juice of the oranges and lemons, and put it into the cask with the spirit. Add a quart of new milk made lukewarm; stir the whole well together, and bung up the cask. Let it stand till very fine, which will be in about a month or six weeks—but it is better to stand for six months—then bottle it. The cask should hold fifteen gallons. This punch will keep for many years. Many persons think this punch made with brandy much finer than that with rum. The best time for making it is in March, when the fruit is in the highest perfection.

One can only imagine that this latter concoction must have had a kick like a mule, while a few pints of Lady Bury's "Very Rare Ale" would surely be enough to lay the strongest man low.

One wonders why *The Lady's Own Cookery Book* never apparently achieved the popularity and success accorded to many of its contemporaries. Perhaps the off-putting title page, with its reference to its having been "adapted to the use of Persons Living in the Highest Style, as well as those of Moderate Fortune" may have had some effect, for after the appearance of the third edition in 1844 the work appears to have gone out of print.

There is no doubt that Lady Bury's cookery book was rapidly eclipsed by the stunning success achieved by what soon turned out to be the most important production in the field of culinary affairs during the mid-1840s. *Modern Cookery in All Its Branches: Reduced to a System of Easy Practice, for the Use of Private Families*, 1845, by Eliza Acton (1799 to

A selection of late-eighteenth-century ice and jelly molds made from beaten copper.

COOKING GAME.

A cottage kitchen of the 1840s

1859), soon swept all contemporary opposition aside and achieved the distinction of becoming a national best seller within a few weeks of its first appearance.

Miss Acton was born in the village of Battle, Sussex, site and scene of the famous Battle of Hastings. She was the daughter of John Acton, a brewer whose business was in the nearby seaside town of Hastings. Later, the family moved to Ipswich, from where young Eliza, on the excuse of suspected consumption of the lungs, was packed off to the South of France with a haste that reflected her family's concern over her well-being. Within a few months she was in Paris, where she became engaged to an officer of the French army soon after her twenty-sixth birthday. Within weeks she discovered him, in true fictional style, in the arms of another woman—or so the tale goes.

Back home in England, with all thoughts of marriage now abandoned, Eliza lived with her married sister Sarah who already had a family of growing children. Amongst these was a girl, Susannah, who in later years is said to have nightly kissed the portrait of Eliza, her supposed aunt, saying "She is the only mother I have known." A suspicion lingers that Eliza's hurried departure for France some time before may well have been due to a condition more prominent than debilitating. Whether, in fact, the poor girl was pregnant or not, has little to do with her later literary and culinary achievements. The first of these, a book of poems, appeared in a small edition under an Ipswich imprint in 1826, when Eliza was twenty-seven years of age.

Regency kitchen implements dating from the 1780s.

What little we know of her life and work is almost wholly derived from the pages of *The Dictionary of National Biography,* her poetical effusions, as she called them, not being of a quality to merit inclusion in *The Cambridge Bibliography of English Literature*. Most of her poems were cliché-ridden and soused in the sentimentalities beloved by the minor writers of the day. They made their appearance in ephemeral publications such as *The Sudbury Pocket-Book* and other annuals and magazines of the period. When she finally plucked up courage to submit a full-length poetical manuscript to a London publisher it was rejected. She had brought it personally to lay before Thomas Longman IV, the proprietor of the old-established firm of Longman, Brown, Green, and Longman, who tempered her disappointment by telling her, perhaps more in jest than earnest, "It is no good bringing me poetry! Nobody wants poetry now. Go home and write me a cookery book, and we might come to terms."

Many another author would have slammed the door behind him, but Eliza was back in London within six months to present Thomas Longman with the completed *Modern Cookery in All Its Branches*. Within weeks of publication, in 1845, a second and then a third edition was called for, with a further three making their appearance before the end of 1846. Revised and augmented, the work proved one of the best money-spinners Longmans had ever commissioned and remained in their current lists until well into the twentieth century. It is quite possible that well-thumbed copies are still in use in the present day.

Although Eliza Acton's book owed something to Lady Charlotte Bury's earlier work, especially as regards its orderliness and ease of consultation, the volume was essentially of her own compilation both in its format and in the recipes she printed. It was, as Mary Aylett and Olive Ordish have

176

already stated in their *First Catch Your Hare*, "the most practical of cookery books. . . . Logical, orderly, concise, she has all the virtues for the kitchen table, and that, after all, is the test of a cookery book. Whatever dark secrets there were in her private life, whatever emotions she chose to release in verse, her feeling, perhaps her deepest longing, for precision and order in her life, is expressed in her culinary writing."

In 1837, she moved to Bordyke House, Tonbridge, Kent, and it was there, in the early months of 1845, that she completed the work with which her name will always be associated. As examples of her many original and extremely practical recipes I have space for only a piquant *soupçon:*

Royalty was frequently pressed into service to puff the products of Victorian manufacturers.

MANUFACTURERS TO THE QUEEN

WM. POLSON & CO'S.
CORN FLOUR.

CLEAR CONSOMMÉ SOUP

Rub a deep stewpan or soup-pot with butter, and lay into it three quarters of a pound of ham freed entirely from fat, skin, and rust. Add four pounds of leg or neck of veal, and the same weight of lean beef, all cut into thick slices.

Set it over a clear and rather brisk fire, until the meat is a fine amber-colour. It must be often moved and closely watched, that it may not stick to the pan, nor burn.

When it is equally browned, lay the bones upon it, and pour in gradually four quarts of boiling water. Take off the scum carefully as it rises, and throw in a pint of cold water at intervals to bring it quickly to the surface. When no more appears, add two ounces of salt, two onions, two large carrots, two turnips, one head of celery, a faggot of savoury herbs, a dozen cloves, half a teaspoonful of whole white pepper, and two blades of mace.

Let the soup boil gently from five hours and a half to six hours and a half: then strain it through a very clean fine cloth, laid in a hair sieve.

When it is perfectly cold, remove every particle of fat from the top; and, in taking out the soup, leave the sediment untouched.

Heat in a clean pan the quantity required for table, add salt to it if needed, and a few drops of chili or cayenne vinegar.

When thus prepared, the soup is ready to serve. It should be accompanied by pale sippets of fried bread, or sippets *à la reine*.

At tables where English modes of service entirely prevailed, clear gravy-soup, until very recently, was always accompanied by dice, or sippets as they are called, of delicately toasted bread. They are now seldom seen, but some Italian paste, or nicely prepared vegetable, is served *in* the soup instead.

Rice, macaroni in lengths or in rings, vermicelli, or *nouilles,* may in turn be used to vary it; but they must always be boiled apart, till tender, in broth or water, and well drained before they are slipped into it. The addition of young vegetables, too, and especially of asparagus, will convert it into superior spring-soup; but they, likewise, must be separately cooked.

It is interesting to note her use of the word *nouilles,* possibly the first printing in any English cookery book. This is the French word from which our present-day term "noodles" has been derived by corruption.

MADEMOISELLE JENNY LIND'S SOUP

The following receipt does not merely bear the name of "Mademoiselle Lind," but is in reality that of the soup which was constantly served to her, as it was prepared by her own cook. We are indebted for it to the kindness of the very popular Swedish author, Miss Bremer, who received it direct from her accomplished countrywoman. We are also informed by Miss Bremer that Mademoiselle Lind was in the habit of taking this soup before she sang, as she found the sago and eggs soothing to the chest and beneficial to the voice.

Wash a quarter of a pound of the best pearl sago until the water poured from it is clear. Then stew it quite tender and very thick in water or thick broth (it will require nearly or quite a quart of liquid, which should be poured to it cold, and heated slowly): then mix gradually with it a pint of good boiling cream, and the yolks of four fresh eggs, and mingle the whole carefully with two quarts of strong veal or beef stock, which should always be kept ready boiling. Send the soup immediately to table.

Each of Eliza's thirty-three chapters, giving a total (in the 1856 edition) of over 1,400 copies and methods of preparation, was headed with paragraphs of market and domestic hints. Chapter II, devoted to fish dishes, started with a warning to young housewives:

See that your cook is well acquainted with the signs of freshness and good condition in fish, as they are most unwholesome articles of food when stale, and many of them are also dangerous eating when they are out of season. The eyes should always be bright, the gills of a fine clear red, the body stiff, the flesh firm, yet elastic to the touch, and the smell not disagreeable. When all these marks are reversed, the eyes are sunken, the gills very dark in hue, the fish itself flabby and of offensive odour, it is bad and should be avoided. The chloride of soda, will, it is true, restore it to a tolerably eatable state, if it be not very much over-kept, but it will never resemble in quality and wholesomeness fish which is fresh from the water.

The application of strong vinegar, or of acetic acid (which may be purchased at the chemist's), will effect this when the taint is but slight . . . but we are very doubtful whether they can by any process be converted into *unquestionably wholesome* food, unless, from some accidental circumstance the mere surface should be affected, or some small portion of them, which could be entirely cut away.

We cannot, therefore, conscientiously recommend the *false economy* of endangering health in preference to rejecting them for the table altogether.

Today, we tend to forget the ever-present problem of keeping food, especially meat, fish, and milk, in fresh and wholesome condition in the days before cold-stores and refrigeration were available. Meat-safes, hung outside kitchen windows, with the close wire-mesh allowing the air to circulate freely while keeping flies at bay, were a common enough sight in Britain and the U.S.A. as late as the mid-1930s. In the 1830s and for much later, deaths from food poisoning were of frequent occurrence, while stomach upsets and gastric ailments were commonplace in even the best regulated households. Sweetening tainted fish and meat was an art practiced, not only by the often hard-pressed housewife, and cooks and chefs in the less than Five Star hotels, but by the shopkeepers who purveyed seemingly fresh food on their slabs and counters. And adulteration of dairy products and other edibles with a variety of "harmless" additives to dilute or add weight to the goods sold, took decades of legislation and prosecutions before the practice was finally brought under control.

Eliza Acton frequently stressed the need for scrupulous cleanliness in both kitchen and dining room, and in all her recipes emphasized that the ingredients used must be perfectly fresh and of good quality:

It is a false economy to use things which have been long stored, as the slightest degree of mustiness or taint in any article will spoil all that are combined with it. Eggs should *always* be broken separately into a cup before they are thrown together in the same basin, as a single very bad one will occasion the loss of many when this precaution is neglected.

Whole chapters were devoted to "Boiled Puddings" and "Baked Puddings," and some of the recipes she printed became the definitive and invariable methods used by families who handed down her secrets from generation to generation.

JOHN BULL'S PUDDING

Roll out a suet crust to half an inch in thickness; line evenly a quart basin (or any other size which may be preferred) and raise the crust from an inch and a half to two inches above the edge.

Fill the lined dish with layers of well-kept rump-steak, neatly trimmed and seasoned with salt and pepper, or cayenne. Pour in some cold water to make the gravy. Roll out the cover, moisten the edge as well as that of the pudding. Draw and press them together carefully to make a lid. Shake out a cloth which has been dipped in hot water, then wrung out and well floured. Tie it over the pudding by gathering the corners together and tying them over the top. Place the pudding in fast boiling water, and let it remain in from three to five hours, according to size.

The instant it is lifted out, stick a fork quite through the middle of the pastry lid to prevent its bursting. Remove the cloth quickly, and cut a small round or square in it to allow the steam to escape, and serve the pudding *immediately*.

Though not considered very admissible to an elegantly served table, this is a favourite dish with many persons, and is often in great esteem with sportsmen fresh from the hunting field, for whom it is provided in preference to fare which requires greater exactness in the time of cooking. If they are late in, an additional hour's boiling, or even more, will have little effect on a large pudding of this kind, beyond reducing the quantity of gravy and rendering it very thick. Two or three dozen of oysters, bearded and washed free from grit in their own liquor (which should afterwards be strained and poured into the pudding), may be intermingled with the meat.

RUTH PINCH'S BEEF-STEAK PUDDING

To make *Ruth Pinch's* celebrated pudding (known also as beef-steak pudding *à la Dickens*) you must make into a very firm

Mr Pinch and Ruth, unconscious of a visitor.

The making of the Ruth Pinch's beef-steak pudding. A scene in Dickens's *Martin Chuzzlewit* pictured by Halbot K. Browne.

smooth paste: one pound of flour, six ounces of butter, half a teaspoonful of salt, and moisten the paste with the well-beaten yolks of four eggs (or with three whole eggs, mixed with a little water). Take a basin which holds a pint and a half, and butter it very thickly before the paste is laid in, as the pudding is to be turned out of it for the table.

Season a pound of tender steak, free from bone and skin, with half an ounce of salt and half a teaspoonful of pepper well mixed together.

Lay it in the crust, pour in a quarter of a pint of water, roll out the paste cover for the basin and close the pudding carefully. Tie a floured cloth over the pudding, and boil it for three hours and a half.

When ready, untie the cloth and invert the pudding over a large plate and take it to table.

Eliza had taken this recipe from the pages of Dickens's *Martin Chuzzlewit*, 1844, Chapter XXXIX, in which Ruth Pinch, sister of the downtrodden Tom Pinch, sets herself up as her brother's housekeeper and

An illustration by Halbot K. Brown for *Bleak House*, 1853, by Charles Dickens, depicting a mid-nineteenth-century ''Dining House.''

decides to attempt a beef-steak pudding. Asked what he would like for dinner, poor Tom had faltered out the one word "Chops!":

"I don't know, Tom," said the sister, blushing, "I am not quite confident, but I think I could make a beef-steak pudding, if I tried, Tom."

"In the whole catalogue of cookery, there is nothing I should like as much as a beef-steak pudding!" cried Tom: slapping his leg to give the greater force to his reply . . .

Ruth . . . [was] as brisk and busy as a bee, tying that compact little chin of her's into an equally compact little bonnet: intent on bustling out to the butcher's, without a minute's loss of time; and inviting Tom to come and see the steak cut with his own eyes. As to Tom, he was ready to go anywhere: so off they trotted, arm-in-arm, as nimbly as you please: saying to each other what a quiet street it was to lodge in, and how very cheap, and what an airy situation.

To see the butcher slap the steak, before he laid it on the block, and gave his knife a sharpening, was to forget breakfast instantly. It was agreeable, too—it really was—to see him cut it off, so smooth and juicy. There was nothing savage in the act, although the knife was large and keen; it was a piece of art, high art; there was delicacy of touch, clearness of tone, skilful handling of the subject, fine shading. It was the triumph of mind over matter; quite.

Perhaps the greenest cabbage-leaf ever grown in a garden was wrapped about this steak, before it was delivered over to Tom. But the butcher had a sentiment for his business, and knew how to refine upon it. When he saw Tom putting the cabbage-leaf into his pocket awkwardly, he begged to be allowed to do it for him; "for meat," he said, with some emotion, "must be humoured, not drove."

Back they went to the lodgings again, after they had bought some eggs, and flour, and such small matters; and Tom sat gravely down to write, at one end of the parlour-table, while Ruth prepared to make the pudding, at the other end . . .

"You *will* call it a pudding, Tom. Mind! I told you not!"

"I may as well call it that, 'till it proves to be something else," said Tom. "Oh, you are going to work in earnest, are you?"

Aye, aye! That she was. And in such a pleasant earnest, moreover, that Tom's attention wandered from his writing, every moment. First, she tripped downstairs into the kitchen for the flour, then for the pie-board, then for the eggs, then for the butter, then for a jug of water, then for the rolling-pin, then for the pudding-basin, then for the pepper, then for the salt; making a separate journey for everything, and laughing every time she started off afresh. When all the materials were collected, she was horrified to find she had no apron on, and so ran *up* stairs, by way of variety, to fetch it. . . . Soon she was kneading away at the crust, rolling it out, cutting it up into strips, lining the basin with it, shaving it off round the rim; chopping up the steak into small pieces, raining down pepper and salt upon them, packing them into the basin, pouring in cold water for gravy; and never venturing to steal a look in his direction, lest her gravity should be disturbed; until at last, the basin being quite full and only wanting the top crust, she clapped her hands, all covered with paste and flour, at Tom, and burst heartily into such a charming little laugh of triumph, that the pudding need have no other seasoning to commend it to the taste of any reasonable man on earth.

Ruth Pinch's beef-steak pudding turned out to be a complete and unqualified success, and its aromatic ghost lingers to this day in attenuated form in modern cookery books. But it is doubtful if any of these copies ever tasted half as good as the original which steamed merrily away in that little lodging house in 1844. Charles Dickens saw to that!

It was with her tongue in her cheek and an amused glint in her eye, that Eliza printed her next recipe, inserting her own italics to drive her point home:

PUBLISHER'S PUDDING

This pudding can scarcely be made *too rich*. First blanch, and then beat to the smoothest possible paste, six ounces of fresh Jordan almonds, and a dozen bitter ones. Pour very gradually to them, in the mortar, three quarters of a pint of boiling cream; then turn them into a cloth, and wring it from them again with strong expression. Heat a full half pint of it afresh, and pour it, as soon as it boils, upon four ounces of bread crumbs. Set a plate over and leave them to become nearly cold; then mix thoroughly with four ounces of macaroons, crushed tolerably small; five ounces of finely minced beef-suet; five of marrow, cleared very carefully from fibre and from the splinters of bone which are sometimes found in it, and shred not very small. Also, two ounces of flour, six ounces of pounded sugar, four of dried cherries, four of the best Muscatel raisins, weighed after they have been stoned; half a pound of candied citron, or of citron and orange rind mixed; a quarter of a spoonful of salt, half a nutmeg, the yolks only of seven full-sized eggs, the grated rind of a large lemon, and last of all, a glass of the best Cognac brandy, which must be stirred briskly in by slow degrees.

Pour the mixture into a *thickly* buttered mould or basin, which contains a full quart. Fill it to the brim, lay a sheet of buttered writing-paper over, then a well-floured cloth. Tie securely, and boil the pudding for four hours and a quarter. Let it stand for two minutes before it is turned out. Dish it carefully, and serve with:

GERMAN PUDDING-SAUCE

Dissolve in half a pint of sherry or of Madeira, from three to four ounces of fine sugar, but do not allow the wine to boil. Stir it hot to the well-beaten yolks of six fresh eggs, and mill the sauce over a gentle fire until it is well thickened and highly frothed.

Pour it over the Publisher's Pudding (or plum, or any other kind of sweet boiled pudding), of which it will much improve the appearance. We recommend the addition of a dessert-spoonful of strained lemon-juice to the wine.

A few pages further on, in complete contrast, Miss Acton gave the recipe for:

MARCH. — Tossing the Pancake.

THE POOR AUTHOR'S PUDDING

Shrove Tuesday, 1837. A George Cruikshank illustration which appeared in *The Comic Almanack* for that year.

Flavour a quart of new milk by boiling in it for a few minutes half a stick of well-bruised cinnamon, or the thin rind of a small lemon.

Add a few grains of salt, and three ounces of coarse sugar, and turn the whole into a deep basin.

When it is quite cold, stir to it three well-beaten eggs, and strain the mixture into a pie dish.

Cover the top entirely with slices of bread free from crust, and half an inch thick, cut so as to join neatly, and buttered on both sides.

Bake the pudding in a moderate oven for about half an hour, or in a Dutch oven over the fire.

What Thomas Longman IV thought of his pudding has not been recorded, but the recipes display Eliza Acton's humor to the full, as did the dish she aptly named:

CURATE'S PUDDING

Wash, wipe, and pare some quickly grown rhubarb-stalks. Cut them into short lengths, and put a layer of them into a deep dish with a spoonful or two of Lisbon sugar. Cover these evenly with part of a penny roll sliced thin: add another layer of fruit and sugar, then one of bread, then another of rhubarb. Cover this last with a thick layer of fine bread-crumbs well mingled with about a tablespoonful of sugar. Pour a little clarified butter over them, and send the pudding to a brisk oven.

Good boiling apples sliced, sweetened, and flavoured with nutmeg or grated lemon-rind, and covered with well-buttered slices of bread, make an *excellent* pudding of this kind, and so do black currants, likewise, without the butter.

The author displayed considerable ingenuity in naming her dishes, and many of her titles became household names in the latter half of the nineteenth century. Many had a modern-sounding ring, as that printed below:

BERMUDA WITCHES

Slice equally some rice, pound, or Savoy cake, not more than the sixth of an inch thick. Take off the brown edges, and spread one half of it with Guava jelly, or, if more convenient, with fine strawberry, raspberry, or currant jelly of the best quality.

On this strew thickly some fresh cocoa-nut grated small, and lightly press over it the remainder of the cake, and trim the whole into good form.

Divide the slices if large, pile them slopingly in the centre of a dish upon a very white napkin folded flat, and garnish or intersperse them with small sprigs of myrtle.

For very young people a French roll or two, and good currant jelly, red or white, will supply a wholesome and inexpensive dish.

Finally, space must be found for the only recipe in which she included her own name:

ACTON GINGERBREAD

Whisk four strained or well-cleared eggs to the lightest possible froth (French eggs, if really sweet, will answer for the purpose), and pour to them, by degrees, a pound and a quarter of treacle, still beating them lightly. Add in the same manner, six ounces of pale brown sugar free from lumps, one pound of sifted flour, and six ounces of good butter, *just* sufficiently warmed to be liquid, and no more, for if it is hot, it would render the cake heavy. It should be poured in small portions to the mixture, which should be well beaten up with the back of a wooden spoon as each portion is thrown in: the success of the cake depends almost entirely on this part of the process.

When properly mingled with the mass, the butter will not be perceptible on the surface; and if the cake be kept light by constant whisking, large bubbles will appear in it to the last.

When it is so far ready, add to it one ounce of Jamaica ginger and a large teaspoonful of cloves in fine powder, with the lightly grated rinds of two fresh full-sized lemons. Butter thickly, in every part, a shallow square tin pan, and bake the gingerbread slowly for nearly or quite an hour in a gentle oven. Let it cool a little before it is turned out, and set it on its edge until cold, supporting it, if needful, against a large jar or bowl.

We have usually had it baked in an American oven, in a tin less than two inches deep; and it has been excellent. We retain the name given to it originally in our own circle.

Eliza Acton's cookery book continued to go through edition after edition during her lifetime and for many decades afterward. By the mid-1850s she had moved to Snowdon House, John Street, Hampstead, London, where she worked on a book which quickly established itself as the definitive work on the subject. *The English Bread-Book for Domestic Use, Adapted to Families of Every Grade,* 1857, was issued by Longmans as a slim little cloth-bound octavo of 204 pages, whose woodcut title page declared that "In no way, perhaps, is the progress of a nation in civilisation more unequivocally shown, than in the improvement which it realises in the food of the community—*Bread to Strengthen Man's Heart!*"

In her preface, Eliza made plain her object in writing the book: the encouragement of home baking of really good and nourishing bread, in the strong hope that it would one day oust the adulterated commercial varieties used so extensively in towns. Countrywomen almost always baked their own, they had no resource to do otherwise, but townswomen who could afford to purchase the commercial variety did so in increasing numbers, despite the cooks which middle-class families invariably kept as members of their establishment. "The adulteration of bread with alum and other deleterious substances, has lately excited the serious attention of the public and the government, and caused searching investigation to be made as to the extent of this fraudulent practice." Eliza Acton told her readers. Chapters were devoted to different methods of making homemade bread and various bread recipes, while the final section of the book detailed methods of making such provincial and foreign loaves as Surrey Cottage Bread; Whole-meal Bread—called in Germany Pumpernickel; the frugal Housekeeper's Brown Bread; Rice Bread; Summer Bread; French Bread; Ginger Loaf; Plain Rolls; Polenta Bread; Cocoa-nut Bread; Turkish Rolls; Newcastle Bread—or Brown Carraway; Oaten-cakes—or, Clapped Bread; Oatmeal Bannocks; Sally Lunn; Potato Bread; Parsnip, and other Vegetable Bread; and dozens of others.

Within a few months of *The English Bread-Book* being published, Eliza, now fifty-eight, was beset with an illness that soon proved to be progressive. It was almost certainly cancer, and, after a long and painful illness, she died in March 1859, at her home in Hampstead. *Modern Cookery* continued to outsell all its rivals until the 1860s and the advent of Mrs. Beeton's classical work on domestic economy; but even then there were households in their thousands who remained faithful to Eliza Acton and the first really practical cookery book published in Britain. Long after she was dead, she was remembered with affection by the children of Victoria's Britain, the high-spot of whose parties, birthdays, or Christmases, was so often those mouth and chin and nose encrusting:

MERINGUES

Whisk, to the firmest possible froth, the whites of six very fresh eggs, taking every precaution against a particle of the yolk falling in amongst them. Lay some squares or long strips of writing paper closely upon a board or upon very clean trenchers, which ought to be nearly or quite an inch thick, to prevent the *meringues* from receiving any colour from the bottom of the oven.

When all is ready, mix with the eggs three-quarters of a pound of the finest sugar, well dried and sifted. Stir them together for half a minute, then with a table or dessertspoon lay the mixture on the papers in the form of a half-egg. Sift sugar over them without delay: blow off with the bellows all which does not adhere, and set the *meringues* in a gentle oven.

The process must be expeditious, or the sugar melting will cause the cakes to spread, instead of retaining the shape of the spoon, as they ought. The whole art of making them, indeed, appears to us to consist in preserving their proper form, and the larger the proportion of sugar worked into the eggs, the more easily this will be done.

When they are coloured to a light brown, and are firm to the touch, draw them out, turn the papers gently over, separating the *meringues* from them, and with a teaspoon scoop out sufficient of the insides to form a space for some whipped cream or preserve. Put them again into the oven upon clean sheets of paper, with the moist sides uppermost, to dry. When they are crisp through they are done.

Let them become cold; fill, and then join them together with a little white of egg so as to give them the appearance of round balls.

Spikes of pistachio nuts, or almonds, can be stuck over them, at your pleasure.

They afford always, if well made, a second course dish of elegant appearance, and they are equally ornamental to breakfasts or suppers of ceremony.

They are made in perfection by the pastry-cooks in France, being equally light, delicate, and delicious. Much of their excellence, it must be observed, depends at all times on the attention they receive in the baking, as well as in the previous preparation. They must, of course, be *quite* cold before the cream or preserve is laid in them.

Chapter Ten

GASTRONOMIC REGENERATORS

The use of mechanical methods of making ice which came into favor in the 1840s opened up several new avenues of culinary endeavour. The first patent for a refrigeration machine was granted in England as early as 1834, and, within a decade, there were dozens of rival methods competing for commercial and domestic buyers.

The original method of freezing and preserving food by chilling depended on natural ice, large blocks being chopped and sawn from frozen lakes and rivers during the winter months. These were carted to ice-pits, deep bottle-shaped man-made caverns, usually brick-lined, whose narrow mouths through which the ice blocks dropped, effectually prevented undue quantities of warm air reaching the cool interiors. The ice inside, piled in large blocks, melted only slowly, and there was usually sufficient left to last through until the next winter's supplies were ready for collection.

During the nineteenth century, an international trade in natural ice was rapidly developed, and it was harvested in large quantities in Scandinavian countries, and in Scotland, for dispatch to London and elsewhere. With the invention of ice-making machines and methods of mechanical refrigeration, this trade gradually declined, though ice was exported to the tropics until well into the 1900s. The first true refrigerated ship, the *Strathleven*, made her maiden voyage in 1879, a development which proved of immense commercial significance to countries in the Southern Hemisphere, enabling Australia, New Zealand, and the Argentine to export large quantities of perishable foodstuffs to Britain and the rest of Europe.

At home, ice-making machines were soon on the market, and most of those intended for domestic use depended on crushed ice and salt as refrigerants. One of the first works on the subject was *The Ice Book: Being a Compendious and Concise History of Everything Connected with Ice from Its First Introduction into Europe as an Article of Luxury to the Present*

JUNE — The unlicensed Victuallers Dinner

George Cruikshank's satirical comment in 1841 on the gross overeating that accompanied so many nineteenth-century dinner parties. Many of the brand names of the gins advertised in the background are still on sale under the same titles today.

time, 1844, by Thomas Masters. He started with a quotation from Shakespeare's *Richard III:*

> Tut! tut! thou art all ice,
> Thy kindness freezes

then went on to inform his readers that he would give them "an account of the artificial manner of producing pure & solid ice, and a valuable collection of the most approved recipes for making superior water ices and ice creams at a few minutes' notice."

The words "ice cream" had been coined over a hundred years previously, and the American *Pennsylvania Magazine of History and Biography* cites an example of their use dated 1744, when describing an *al fresco* lunch as including ". . . some fine ice cream, which, with the strawberries and milk, eat most deliciously." The first printed recipe in an English cookery book I know of is found in Mrs. Raffald's *The Experienced English House-Keeper,* 1769, and reads as follows:

TO MAKE ICE CREAM

Pare, stone, and scald twelve ripe Apricots, beat them fine in a Marble Mortar, put to them six Ounces of double refined Sugar, a Pint of scalding Cream. Work it through a Hair Sieve, then put it into a Tin which has a close Cover, set it in a Tube of Ice broken small, and a large quantity of Salt put amongst it. When you see your Cream grow thick around the Edges of your Tin, stir it, and set it in again 'till it all grows quite thick.

When your Cream is all Froze up, take it out of your Tin, and put it in the Mould you intend it to be turned out of. Then put on the Lid, and have ready another Tub with Ice and Salt in as before. Put your Mould in the Middle, and lay your Ice under and over it. Let it stand four or five Hours. Dip your Tin in warm Water when you turn it out. If it be Summer, you must not turn it out 'till the Moment you want it.

You may use any Sort of Fruit if you have not Apricots, only observe to work it fine.

By the 1850s, a course of dessert consisting of various molded forms and flavors of ice cream, with perhaps a refreshing *sorbet* ice served between courses, had become almost commonplace at middle-class dinner parties. "At dessert, you must cut the ice with a spoon, and eat the mimic fruits particle by particle," Charles Pierce informed the readers of his *The Household Manager*, 1857. "The epicure considers ice as acting upon the palate in effect as milk and apples do," he went on, "and therefore *degustateurs* and *gourmets* employ it to restore the taste after exhaustion by degustation, and to impart tone to the stomach."

So popular did ice cream become, that books solely devoted to its manufacture in the home were available from the early 1830s onward. *How to Make Ices*, 1831, was a privately printed booklet issued by Biertumpfel & Son, London, complete with illustrations; but the definitive work on the subject in Victorian days was *The Book of Ices* (c. 1880), by Mrs. A. B. Marshall, the proprietor of Marshall's School of Cookery, Mortimer Street, London. Before the turn of the century this work, complete with its color-printed full-page plates of ices molded into shapes as varied as gliding swans, growing pineapples, or baskets piled high with fruit, had passed through nearly twenty editions and was still in popular use up to the outbreak of World War I.

Meanwhile, back in the 1840s a book was shortly to appear which would have a profound effect on the cooking and eating habits of several generations of Britons. *The Gastronomic Regenerator: a Simplified and Entirely New System of Cookery*, 1846, was by Alexis Soyer (1809 to 1858), and marked yet another departure from the accepted mien of cook books. Soyer's biographer, Helen Morris, had this to say about her subject in *Portrait of a Chef*, 1938:

Among the less eminent Victorians was a man who wrote a book which sold a quarter of a million copies and who was caricatured in one of Thackeray's novels; who figured more often in the pages of *Punch* than many a Cabinet Minister; who was a dandy and a "card"; who saved the lives of thousands of soldiers and benefitted hundreds of thousands; who drew the breath of his being from the French Romantics and who won the respect of Victorian England for his practical resourcefulness and powers of administration. He

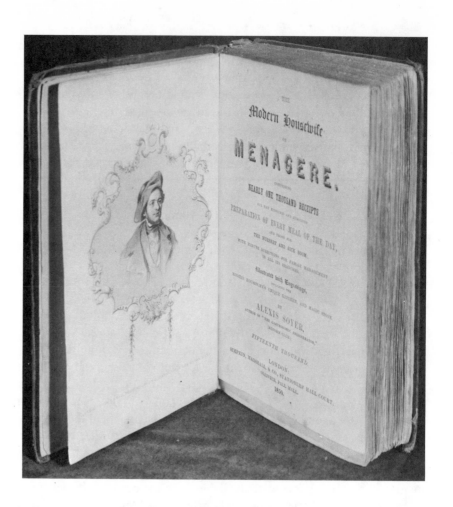

The portrait-frontispiece was taken from a painting of Alexis Soyer made by his wife.

was only a cook, but he cooked for princes and paupers, and his cooking had not a little to do with the growth of a great political party.

Alexis Benoit Soyer was born at Meaux-en-Brie, a small town on the Marne, some twenty-five miles north of Paris. He was the youngest son of a small shopkeeper, whose wares, offered for sale, included the famous locally-made Fromage de Brie, a sought-after delicacy today as much as in Soyer's time.

At the age of nine, Alexis was sent to the cathedral school at Meaux for training as a chorister and, ultimately, his mother hoped, as a priest. A series of practical jokes, culminating in the sudden ringing of the massive bass bell of the church at midnight—the signal of fire, invasion or revolution—roused the whole town from their beds, and resulted in Alexis's immediate expulsion from the church school the morning after. Within a week, at the age of twelve, he was packed off to Paris, soon finding himself apprenticed to his elder brother Philippe, cook at the house of Grignon, in the Rue Vivienne, a restaurant which boasted no less than twenty dining rooms.

Here Alexis served much of his time, leaving at the age of sixteen to work as second cook to the well-known chef and restaurateur M. Douix, on the fashionable Boulevard des Italiens. Within a few months he proved himself so adroit and skillful that, despite his tender age, his master promoted him to be head cook. With a kitchen staff of over twenty, most of whom were many years his senior, young Soyer cannot have found things easy to manage. At seventeen, he commanded twelve undercooks, and only by proving his own culinary skill and enterprise was he able to earn their respect and some degree of obedience. Despite the jealousy of some of the older men, he succeeded to an extent that brought praise from M. Douix and a substantial rise in wages. Soyer's unfailing wit and obvious intelligence, and such endearing attributes as an uncanny ability to mimic the celebrated comedians and actors of the day, as well as the howls of laughter which followed the more successful of his practical jokes (he had a weakness for these all his life) made him such a likable figure in the kitchen and restaurant that everybody wished to call him friend.

Why then, with a successful career obviously opening before him in the capital, did he suddenly decide to leave Paris and emigrate to England? The answer lies in the revolutionary conditions prevailing in France at that time, and the temptation afforded by the very high rates of pay, offered by English lords and ladies and the wealthier of the landed gentry, to the first-class French chefs to supervise their kitchens. French cooking had

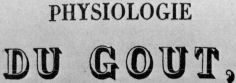

PHYSIOLOGIE
DU GOUT,
OU
MÉDITATIONS DE GASTRONOMIE
TRANSCENDANTE;

OUVRAGE THÉORIQUE, HISTORIQUE ET A L'ORDRE DU JOUR,

Dédié aux Gastronomes parisiens,

PAR UN PROFESSEUR,
MEMBRE DE PLUSIEURS SOCIÉTÉS LITTÉRAIRES ET SAVANTES.

Dis-moi ce que tu manges, je te dirai qui tu es.
APHOR. DU PROF.

TOME PREMIER.

PARIS,
CHEZ A. SAUTELET ET Cᵉ LIBRAIRES,
PLACE DE LA BOURSE, PRÈS LA RUE FEYDEAU.
—
1826.

One of the most important and most readable of culinary histories, written by Anthelme Brillat-Savarin, and shown here as a first edition.

193

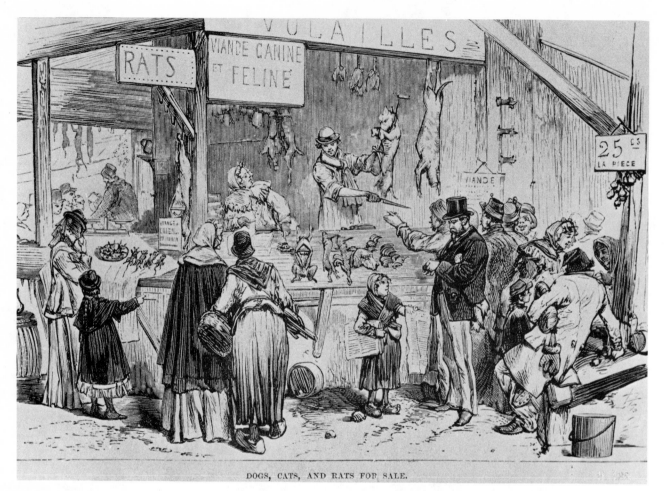

DOGS, CATS, AND RATS FOR SALE.

A butcher's shop in Paris during the siege of the city in 1870 by the German army.

become as fashionable in Britain as Empire furniture, and some of the more famous chefs received salaries that in those days would have meant their financial independence within less than seven years. Many were as temperamental as prima ballerinas, and not even an offer of the equivalent of £1,000 a year could keep the famous Marie Antoine Carême (1784 to 1833), in the employment of then Prince Regent, later George IV. *"C'est que la cuisine de son altesse royale est trop bourgeoise!"* he said, disdainfully, as he packed his bags and left England for the Czar's palace in Moscow. Carême, long famous for the artistic nature of his elaborately prepared dishes, published *Le pâtissier royal,* 2 volumes, 1815, and *Le Cuisinier Parisien,* 1828, among several other notable culinary works, all of which had a profound influence on the recipes and composition of later English and Continental cookery books. His *L'art de la cuisine française au dix-neuvième siècle,* 3 volumes (1833–1835) established itself as the standard work on French cuisine and was translated into several European languages, appearing in English as *French Cookery,* 1836, complete with "73 plates illustrative of the art," under the imprint of John Murray.

This work, and all other contemporary and later histories of gastronomy and cooking in general, and French cookery in particular, owed a debt to the classical treatise of Anthelme Brillat-Savarin (1755 to 1826), who published his *Physiologie du Gout, ou méditations de gastronomie transcendante,* 2 volumes, 1826; a second edition making its appearance in 1828, and a third in 1829 (see illustration, page 191). In 1793, Brillat-

Savarin became mayor of his hometown, Belley, but, during the Reign of Terror, he was forced to flee from France to Switzerland, and subsequently to America. There he earned a living by playing in the orchestra at a New York theater, but returned to his native France upon the fall of Robespierre. For over twenty-five years he worked on his great classic of gastronomy, only to die some months before the work was published. Translated into almost every European language, this witty and authorative compendium on the art of dining has never been out of print since its first appearance some one hundred and fifty years ago. The first edition, if in good condition in a contemporary binding, will now cost the collector anything up to $1,000; but, for those wishing to read the text, modern English translations, under such titles as *Physiology of Taste,* or *The Philosopher in the Kitchen,* can be obtained in paperback form for less than $6.

Alexis Soyer's departure from France was undoubtably accelerated by his narrow escape from death at the hands of an infuriated mob during an incident which occurred in the kitchens of the French Foreign Office. He had been seconded there, together with several other helpers, at the request of the foreign minister, Prince Polignac, who had arranged to give a lavish banquet to members of the various diplomatic missions in Paris. This ostentatious display of gastronomic expertise took place in late July 1830, the day after the reactionary *ordonnances* of Saint Cloud fired tempers in Paris to an extent that led to bloody revolution in the streets, toppled the hated Charles X, and ended the Bourbon monarchy.

While these events were going on, Soyer and his companions were hard at work in the kitchens of the Foreign Office building preparing the banquet for the tables so carefully laid upstairs. The first warning they had of trouble was the gradually increasing roar of an angry mob approaching, followed by the battering down of the outer doors leading to the kitchens and cellars. A rush took place by the *chefs* and their helpers for the upper stairs, but a volley of shots killed two cooks outright before Soyer and most of the rest of the staff had time to disappear. In the comparative silence that followed this incident, there was a cry from the back: "I'm with you!" shouted Soyer, and, with great presence of mind, promptly leapt on the highest kitchen table and started to sing *"La Marseillaise"* at the top of his voice. Others around him took up the revolutionary anthem, the keys of the wine cellars were tossed to the leader of the rioters, and Alexis Soyer and his companions were able to make a hasty escape out of the building before the inevitable conflagration ensued.

The chaos resulting from the riots had a disastrous effect on the Paris restaurant trade: Alexis found himself without a job for the first and only time in his life, and within days had accepted an invitation from his brother Philippe to join him in England as a chef in the palatial home of the Duke of Cambridge.

The only thing which made Soyer hesitate was the tales he had been told by his compatriots of the utter lack of understanding by most of the British of the subtler nuances of French wines, and the carefully prepared sauces which accompanied many of the dishes prepared by the foreign chefs. Allied to what seemed an inability to comprehend the craftsmanship and culinary skill which ultimately resulted, after hours or even days of hard work, in a dish fit to crown a royal table, this was enough to make any master chef ask himself if the tempting salaries offered compensated for the loss of proper respect he felt he might suffer from such an unappreciative audience. One such returning émigré, nicknamed "Felix," had served the Duke of Wellington, only to leave in tears after an hysterical outburst in front of the wide-eyed kitchen staff: "I serve him a dinner which would make Ude or Francatelli* burst with envy, and he says—nothing! I go out and leave him a dog's dinner half-dressed by an under-cookmaid, and he says—nothing! I cannot live in the same house with such a man—were he a hundred times as great a hero!"

Not all the English aristocracy were as gastronomically tone-deaf as the hero of Waterloo. It is recorded that the Duke of Buckingham (1776 to 1839), facing the temporary embarrassment of financial ruin, expressed the utmost horror when it was suggested by his creditors that, as he had a French chef and an English roasting-cook, he might well be persuaded to dismiss his Italian confectioner. In a voice which silenced not only the room but the entire mansion, his Grace brought his cane down with a crash on the writs and summonses littering the table and cried out, "Good God Almighty! Mayn't a man have a biscuit with his glass of sherry?" The munificence with which he had entertained members of the royal family of France on one of his many estates was reported as being the main cause of the noble Duke's lack of cash. In the event, he boarded his newly commissioned yacht, the *Anna Eliza*, and disappeared from the sight of his creditors for a two-year cruise. Historians tell us that he was finally brought low "by violent attacks of the gout."

Early in 1831, Alexis Soyer joined his brother in London, working as cook first for the newly constituted household of the young Prince George of Cambridge, and later for the Duke of Sutherland, the Marquis of Waterford, and then for the wealthy Mr. William Lloyd of Aston Hall, near Oswestry. At this latter establishment he stayed for more than four years, making Lloyd's dinner parties so famous that the host's friends frequently begged leave to borrow his estimable French cook when a wedding banquet had to be arranged or some other special entertainment was in hand.

His sumptuous entertaining ultimately led to Lloyd losing his jewel of a chef. The well-known imbiber and gourmet, the Marquis of Ailsa, poached Soyer's services; but, within twelve months lost him to the committee of the rapidly expanding Reform Club, Pall Mall, London. In 1836, Soyer was appointed *chef de cuisine,* at a salary far too tempting to let him stray elsewhere. And it was here that he made a nationally famous name for himself, building a reputation not only as a superlative chef; but as a writer on almost every aspect of cookery and domestic economy and as an inventor and manufacturer of utensils and cooking stoves far in advance of similar devices then available.

His first literary work, *Délassements Culinaires,* 1845, with the title translated as "Culinary Recreation," was a slim little volume of adulatory sketches in the form of a kitchen ballet. The book was spiced, in the words of a contemporary reviewer, with "poetry, pastry and politics," and boasted such recipes as *La Crème de la Grande Bretagne*. Ingredients needed for this particular dish were "a Smile from the Duchess of Sutherland, a Mite of

---

*Louis Eustache Ude was one of the most illustrious of nineteenth-century chefs; Charles Elmé Francatelli, a native-born Englishman, was sometime chef to Queen Victoria and chef of the Reform Club in London.

Gold from Miss Coutts, a Figment from the Work of Lady Blessington, a Ministerial Secret from Lady Peel, Piquante Observations of the Marchioness of Londonderry, and a gentle shower of Reign from Her Most Gracious Majesty.''

After seeing this sycophantic pamphlet safely through the press, Soyer turned his attention to more serious affairs, this time of the stomach rather than the stage: ''After all, my principal business is with the palate.'' He told his readers. Leaving the transcription of his recipes to his first kitchenmaid, and the preparation of the ingredients to his senior apprentice, Alexis supervised and edited the gradual accumulations of written sheets that were shortly to make their appearance as *The Gastronomic Regenerator*. The book was well advertised and very well reviewed, and within a few months of its publication in 1846 two thousand copies had been sold at the high price of a guinea apiece. His London publishers, Simkin, Marshall & Co., must have been well satisfied, for the book ran through five large editions in less than two years (fifth edition dated 1848), and the work was still in print during the 1870s.

It contained well over two thousand recipes, and only ten months elapsed from the time he started work on the scheme to the day when the completed manuscript was handed to his publishers. As the *Times* reviewer wrote: ''For ten months he laboured at the pyramid which the remotest posterity shall applaud; and during the whole of that period he was intent upon providing countless meals at the Reform Club which a living generation have already approved and fully digested. Talk of the labours of a Prime Minister or Lord Chancellor! Sir Robert Peel was not an idle man. Lord Brougham was a tolerably busy one. Could either, we ask, in the short space of ten months . . . have written the *Gastronomic Regenerator,* and furnished 25,000 dinners, 38 banquets of importance, comprising above 70,000 dishes, besides providing daily for sixty servants, and receiving the visits of 15,000 strangers, all too eager to inspect the renowned altar of a great Apician temple? All this did M. Soyer.'' Who it was that fed the *Times* critic his background information is only too easy to guess!

Soyer had dedicated *The Gastronomic Regenerator* to the Duke of Cambridge in the most fulsome terms, following this with two closely printed double-column pages of ''distinguished persons who have honoured the author with their approbation . . .'' The names of princes, archdukes, dukes, duchesses, marquises, earls, counts, lords, barons, and knights, follow each other by the score, with an apologetic list of mere esquires waiting patiently at the end of the very long queue. In deference to his noble patrons, sections of his book were devoted to recipes and instructions intended only for ''the kitchens of the wealthy.'' Throughout the work there are frequent references to the chefs and cooks of large establishments for whom the work was obviously intended, the price of the volume putting it far beyond the reach of the average British household. The culinary hints and instructions he gave were interspersed with remarks addressed to ''the real gourmet'' or ''the real epicure,'' and *The Gastronomic Regenerator* must have had a strong snob-value appeal amongst chefs and patrons alike. Typical are Soyer's remarks about soufflé:

All kinds of soufflé or fondu must be well done through, or they would be very indigestible, clog the delicate palate, and prevent the degustation of the

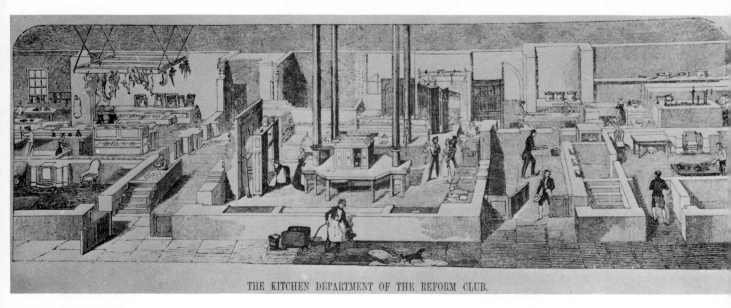

THE KITCHEN DEPARTMENT OF THE REFORM CLUB.

The kitchens built to Alexis Soyer's own design. A folding pull-out illustration to *The Gastronomic Regenerator*.

generous claret which flows so freely after dinner on the table of the real epicure.

As might be expected, much space is given to the recipes for the exotic sauces for which the Reform Club was famous, many of which had been invented by Soyer himself. Eight of his favorites he termed "Foundation Sauces," and frequent use is made of them in the recipes which follow:

SAUCES

To facilitate and simplify the making of all kinds of made dishes, I have throughout this work principally referred to the Brown Sauce (No.1), and the White Sauce (No.7), which are the two sauces I daily and principally use. The others are of course very good, and sometimes necessary; but being more complicated, I would recommend that they be left to culinary artists, who can easily surmount this difficulty.

BROWN SAUCE

Put a quarter of a pound of butter in a large thick-bottomed stewpan. Rub it all over the bottom, then peel and cut ten large onions in halves, with which cover the bottom; then take two pounds of lean ham cut into pieces, which lay over the onions.

Have ready cut in large slices twenty pounds of leg of beef and veal, put it over the ham, and place the stewpan over a sharp fire. Let it remain a quarter of an hour, then with a large wooden spoon move the whole mass round, but keeping the onions still at the bottom.

Keep it over the fire, stirring it occasionally, until the bottom is covered with a light brown glaze, then prick the meat with a fork, take off the stewpan, and put some ashes upon the fire to deaden its heat. Place the stewpan again over it, and let it stand half an hour longer, stirring it twice during that time.

The bottom will then be covered with a thick but clear brown glaze. Fill it up with fourteen quarts of water or sixteen of light stock, then add three turnips, two carrots, four blades of mace, and a bunch of ten sprigs of parsley, six sprigs of thyme, and four bay-leaves. Leave it over the fire until it boils, then place it on the corner, add a quarter of a pound of salt; skim off all the fat, and let it simmer for two hours, adding two quarts of cold water by degrees to clarify it and keep it to its original quantity.

Then skim it again, and pass the stock through a fine cloth into a basin (by filling up the stewpan again with water you will have then an excellent second stock for other soups and sauces).

If by any misfortune the stock should become thick, clarify it. Do this by whisking the whites of eight eggs with their shells for about half a minute; then add a quart of cold stock, whisking all well together. Have your stock which has become too thick ready boiling, then whisk into it the egg mixture. Continue whisking it over a clear fire until it simmers and the eggs separate from the stock, which will then be quite clear. Then pass it through a thin but very fine cloth into a basin and it is ready for use. This is a new mode of clarifying and cannot fail.

Having clarified your stock, if this is necessary, proceed as follows:

Put one pound of butter into a deep stewpan (which is always the best for this purpose), place it over the fire, stirring it until it melts. Then stir in a pound and a half of the best flour, mix it well, and keep stirring it over the fire until it assumes a brownish tinge. Then take it from the fire, and keep stirring the roux until partly cold. Pour in the stock quickly, still stirring it. Place it over a sharp fire, stirring it until it boils, then place it at the corner of the stove, and let it simmer an hour and a half. By keeping it skimmed you will take off all the butter, and the sauce will become clear and transparent.

Place it again over a sharp fire, and keep it stirred until it adheres to the back of the spoon, then pass it through a tammie* into a basin, stirring it round occasionally until cold.

WHITE SAUCE—OR BÉCHAMEL

Cut twelve pounds of knuckle of veal into large dice, with two pounds of lean ham. Well butter the bottom of a large stewpan, into which put the meat (some of the bones of the knuckles may be included in the weight of the meat, but not much). Add three large onions, one carrot, a blade of mace, four cloves, and a bunch of parsley, two sprigs of thyme, and two bay-leaves.

Pour in half a pint of water and place the stewpan over a

*Tammie: a strainer; usually made of a fine worsted cloth.

sharp fire, stirring it occasionally, until the bottom is covered with a clear white glaze. Then fill it up with ten quarts of stock, or nine of water. Add three ounces of salt, and when upon the point of boiling, place it on the corner of the fire.

Let it simmer two hours and a half, keeping it skimmed, and adding cold water occasionally to keep up the quantity.

Pass the whole through a fine cloth into a basin.

In another stewpan have one pound of fresh butter: melt it over the fire ten minutes, but do not let it change colour; then take it from the fire, stirring it until half cold. Pour in the stock, stirring it quickly all the time; place it over a sharp fire, keep stirring, and boil for half an hour. Add two tablespoons of chopped mushrooms, and a quart of boiling milk: boil it ten minutes longer, then pass it through a tammie into a basin.

Stir it occasionally until cold, and use it where required. The sauce is easily made, is full of flavour, and has a very good appearance.

A glance at these complicated and extravagant recipes, resulting in a few quarts of what Soyer called his "simple Foundation Sauces," reveals the difficulties the mistress of a middle-class household would encounter if she used *The Gastronomic Regenerator* as her standard cook book. To make the Brown Sauce, or White Sauce, or any other of his "foundation sauces" could take up to three days of constant boiling, skimming, and straining, before the translucent effect he desired was achieved. Clarifying and clearing his soups was an equally prolonged and painstaking process, often involving the use of his famous "tammie." This finest of all strainers, specially made from high quality worsted cloth, involved the use, in large kitchens, of a taughtening machine which gradually twisted the tube of cloth tighter and tighter to wring the drops of almost clear liquid through. To twist the cloth by hand sufficiently was all but impossible, and even with the use of a mechanical tammie a proportion of the liquid was unable to filter its way through. But, as Mary Aylett and Olive Ordish pointed out in *First Catch Your Hare,* "All these things were routine in the Victorian professional kitchens, where sauce-cooks prepared one ingredient, vegetable cooks another, and so on, until all the chef had to do was to assemble the finished product." For the ordinary housewife or the cook of a small establishment, such refinements were quite impossible and Soyer's *Gastronomic Regenerator* no more than an intriguing revelation of how the upper crust dined.

The use to which these sauces were put can be seen by Soyer's recipe for:

SOLE AU GRATIN

Cut the fins off a fine fresh sole, make an incision in the back, then butter a sauté-pan and put two teaspoonfuls of chopped onions in it with half a glass of white wine. Lay in the sole, cover

MY TABLE AT HOME.
Une réunion Gastronomique sans dames, est un parterre sans fleurs,
L'océan sans flots, une flotte maritime sans voiles.

it with Brown Sauce, and sprinkle some brown bread-crumbs over it, together with a few small pieces of butter.

Place it in a moderate oven for twenty minutes to half an hour (try when done as before). Take it out of the sauté-pan and dish without a napkin. Then put four spoonfuls of stock and two of Brown Sauce in the sauté-pan, boil it for five minutes keeping it stirred. Add the juice of half a lemon, a teaspoonful of chopped mushrooms, one of chopped parsley, one of·essence of anchovies, and a little sugar and cayenne pepper.

Pour the sauce round the fish, place it again in the oven for a quarter of an hour, pass the salamander* over it and serve hot.

When one remembers the days of effort required to make Soyer's famous brown sauce, used here in such nonchalant fashion, one realizes why Reform Club dinners attained a fame which was international. Even that humble dish from the cottage garden, boiled carrots, later immortalized in song, attained a dignity in Soyer's hands which set them far above themselves:

*Salamander: an iron plate, usually circular, which was made red-hot then passed over any dish which required rapid browning, such as a pudding, pie crust, or, as here, a fish dish.

Alexis Soyer dining at home. An illustration from *The Gastronomic Regenerator*, 1846.

Scrape forty young carrots, which put into a stewpan with a teaspoonful of sugar, four young onions, a bunch of parsley, and a bay-leaf.

Just cover them with a good white stock and stew till the carrots are tender. Carefully take them out and dress in the form of a dome by sticking them into a bed of well-mashed potatoes. Strain the stock they were stewed in through a napkin into a stewpan; add to it half a pint of Brown Sauce, and reduce it till it adheres to the back of the spoon.

Add two pats of butter, sauce all over and serve.

Even boiled potatoes take on an exotic and regal presence of their own as Alexis translates them into the magical:

POMMES DE TERRE À LA MAÎTRE D'HOTEL

There is no potato to equal the French red kidney potato, which will keep as it is cut, while a round mealy potato would crumble to pieces.

Being rather difficult to procure, obtain some waxy kidney potatoes, which boil and stand by to get cold. Peel and cut them into slices, which put in a stewpan, with a little pepper, salt, and about half a pint of stock. Set them upon a fire, and let them boil two or three minutes; then add three quarters of a pound of fresh butter. Keep shaking the stewpan around over the fire until the butter is melted, it will thus form its own sauce. Finish with a tablespoonful of chopped parsley and the juice of a lemon.

Turn out upon your dish and serve.

The Gastronomic Regenerator had brought Soyer's name before a much larger public, and the success of the book amongst his wealthy patrons and their friends seems to have had an inflationary effect on the little man. In the 1847 edition, in addition to a portrait of his late wife, he conducted an imaginary dialogue betweeen himself and Lord Melbourne, setting out his ideal of the perfect meal, while discoursing about gourmets and gourmands. He prepared his meals and banquets, as one newspaper reviewer pointed out ". . . for highly selective parties of connoisseurs—none of your gobble and gulp people!"

Soyer was fast becoming a comparatively wealthy man, and he took to dressing the part of every Britisher's idea of an *outré* Frenchman, while living the life of a man-about-town. He was frequently the target of cartoonists in *Punch* and elsewhere, while in *The History of Pendennis,* 2 volumes, 1849, W. M. Thackeray lampooned him under the pseudonym of M. Mirobolant (see illustration, page 203):

The *chef* of the kitchen, Monsieur Mirobolant . . . walked amongst them . . . in his usual favourite costume, namely, his light green frock or paletot, his crimson velvet waistcoat, with blue glass buttons, his pantalon Écossais, of a

Mirobolant fascinates the natives.

W. M. Thackeray's caricature of Alexis Soyer in *The History of Pendennis*

very large and decided check pattern, his orange satin neckcloth, and his jean-boots, with tips of shiny leather—these, with gold embroidered cap, and a richly-gilt cane, or other varieties of ornament of a similar tendency, formed his usual holiday costume, in which he flattered himself there was nothing remarkable (unless, indeed, the beauty of his person should attract observation), and in which he considered that he exhibited the appearance of a gentleman of good Parisian ton . . .

Having fallen in love with an English Miss of good standing, Mirobolant confides in a fellow countrywoman, the milliner Madame Fribsbi, how he had tried to win the heart of his beloved:

. . . the charming Miss entertained some comrades of the pension; and I advised myself to send up a little repast suitable to so delicate young palates. Her lovely name is Blanche. The veil of the maiden is white; the wreath of roses which she wears is white. I determined that my dinner should be as spotless as the snow.

At her accustomed hour, and instead of the rude *gigot à l'eau,* which was ordinarily served at her too simple table, I sent her up a little *potage à la Reine—à la Reine Blanche,* I called it—as white as her own tint—and confectioned with the most fragrant cream and almonds. I then offered up at her shrine a *filet de merlan à l'Agnes,* and a delicate *plat,* which I have designated

For Pots and Pans.   For Mantels and Marble.   For Fire-irons and Gas Globes.   For a thousand things in the Household, the Factory, the Shop, and on Shipboard.

WILL DO A DAY'S WORK IN AN HOUR.

Sold by Grocers, Ironmongers, and Chemists everywhere. If not obtainable near you, send 4d. in stamps for full-size Bar, free by post, or 1s. for three Bars, free by post (mentioning the "Graphic"), to

B. BROOKE & CO., 36 to 40, York Road, King's Cross, London.

The catch phrase: "Brooke's Soap won't wash clothes," invented by the proprietor of the company, coupled with the trademark "Monkey Brand," ensured the product's success in the 1880s.

as *Eperlan à la Sainte-Thérèse,* and of which my charming Miss partook with pleasure. I followed this by two little *entrées* of sweet-bread and chicken; and the only brown thing which I permitted myself in the entertainment was a little roast of lamb, which I laid in a meadow of spinaches, surrounded with croustillons, representing sheep, and ornamented with daisies and other savage flowers.

After this came my second service: a pudding *à la Reine Elizabeth;* a dish of opal-coloured plover's eggs, which I called *Nid de tourtereaux à la Roucoule;* placing in the midst of them two of those tender volatiles, billing each other, and confectioned with butter; a basket containing little *gâteaux* of apricots, which, I know, all young ladies adore; and a jelly of marasquin, bland, insinuating, intoxicating as the glance of beauty. This I designated *Ambroisie de Calypso à la Souveraine de mon Coeur.* And when the ice was brought in—an ice of *plombière* and cherries—how do you think I shaped them, Madame Fribsbi? In the form of two hearts united with an arrow, on which I had laid, before it entered, a bridal veil in cut-paper, surmounted by a wreath of virginal orange-flowers. I stood at the door to watch the effect of this entry. It was but one cry of admiration. The three young ladies filled their glasses with the sparkling Aÿ, and carried me in a toast. I heard it—I heard

Miss speak to me—I heard her say, "Tell Monsieur Mirobolant that we thank him—we admire him—we love him!"

My feet almost failed me as I spoke.

The reader may wonder where Thackeray managed to glean so much authentic culinary information and the easy ability to make use of so many *termes de la cuisine,* but the knowledge that he knew Soyer and had often attended his soirées held in ostentatious splendor at Gore House explains the phenomenon.

Gore House, a magnificent mansion then standing just outside Hyde Park, opposite the gate where the Albert Hall is now, nearly proved Soyer's undoing. In 1849 he had published *The Modern Housewife or Ménagère,* a book which sold well over fifteen thousand copies in less than nine months, and the second issue, dated 1850, did almost as well in sales. *The Gastronomic Regenerator,* selling at no less than a guinea a copy, had now entered its sixth edition; while his various sauces and relishes, marketed privately under his own name, were now to be found in grocers and provision merchants throughout the country. His now famous *Soyer's Sauce,* marketed by Crosse & Blackwell, was selling especially well, thanks largely to the immense amount of publicity he seemed able to command for any of his new projects. His friends at the Reform Club saw to that, as *John Bull* soon pointed out:

29th April, 1848.

Amongst the very few good things for which we have been indebted to the French during the last few weeks is to be reckoned a new sauce from the laboratory of Professor Soyer, of the Whig College, commonly called the Reform Club. We beg to acknowledge the receipt of a specimen, which arrived a few days since at our office, with a communication highly characteristic of the learned Sauce-rer. John Bull is not addicted to kickshaws, but gratitude compels him to notify the pleasure which he derived from his last steak, seasoned as it was with the specimen above referred to.

"The great Napoleon of Gastronomy," as *The Sun* called him, had seen to it that every newspaper and magazine editor in London and the provinces had received a free sample bottle of *Soyer's Sauce* the week before he placed the product on the market. The editor of *Punch,* in the issue for May 25, 1848, wrote a column on the bottle then standing on his desk:

M. Soyer has invented a new sauce—a day or two ago there was a magnificent article upon it in the *Chronicle,* written by Mr. Disraeli—a new sauce of such wondrous power, that with it Colonel Sibthorpe has already professed himself ready to swallow the Charter! It is a New Devouring Element! You all know Soyer the Philanthropist, who pretends to be so full of his fellow-creatures? Can you doubt it after the following? Read it, and feel "like goose's flesh" all over!—*"Soyer's New Sauce for Ladies and Gentlemen!!!"* Was there ever such a cannibal? And this is the man who would wish to redress our society and our dinners! Why, it is regularly setting man against wife, son against mother-in-law, pauper against beadle, boots against cook! No lady, no gentleman is safe. The aristocracy is on the verge of the sauce-boat. We denounce Soyer as the greatest *traiteur* in England, or even Ireland, and the latter is saying, at present, an immense deal.

Soyer's Nectar "complete in the new-shape bottle," was also heavily advertised and publicized, the ingredients selected and mixed under the personal supervision of the master—or so his advertisements informed the public:

SOYER'S NECTAR

A rumour has got into circulation that M. Soyer, in consequence of his numerous engagements, does not attend to the manufacture of the above. Such is not the case! The ingredients are manufactured every morning, under his *personal* supervision, at his factory, Rupert-street, and afterwards bottled, with the addition of aerated water, at his factory, Whittlebury-street, near the Euston-square station, which he has established for the sake of obtaining the purest water in London, from the Artesian Well belonging to the North Western Railway Company.

The receipts annexed are a few in which the Nectar can be used to advantage . . .

SOYER'S NECTAR COBBLER

Scrape one ounce and a half of Wenham Lake ice into a long glass, to which add a glass of Madeira; then pour the contents of a bottle of Nectar over all, and imbibe it through a straw: it is excellent.

NECTAR CLARET COBBLER

A George Cruikshank drawing emphasizing the horrors of the most awful calamity that can beset a hostess during the course of a carefully prepared meal.

Is excellent after dinner, and should be made as above, only with double the quantity of Claret, and one pinch of finely-grated cinnamon.

These were but two of his money-spinners; his later advertisements quoted Leigh Hunt's satirical remark (but in seeming earnestness) "With this sauce a man might eat his father!" *Soyer's Portable Magic Stove,* guaranteed "entirely fire-proof!" was "the most useful, ingenious, simple, and economical *Cooking Apparatus* ever invented" according to its inventor, and sold at "Thirty Shillings, complete." With these, and Soyer's Relish, Soyer's Paste, and Soyer's Demi-Glaze, he was now in receipt of an income of several thousands of pounds a year and Alexis became determined to enlarge his financial empire by acquiring his own large and exclusive restaurant.

Plans for the Great Exhibition of 1851 were already well advanced during the early part of 1850, and the Committee of Management invited tenders to be submitted for the sole catering rights. In the event, the contract went to a name famous in the present day, Messrs. Schweppes, who paid £5,000 for the catering rights. It turned out to be one of the most profitable deals they had ever negotiated, and the firm's records show that they sold food and drink to the value of well over £75,000 to a total of over six million people. In the light-refreshment range, they sold 934,691 Bath buns and 870,027 plain; 1,092,337 bottles of lemonade, soda-water, and gingerbeer at sixpence a glass; and sandwiches and cakes by the hundreds of thousands.

Alexis Soyer had declined to tender, but the news of the coming exhibition decided him on a course of action late in 1849 that led to resigning his position as chef at the Reform Club. Once free of this engagement, the news of which "shocked and prostrated many long-standing members," he set about organizing a magnificent restaurant of his own. He chose Gore House, which he leased from the creditors of the bankrupt Lady Blessington, hoping that its close proximity to the coming Great Exhibition in Hyde Park would pack the place with diners for at least the first twelve months, by which time much of the capital cost would have been regained and the restaurant established as one of London's showplaces.

Thousands of pounds he had made and saved during the last successful years were spent in costly alterations and decoration. Young George Augustus Sala, artist, journalist, and designer, was commissioned to devise vast murals for the walls and staircases, as well as many other expensive novelties. Much of the interior of the mansion was torn out and rebuilt, and extra ground was bought to enable a massive edifice, named The Monster Pavilion of All Nations, to be built as an annex, in which fifteen hundred people could dine at a single sitting. Over the massive doorway of the main building he had carved an epigram by Martial: *Say how many you are, and at what cost you wish to dine: Add not a word—your dinner is arranged!* This, in fact, was one of the most successful facets of the enterprise: a client could let Soyer's manager know some hours or days beforehand that he wished a table for, say, eight guests, at not more than six shillings a head. The rest was left entirely in the hands of Soyer's chefs and headwaiters, and the client knew he would receive a far better dinner than any personally selected menu of his own designing. The bill, when it came, would amount to exactly the stipulated forty-eight shillings, for a seven course meal of excellent quality with wines well matched to the food served.

Despite the high influx of foreign and provincial visitors which the Great Exhibition brought almost to the doorstep of Soyer's complex of restaurants in the grounds and mansion of Gore House the venture was not a financial success. Much of the capital required for the massive facelift he had given the property had been advanced by wealthy members of the Reform Club, and these advances were supposed to be repaid from the profits at each year's end. But at the end of the first year's trading, despite the thousands of patrons who dined there after a day at the Great Exhibition, the books of the company disclosed a loss of some seven thousand pounds. When the Great Exhibition closed, so did Soyer's restaurant, and the little Frenchman found the small fortune he had accumulated had vanished as quickly as the crowds of visitors who had once thronged the aisles and avenues of Prince Albert's Crystal Palace.

Only the fact that his sauces and relishes were still selling thousands of bottles every month and that Soyer's Magic Stove—lit and used with great success by "a noble marquis and his company on the very apex of one of the Great Pyramids," as well as by Captain Austin and his shipmates in their expedition to the Arctic in search of the missing Sir John Franklin—had proved to be a money-spinner beyond all expectations, kept his head above the waters of financial disaster. In 1852, sales of his Magic Stove, now selling at thirty-five shillings each, were so brisk that the factory could not keep pace with the demand.

Punch and other magazines carried frequent references, including a tribute from a Mr. Lee Stevens:

> *Soyer, no more to one small class confined,*
> *With magic stove now cooks for all mankind.*
> *Pall Mall but just sufficed for his rehearsal,*
> *The world his Club, his guests are universal.*

In the following year Soyer published the book by which he hoped to be remembered by posterity: *The Pantropheon; or, The History of Food, and Its Preparation, from the Earliest Ages of the World*, 1853. The work was embellished with forty-two steel-engraved plates "illustrating the greatest gastronomic marvels of antiquity," and its success must have exceeded Soyer's most optimistic expectations. In less than five years 200,000 copies were sold, and with his royalties from these sales and his income from the sauces and relishes he had marketed, Alexis Soyer gradually repaired his depleted finances.

Not all Soyer's recipes were the costly extravaganzas he served to his wealthy patrons at the Reform Club and elsewhere. Many of those taken from *The Modern Housewife* have a parsimonious ring and seem to derive from the dishes served to the catering staff at one or other of his restaurants. Little or nothing was allowed to go to waste, and yesterday's leftovers from the club rooms upstairs were served for kitchen lunches below stairs:

HODGE-PODGE

Cut two pounds of fresh scrag of mutton into small pieces, which put in a stewpan with three quarts of cold water and a tablespoon of salt. Set it upon the fire, and when boiling place it at the corner to simmer, keeping it well skimmed. Let it simmer an hour, then add a good-sized carrot, two turnips, two large onions cut into small dice, and six cabbage-lettuces if in season (the whole well washed). Let the whole simmer until quite tender.

Skim off the fat, and serve either with the meat in the soup or separately. If in season, a pint of green peas boiled in the soup is a great improvement.

FRENCH CABBAGE SOUP

Put a gallon of water into a saucepan, with two pounds of streaky pickled pork or bacon, whichever most convenient; to which add a couple of pounds of white cabbage, cut in strips (using every part but the stalk, and previously well washed). Add two large onions, a carrot, a turnip, and a head of celery. Let the whole boil three or four hours, until the pork is tender, skimming off all the fat.

Season with a little black pepper, brown sugar, and salt, if required (which is not very frequently the case, the pork or bacon generally being sufficiently so). Lay slices of bread in your tureen (about one pound), pour the soup over; keep the tureen covered ten minutes until the bread is soaked, and it is ready to serve.

The pork or bacon may be either served separate or cut into small square pieces, and served in the soup. A few mealy potatoes are sometimes introduced, or a quart of large green peas, or a pint of dry split peas.

You must observe that vegetables in France are much more used than in this country, as there are but few poor people there who do not possess a little garden in which they grow their own. It is also frequently made *maigre* by omitting the pork or bacon, adding more vegetables of all kinds, and a quarter of a pound of butter, and frequently where they get nothing else but cabbage they make it only of that.

Now, setting all national feeling aside respecting the poverty of their meals, I have known strong healthy men make a hearty meal of it, preferring it to meat of which they scarcely ever partake.

There followed a number of recipes of similar character, headed with titles such as: Remains of Ox-Tongue; Remains of Salt Beef; A Made-Dish from Veal Joints that Have Been Previously Served; Irish Stew, with a note saying, "I hope you will not blame my apparent vulgar taste in saying I am fond of it"; Remains of Roast or Boiled Lamb with Peas; Croquettes of Fowl, starting with the instruction: "Take the lean of the remains of a fowl from a previous dinner . . ."; Hashed Wild Duck; and, no doubt with memories of poultry and game left hanging uneaten until well past their prime, a smell-disguising recipe headed simply:

TURKEY—IF OLD

The French stew it exactly like ribs of beef . . . but as this is a large *pièce de résistance,* I will give you the receipt in full.

Put a quarter of a pound of butter in a convenient-sized saucepan, such as will comfortably hold the old gentleman; cut one pound of lean bacon in ten or twelve pieces and place for a few minutes in the pan on the fire. Then add your turkey trussed as for boiling, breast downwards. Set it on a moderate fire for one hour until it is a nice colour. Then add two tablespoonfuls of flour, and stir well round until it forms a roux. Then add two quarts of water or broth.

When you have it on the point of boiling, add fifty pieces of carrot the size of walnuts, the like of turnip, ten button onions, a good bouquet of sprigs of thyme, two bay-leaves, and ten of parsley, a small glass of rum, a clove, a piece of garlic, and let it stew gently for four hours. If you use water, season in proportion. Take the turkey out, and put the vegetables and sauce in a smaller stewpan, which ought to be nearly full. Let it simmer on the corner of a fire, so that the fat rises and can be removed. Gradually reduce the whole to a demi-glaze.

Dish up the turkey and serve it with the sauce poured over it. Small new potatoes, about twenty, when in season, may be added to the sauce, or roasted chestnuts.

The remains are excellent when cold, or will warm again with the addition of a little broth or water.

Where the leftovers came from in such abundance is quickly made obvious when one reads his special recipe for mutton cutlets. In the original recipe, as his footnote tells, the discards were thrown away, but this certainly did not happen when Soyer himself was in charge of the kitchen:

CUTLETS À LA VICTIME

Cut three cutlets from the neck of mutton, about half an inch thick, trim one very nicely, free from fat. Leave the other two as cut off.

Put the trimmed one between the two, flatten them together so that the fat of the outside ones meet over the middle one. Tie them together thus, and broil over a very strong fire for ten minutes. Remove from the fire, cut the string, and dish up the middle one only on a very hot dish with a little salt sprinkled over it.

If wanted roasted, proceed as above.

In his footnote, Soyer explains his source of this wasteful and extravagant recipe, telling his readers that he certainly did not recommend it on the score of economy ''as it is the very tip-top of extravagance.'' It was the invention of the ''culinary artist'' of Louis XVIII of France:

It was first partaken by that intellectual monarch and gourmet, who, at the end of a stormy reign, through a serious illness, was rendered completely paralysed. At the same time, the functionary organs of his digestion were much out of order.

Being a man of great corpulence, and a great admirer of the festive board, much food was required to satisfy the royal appetite. The difficulty which his physicians experienced was to supply this continual train of food in the smallest possible compass as the strain of passing it down his royal throat without choking his majesty (due to his paralysis) was taxing their energy to the utmost. "Fine and succulent food in tiny cutlets," was the order passed to the *chef* in the Tuileries' kitchen, and neither they nor his majesty would brook the least delay.

The head-cook, at his wit's end to supply the deficiency, begged a few hours' delay, the order being further complicated by the head physician insisting that only mutton entirely deprived of fat would be acceptable as a specific.

After a profound study by the *chef* and his satellites, a voice was heard from the larder, which was a considerable distance from the kitchen, crying, "I have found it! I have found it!" A young man by the name of Alphonse Pottier dashed up to the *chef* waving three prime mutton cutlets, tastefully trimmed and tied together. With a wave of his hand the *chef* indicated that no comment was to be made until the recipe had been explained and a trial had been made, and young Alphonse immediately proceeded to prepare his dish. With a small skewer he fastened his three tied cutlets to a spit, and placed them, to the astonishment of all present, close to the bars of the grate. The two outside cutlets soon got brown; from brown they soon turned black. Everyone gazed at each other in astonishment, whilst Pottier, with a composed countenance, terminated his scientific experiment. He took them off the spit, drew the skewer out, cut the string, threw the two burnt cutlets away, and smilingly placed the middle one tenderly on a hot plate. It seemed to have absorbed all the nutriments of the other two, and could be rolled into a compass small enough to satisy the physicians' and his majesty's needs. It was served and immediately approved: a dish of twelve was despatched to the royal bedchamber, to be returned gratifyingly empty. His Majesty, though unable to speak, was said by his physicians to have signified his approval and gratification in the only way left open to him!

What that way may have been, Alexis Soyer did not attempt to elucidate to his lady readers.

The final recipes given are taken from *The Modern Housewife,* and display his ingenuity with some of the most simple dishes and beverages consumed in every middle-class household, not only in the Victorian era, but in the present day. What he would have said about our instant coffee is best left to the imagination.

EGGS AU BEURRE

New-laid eggs should not be used until they have been laid about eight or ten hours, for that part which constitutes the white is not properly set before that time, and does not until then obtain that delicate flavour.

Nothing being more offensive than eggs in a state of decomposition, it is very important that every person should know how to detect them (especially in winter, when a much greater quantity are used in London). If, by shaking them, they sound hollow, you may be certain they are not new-laid, and not fit to be boiled for breakfast, but, if broken, they may prove fit

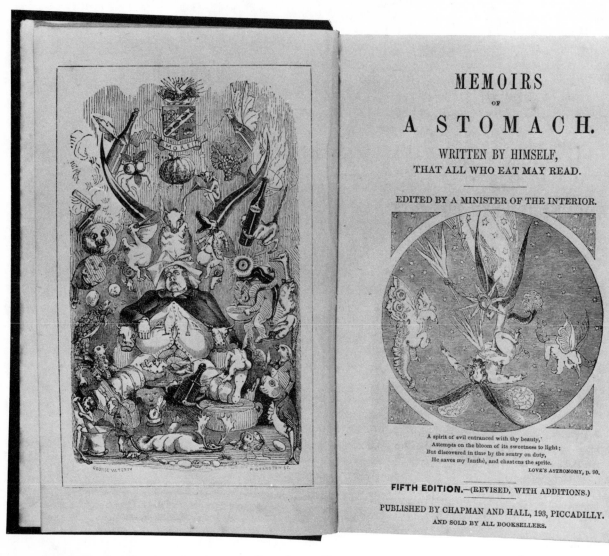

MEMOIRS
OF
A STOMACH.

WRITTEN BY HIMSELF,
THAT ALL WHO EAT MAY READ.

EDITED BY A MINISTER OF THE INTERIOR.

A spirit of evil entranced with thy beauty,
Attempts on the bloom of its sweetness to light;
But discovered in time by the sentry on duty,
He saves my Ianthé, and chastens the sprite.

LOVE'S ASTRONOMY, p. 90.

FIFTH EDITION.—(REVISED, WITH ADDITIONS.)

PUBLISHED BY CHAPMAN AND HALL, 193, PICCADILLY.
AND SOLD BY ALL BOOKSELLERS.

A popular ''yellowback'' of 1853. The anonymous author was Sydney Whiting, who informed his readers that: ''The stomach's curse, is midnight verse.''

for other culinary purposes, except for soufflés, for which eggs must be very fresh.

For Eggs au Beurre—let the eggs boil for six minutes instead of three, then take them out, dip them for two seconds in cold water, crack them and peel off the shells, and lay them in a hot plate (they will remain quite whole if properly done).

Cut each egg in halves lengthwise, spread a little fresh butter and sprinkle a little salt over the interior, and eat them very hot. Eggs done in this manner are delicate and digestible.

TO MAKE COFFEE

Coffee, which has now come so generally into use, originally came from Arabia, where it has been known from time immemorial, but was brought into use in England in 1653 . . . The new system of making coffee which I give here, was found out by the author after travelling by night in a railway train. Arriving in due time at a station where the train was to stop for a full five minutes, I decided to restore exhausted nature after a long and tedious journey by purchasing a cup of coffee. I was obliged to use a certain portion of manual strength in pushing through the crowd to get at what is called the refreshment room.

After waiting for nearly two minutes for my turn to be served with some of the boiling liquid which they called coffee, I found it as bad as any human being could possible make it . . . it tasted anything but palatable; but having a long journey before me, and requiring some thing to eat and drink, I was obliged to put up with it. But before I could partake of half the cup, or finish masticating some stale toast or over-buttered muffin, the unsociable bell violently rang to acquaint the passengers that the train was about to start. Every one being perfectly aware that railway trains, like time, wait for no one, I hurried back, this fortunately letting me escape the swallowing of the thick part which was deposited at the bottom of my cup. Rushing out of the refreshment room, I jumped into the wrong carriage, the fidgety train having changed its place, and the time being too short to rectify this mistake, I was obliged to make fresh acquaintance with my new *compagnons de voyage,* who happened to be as much dissatisfied with the steaming-hot refreshment as myself who had patronised the steaming Mocha.

As soon as I arrived at the Reform Club I tried several experiments to simplify the present methods of making coffee. In this I succeeded, and I do strongly advise my readers to give my recipe a trial. I also recommend all providers of refreshment at railway stations not to make the coffee boiling hot, but to keep the *cafetière* in a *bain-marie,* which would prevent all the above inconvenience, both as regards quality and heat.

Put two ounces of ground coffee into a stewpan, which set upon the fire, stirring the powder round with a spoon until it is quite hot. Then pour over it a pint of boiling water; cover over closely for five minutes, pass it through a cloth, warm again, and serve.

WHITE COFFEE

Put two ounces of unground coffee, slightly roasted, into a clean stewpan, which set upon a moderate fire, slowly warming the coffee through, shaking the stewpan round every half minute.

When very hot, which you will perceive by the smoke rising from it, pour over half a pint of boiling water. Cover the stewpan well, and let it infuse by the side of the fire for fifteen minutes. Then add half a pint of boiling hot milk, pass the coffee through a small fine sieve in to the coffee-pot or jug, and serve with white sugar-candy or crystallized ginger.

Soyer's next idea was to open a college of domestic economy, but he reluctantly abandoned this when he failed to raise sufficient capital. Asked by the owner of the Hall of Commerce, in the City, if he would like to rent the building for use as a restaurant for the hundreds of City gentlemen who passed its doors every lunchtime, he toyed with the scheme for some time before finally turning it down. He had visualized the hall sumptuously furnished in the style of Gore House, but a tour of central London eating houses had convinced him that all members of the Stock Exchange, and of the finance houses, required was a quick lunch served and consumed in so

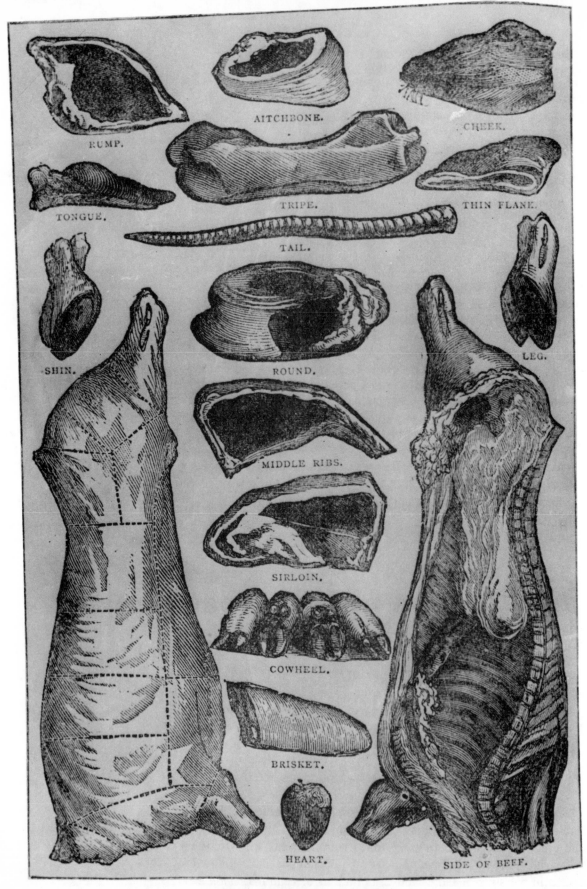

RUMP.

AITCHBONE.

CHEEK.

TONGUE.

TRIPE.

THIN FLANE.

TAIL.

SHIN.

ROUND.

LEG.

MIDDLE RIBS.

SIRLOIN.

COWHEEL.

BRISKET.

HEART.

SIDE OF BEEF.

THE JOINTS OF BEEF.

A typical full-page illustration from a late-nineteenth-century cook book.

many minutes—then back to the office for a midday snooze. A graphic picture of the chop houses of the 1850s is given by Robert Surtees in his novel *Handley Cross,* 1854, in which Mr. Jorrocks sets the scene in his own inimitable style:

Now for a chop-house or coffee-room dinner! Oh the 'orrible smell that greets you at the door! Compound of cabbage, pickled salmon, boiled beef, sawdust and anchovy sarce. ''Wot will you take, sir?'' inquires the frowsty waiter, smoothin' the filthy, mustardy, cabbagey cloth, ''soles, macrel, vitin's—werry good boiled beef—nice cut. Cabbage, cold 'am and weal, cold lamb and sallard.''

Hah! The den's 'ot to suffocation—the kitchen's below—a trap-door vomits up dinners in return for bellows down the pipe to the cook. Flies settle on your face—swarm on your head; a wasp travels around; everything tastes flat, stale and unprofitable.

Soyer's Shilling Cookery made its appearance in 1854, a book he had designed for ''the artisan, mechanic, and cottager.'' Once more he was gratified to learn that he had written a best seller: the whole of the first printing of ten thousand copies were sold on the day of publication, and a further sixty thousand were disposed of in less than seven weeks. This little shilling booklet, with sales soon totaling over a quarter of a million copies, repaired Alexis Soyer's fortunes to an extent that left him once more financially independent and looking round for fresh fields to conquer.

These he found in the Crimea! Things had been going badly there for the British Army, ravaged by disease and near starvation. Soyer wrote to *The Times* in February, 1855, volunteering to proceed to Scutari at his own expense to advise on the cooking and catering arrangements for the troops at the front, and a harassed government was only too thankful to accept. Within a few weeks of his arrival he had completely reorganized the cooking and rationing arrangements at Florence Nightingale's barracks hospital, before going on to Balaclava itself to direct the catering for the army in the field. It was here that he invented the famous field kitchen which was in use for nearly a hundred years, and with which troops in the field were fed from almost up to World War II.

The strain of months in the disease-ridden climate of the Crimea began to take its toll, and Soyer was invalided home. No longer a young man, he recovered sufficiently on his way back to England to visit Paris for an interview specially requested by Napoleon III. In May 1857, he was once more in London, and within weeks had issued what proved to be his final book. *Soyer's Culinary Campaign,* 1857, was published as being ''historical reminiscences of the late war, with the plain Art of Cookery for military and civil institutions.''

One of his last public engagements was to demonstrate a mobile cooking range at the United Services Club, and to supervise the building of the new kitchens at Wellington Barracks, London.

He died at his house in St. John's Wood, on August 5, 1858, at the age of forty-nine, and was buried in Kensal Green cemetery. ''His death,'' wrote Florence Nightingale, ''is a great disaster. Others have studied cooking for the purposes of gormandizing, some for show, but none but he for the purpose of cooking large quantities of food in the most nutritious manner for great numbers of men. He has no successor.''

His close friend, George Augustus Sala, wrote his obituary notice:

He was but a Cook; but he was my dear and good friend.
He quacked, certainly—puffed himself and his eccentricity in all kinds of ways—in dress, manners, speech, mode of life; but he never derogated one iota from his dignity as an honest man.

He was no vulgar charlatan, for he was full of inventive ingenuity; and to the soldier's and poor man's kitchen his maxims, if properly carried out, would be even now inestimably beneficial. He was an original. He didn't do anybody any harm . . . he knew his own place, exacted the meed of respect due to him, and when the grandees came to see him in his kitchen, let them know that not alone *savetier,* but *cuisinier,* was *maître chez soi.* Peace be to his ashes; for he was the worthiest of souls.

Chapter Eleven

THE BEETON ERA

"I must frankly own, that if I had known, beforehand, that this book would have cost me the labour with it has, I should never have been courageous enough to commence it. What moved me, in the first instance, to attempt a work like this, was the discomfort and suffering which I had seen brought upon men and women by household mismanagement. I have always thought that there is no more fruitful source of family discontent than a housewife's badly-cooked dinners and untidy ways. Men are now so well served out of doors—at their clubs, well-ordered taverns, and dining-houses, that in order to compete with the attractions of these places, a mistress must be thoroughly acquainted with the theory and practice of cookery, as well as be perfectly conversant with all the arts of making and keeping a comfortable home."

These were Isabella Beeton's opening words in the first edition of what was eventually to become her internationally famous cook book, and in them lies the secret of her unparalleled success as a writer on domestic economy and culinary affairs. She set out with the avowed intention of teaching housewives the art of making their men appreciate their own homes to an extent that turned them into willing inmates, and by so doing she soon had the feminine legions on her side. They became her intimates and partners in a code of domestic enterprise that eventually wrought a radical transformation in the home life of the newly emancipated middle classes of Britain—though she was not to be permitted to live to see the changes she had inspired. "Dear, Dear Mrs. Beeton," a bride of some twelve months' standing wrote in *The Englishwoman's Domestic Magazine*, "your sound advice and practical commonsense persuaded me to attempt dishes that instantly brought forth comment and praise from a spouse not given to such outward shows of domestic affection. Your treasured book has done *so* much to restore harmony in what I am determined to make a *truly* happy home. I call you dear Mrs. Beeton, and dear to me you are!"

An example of the carefully drawn hand-colored illustrations depicting the fashions of the day that accompanied each issue of *The Englishwoman's Domestic Magazine*.

These were sentiments Isabella herself would have echoed in the months preceeding her own marriage. ''Why has no one written a book—a *good* book for brides? A book to help them manage a household and learn all the things they simply *must* know if they are to succeed in married life!'' were questions she posed to her sisters at Epsom during the weeks of her engagement to her beloved Samuel. Her answer was to write the book herself, and as *The Book of Household Management,* 1861, it not only proved itself an indispensable adjunct to any bridal bottom drawer, but the definitive work on Victorian cookery and domestic economy for generations yet to come.

Isabella Mayson was born at 24 Milk Street, off Cheapside, in the City of London, on March 14, 1836. Here, within the sound of Bow Bells, she spent the first five years of her life, qualifying, in the words of a correspondent to *Ainsworth's Magazine,* as ''one of our pretty, young cockneyesses.''

With her family background, this attribute would be the last which Isabella would ever have wished to acknowledge, for she was always intensely proud of her ancestoral connection with Cumberland and the North of England, treating her residence in the City as no more than a geographical accident of birth. Her father, Benjamin Mayson, son of the Reverend John Mayson, rector of Orton, Cumberland, had migrated to London in his youth, and now kept a dry-goods store at 24 Milk Street; while Isabella's mother, Elizabeth Jerram (1815 to 1871), was the daughter of a William Jerram who kept a posting house and stables on the Portsmouth Road. William Jerram subsequently died of glanders, caught from one of his infected horses, the animals which were so often to feature, for good and ill, in the lives of his descendants.

In 1841, when Isabella Mayson was only five, her father died, leaving his wife with four young children to look after, three girls and a boy. Isabella was the eldest. Fortunately for all concerned, within two years Mrs. Mayson had married again, this time to a widower who also had four children to support, a Mr. Henry Dorling. After only a few days courting, the handsome and prosperous Mr. Dorling had so swept the widow Mayson off her feet that she was persuaded to post off to Scotland with him, where they were married in equally romantic fashion, over the anvil at Gretna Green. In the same year, probably to appease the Reverend John Mayson, they were remarried at Islington, after which the whole family, parents and eight assorted children, left in the very best of spirits to start a new life at Epsom. It was here that Dorling's father had established a printing business many years before, and Henry had recently achieved his heart's ambition by being appointed Clerk of the Epsom racecourse.

Henry Dorling turned out to be an excellent father to all the stepchildren, and to the thirteen subsequent children he fathered by his new wife. This made a total of twenty-one in all, not counting those who died at or shortly after birth. As she grew to girlhood, much of the social and domestic arrangements for the ever-expanding family devolved on Isabella. Dorling had moved them all into the recently built and well-furnished living quarters that comprised one section of the massive Epsom Grandstand of which he was in supreme charge, and it was here that Isabella and the rest of the rapidly growing family lived and worked. It seems to have been a singularly

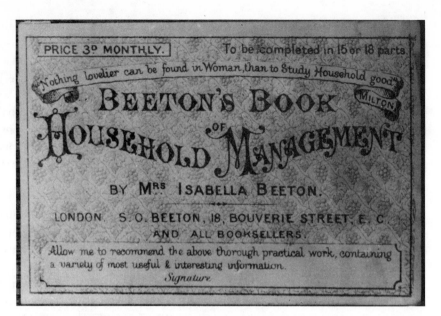

united and happy family, despite its diversity and size, Henry always sticking to the promise made to Elizabeth, that "... his four little Maysons were always to be treated exactly the same as his four little Dorlings." The same rule presumably applied to the thirteen later offspring.

As the eldest girl, a great deal of the cooking needed to satisfy so many hungry mouths and youthful appetites fell directly onto Isabella's shoulders; but domestic science in all its many aspects was to the eldest Miss Mayson a fascination and delight from long before her teen-age days. Cooking exciting and often novel dishes for the family dinner, as well as serving superbly cooked and presented meals of traditional character, were tasks she enjoyed as a consuming hobby rather than mere daily domestic chores. Mrs. Dorling herself, and her mother, "Granny" Jerram, were both capable women and first-class cooks in their own rights; but as Isabella grew to womanhood every form of household management, including detailing the servants in their duties, dealing with the host of tradesmen who not only served the family but supplied the various bars and dining rooms of the Grand Stand, coping with illnesses and other domestic emergencies, became part of normal everyday life for the bustling young Miss Mayson.

The family and all the children lived in the Grandstand the whole year round, except at the time of race meetings when they had to be found rooms with various relatives and friends in Epsom. "I am going to the Stand this afternoon," wrote Isabella on the eve of one of these meetings, "to assist in bringing down that living cargoe of children into the town, where they will remain ten days."

After a year at a finishing school at Heidelberg, Germany, where, among many other accomplishments, she learned to speak fluent French and German, Isabella returned home to Epsom as a good-looking and talented young lady of nineteen. She had developed a love of music and used to go by train to London to take lessons on the pianoforte from the celebrated Sir Julius Benedict. She had also acquired a taste for the exotic fancy pastries so beloved by the Germans for afternoon tea, and she rather shocked her friends in the town by paying for pastry-making lessons from a local confectioner well versed in the art.

The day cook gave notice. A satire by Sol Eyting of the complete reliance by upper- and middle-class housewives of the 1880s on their domestic staffs.

It was probably on one of her music-lesson trips to London that Isabella again met Samuel Orchart Beeton. I say *again,* for young Samuel was born on March 2, 1831, in Milk Street, and the Beetons, also an old City family, had been friends with the Maysons and the Dorlings from their earliest days. Samuel was born in the Dolphin Tavern, Milk Street, a few doors from Isabella's first home, and visited there frequently as a boy after he had moved to live with his grandmother at Hadleigh, Suffolk. The two must have met as children on several occasions; but, in the meantime, Samuel had grown to be a handsome young man with what were thought to be excellent prospects as both publisher and printer. In 1852, he had entered the offices of Charles H. Clarke & Company, Fleet Street, the well-known booksellers and publishers, where he bought a junior partnership for himself. This was the year when Clarke & Company managed to scoop the entire British publishing trade by bringing out the first English edition of Harriet Beecher Stowe's *Uncle Tom's Cabin,* a pirated version based on a copy of the tenth American edition brought over from the U.S.A. by a young employee of the publishing house of Putnam in New York. The work had originally appeared in two volumes under the imprint of John P. Jewett & Company, Boston, and the version Clarke & Company printed was completely unauthorized. Nevertheless, it soon revealed itself to be an all-time best seller, no less than twenty-eight pirated versions appearing in Britain during the year 1852 under as many various imprints. Clarke & Company, with their noses just in front of the rest of the trade, reaped by far the largest benefit, and their illustrated version (their original English edition was rushed out without any plates) continued in print for almost a decade.

From this stroke of unlooked-for good fortune young Samuel Beeton was one of the lucky benefactors, and the prosperity of the firm enabled it to undertake business ventures whose initial success was by no means assured. One of these, with S. O. Beeton installed as editor, was the launching of *The Englishwoman's Domestic Magazine* in 1852, a periodical whose objective, according to its twenty-one-year-old editor, was the "improvement of the intellect, the cultivation of the morals, and the cherishing of domestic virtues. In carrying out this object," he went on, "we have endeavoured to adopt a tone of morality free from severity, and to blend amusement with instruction."

As a woman's magazine, its circulation figures exceeded all expectations, reaching 25,000 copies a month in less than a year, and double that by 1859 in spite of the difficulties brought on by the Crimean War. Much of its success was due to Beeton's avant-gardism, his flair for sensing the public taste in advance of his competitors, and his ability to offer the most novel inducements to potential readers as a method of securing regular orders. One of the most successful of these was the "giving away" of dress patterns with many numbers, and the well-patronized column he entitled "Cupid's Letter-Bag" where the young and not-so-young amongst his lady readers could pour out their problems to a sympathetic ear.

Samuel's ambitions would not allow him to stay in partnership for any longer than it took to save the necessary capital to branch out on his own, and in 1855 he and Clarke parted company. It was agreed between them that Beeton should be allowed the sole copyright in *The Englishwoman's Domestic Magazine,* and *The Boy's Own Magazine,* another of Samuel's conceptions, while Clarke retained all the rest of the company's list. Beeton moved into offices in 18 Bouverie Street, and before long books and magazines were issuing from the press under his own personal imprint.

It was at this juncture of their affairs that the friendship between Isabella Mayson and the now twenty-four-year-old Samuel Beeton "blossomed into romance" as her sister put it. Samuel proposed to Isabella at Epsom, at the time of the Spring Meeting in 1855, and to mark the occasion the trainer of that year's Derby winner, Robert Sherwood, whose horse Wild Dayrell had trounced the rest of the field to come home at even money, presented the bride-to-be with a full-length bolt of dress material. It was in this dress of red-striped silk that Isabella posed for the first photograph taken of her the original of which is now in the National Portrait Gallery, London.

They were married in 1856 at Epsom Parish Church, just before the Summer Meeting, and went to live in their newly furnished home at Pinner. Sam left by train every morning for a day at the office while his wife stayed at home to manage the house and garden. Before long she was reading the proofs for the cookery section of *The Englishwoman's Domestic Magazine,* later proofreading the whole of each months' new issue, devising the format, writing articles, and finally acting as editor in all but name. All this was between and during pregnancies, and while superintending the needs of her very efficiently run household, translating all the French and German correspondence her husband received at the office, and devising dress pat-

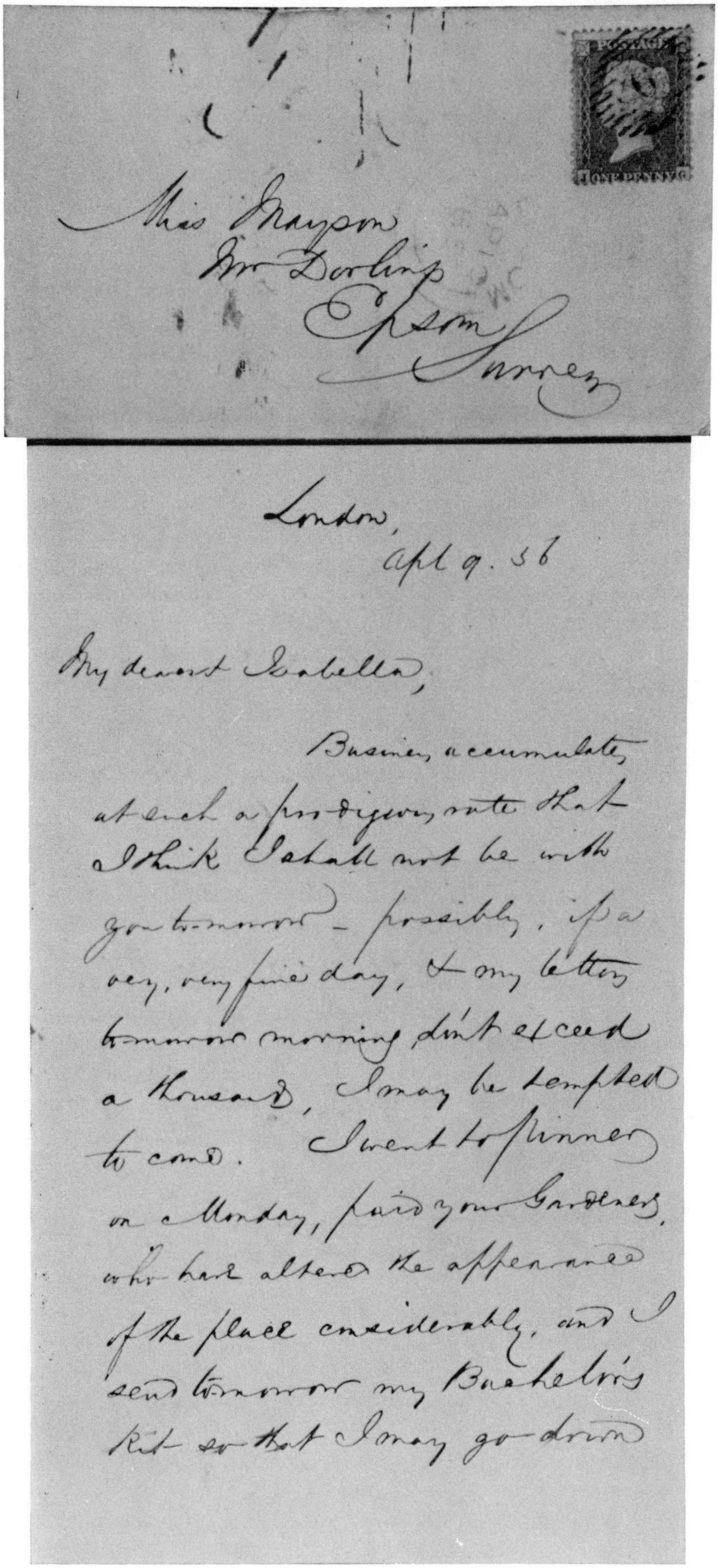

Miss Mayson
Mr Dorling's
Epsom
Surrey

London,
Apl 9. 56

My dearest Isabella,

Business accumulates at such a prodigious rate that I think I shall not be with you tomorrow — possibly, if a very, very fine day, & my letters tomorrow morning don't exceed a thousand, I may be tempted to come. I went to dinner on Monday, paid your Gardeners, who had altered the appearance of the place considerably, and I send tomorrow my Bachelor's Kit so that I may go down

A letter, dated April 9, 1856, from Samuel Beeton to his fiancée Isabella Mayson.

terns for Sam to include in each monthly issue.

In May 1857, their first child, Samuel Orchart, was born, only to die "of a fever" in August that same year. A second son, bearing the same name, was born in September 1859, but lived only until the winter of 1862; both of them felt his death very deeply. Isabella was well advanced in pregnancy again when this loss occurred, and the birth of their third child, Orchart, who survived to live to 1947, did much to alleviate the sorrow of bereavement.

In the meantime, both had buried themselves in literary work. Mrs. Beeton had taken over almost complete control of the *Domestic Magazine* and was continually suggesting to Sam new methods of increasing its circulation. In September 1859, she first conceived the idea of issuing a separately-printed supplement devoted entirely to cookery and domestic economy, divorcing it completely from the novels and romances, fashion hints, plays, puzzles, and charades, which formed so large a part of the mother work. It would eventually comprise a complete cookery book and would be issued in fifteen or eighteen monthly parts at 3d each, in a binding of printed paper wrappers. In the event, so popular did the work become, that a total of twenty-four monthly parts were issued, followed by a cloth-bound volume complete with colored plates.

The first monthly issue of *Beeton's Book of Household Management,* "edited by Mrs. Isabella Beeton," made its appearance on November 15, 1859. Priced at threepence a copy, it was published in a binding of light-brown wrappers printed in black; later issues containing inserted color-printed full-page plates (one of these was inserted in alternate months, making twelve in all), and with various tipped-in advertisement slips puffing other titles at present issuing from S. O. Beeton's press. With the final, twenty-fourth, issue, a series of extras was inserted for those wishing to have the parts bound up to form a single volume. These comprised a printed title page; the contents leaf; analytical index—including a list of the colored plates; and a specially designed color-printed lithographic frontispiece and a title page. Of these latter embellishments Isabella was especially proud. The well-known artist H. Noel Humphreys was commissioned to design the ornamental title page, with H. G. Hine supplying the drawing for the scene of rustic bliss used for the frontispiece. Why this particular scene, depicting haymaking in the background, with a party of countrymen and women quaffing flagons of cider outside an ivy-covered cottage, should have been chosen as the frontispiece for a book devoted to cookery and household management is difficult to understand. The most likely explanation is that this lithograph happened to be in stock and was used as a "filler," thus saving the expense of a specially commissioned drawing. The colored-plates, printed from three-color blocks only, were supplied and printed by William Dickes, the lithographic plates being drawn by H. N. Woods, from the designs supplied by the artists.

By the time the third monthly issue had made its appearance it was obvious to Samuel Beeton that his wife had compiled a work that had almost immediately "caught on" (to use his own expression), with a female readership far wider than expected. The print of later parts was increased by several thousand copies, the series extended to twenty-four, and arrangements made to bring out a single-volume edition as soon as the monthly issues were completed. Both of them were delighted with the success of the venture, and plans were laid for other ambitious publishing schemes with Isabella in complete charge.

There are many pointers to the reason for the book's astonishing popularity, chief of which were undoubtedly its ease of reference, its clarity of instruction, and its ability to answer questions on every conceivable aspect of household management and domestic affairs. The first edition extended to 1,112 pages, and contained well over three-quarters of a million words. A total of 2,751 numbered recipes and household hints and instructions were given, and each of the recipes carried a legend at the end giving its average cost, the time necessary for cooking, the amount of persons it was sufficient for, and, where applicable, the months when the meat, game, or fish, was in season. This was a new innovation and one much appreciated by her many thousands of readers.

On October 15, 1861, the bulky single-volume edition made its appearance, priced at 7/6d a copy. It was issued as a fat little octavo, over two-and-a-half inches thick, bound in brightly-hued purple cloth stamped in gold and blind. For those who wished to bind up the issues they had saved each month, there were half-calf binding cases available at the bargain price of 1/6d each. Most of the original purchasers seem to have taken advantage of these, or commissioned their own individual leather bindings, for copies of the first edition still clothed in their original publisher's cloth bindings are now of the utmost rarity. The purple bead-grained cloth in which the volume was originally issued was particularly subject to soiling and fading, and the text and plates were far too heavy for the cloth binding in which they were cased. Dropped once in a stone-flagged Victorian kitchen, the book would inevitably split its hinges and spring sections of text. Greasy-fingered cooks and a plethora of other hazards ensured that the leaves became dog-eared and soiled after a few years of use. No one imagined that a copy of ''Mrs. Beeton's Cookery Book'' as it soon came to be called, would one day be eagerly sought by collectors, or that the first edition would ever be worth more than its face value. So the volume was treated to all the affectionate insults and outrages reserved for a much-used and much-loved text.

Only one copy is known to have been spared the misfortunes attendant on any work which spends most of its life on a shelf in a steam- and fume-filled kitchen, or on top of a conveniently placed cupboard within reaching distance of floured and greasy hands. The day he received the first of the cloth-bound volumes from Cox & Wyman, his printers in Great Queen Street, just off Lincoln's-Inn Fields, Samuel Beeton commissioned a velvet-lined leather drop-sided box to be made. In this he placed the brand-new copy of his wife's book, wrapped the whole in brown paper, and presented it to her that evening at their Pinner home. Happily, this volume has survived in excellent condition to the present day, its spine and sides unfaded and with its text and colored full-page plates as clean and unsullied as when they left the printers in 1861. (See illustration, page 229.)

The first issue of the volume edition bore the old address of ''S. O. Beeton, 18 Bouverie St., London. E.C.'' on its colored lithographed title page, although by this time, as the printed title page clearly pointed out, the firm had moved to more imposing premises at 248 Strand, W.C. The explanation is that the lithographed plates had been prepared some weeks

225

Samuel Beeton's publishing
house at 248, The Strand, London, in 1861.

beforehand and were far too expensive to scrap or alter, while the printed
title page was not set up in type until the last moment—well after the
printing of the rest of the text. Later, with the book still selling well, a new
colored lithographed title page was prepared, incorporating the Strand address. Copies of the first edition, dated 1861, bearing the Strand address on
the lithographed title page, are of later issue than those bearing the Bouverie
Street address.

To peruse the book in any depth is immediately to realize why
Isabella confessed that she had spent at least four years in collecting material
for its various sections and amassing the hundreds of well-tried and trusted
recipes with which she filled its pages. The printed title page gives some
indication of the scope of the work, issued in this format as *The Book of
Household Management,* 1861, by Mrs. Isabella Beeton. It told its readers
that the volume comprised information ". . . for the Mistress, Housekeeper, Cook, Kitchen-Maid, Butler, Footman, Coachman, Valet, Upper
and Under House-Maids, Lady's-Maid, Maid-of-all-Work, Laundry-Maid,
Nurse and Nurse-Maid, Monthly, Wet, and Sick Nurses, Etc. Etc. Also
Sanitary, Medical, & Legal Memoranda; with a History of the Origin,
Properties, and Uses of all things connected with Home Life and Comfort."
Chapter One opened with a bang:

As with the Commander of an Army, or the leader of any enterprise, so it is
with the mistress of a house. Her spirit will be seen through the whole
establishment; and just in proportion as she performs her duties intelligently,
and thoroughly, so will her domestics follow in her path . . . In this opinion
we are borne out by the author of *The Vicar of Wakefield,* who says: "The

modest virgin, the prudent wife, and the careful matron are much more serviceable in life than petticoated philosophers, blustering heroines, or virago queens. She who makes her husband and children happy, who reclaims the one from vice and trains up the other to virtue, is a much greater character than ladies described in romances, whose whole occupation is to murder mankind with shafts from their quiver, or their eyes.

Much of the early part of the book is devoted to etiquette, not only while dining and entertaining, but in the mistress's relations with the servants of the household, and with the various categories of tradesmen and shopkeepers with whom she might come in contact. Typical of Isabella's hints to diners is her instruction on how to use the finger-bowl:

When dinner is finished, the dessert is placed on the table, accompanied with finger-glasses. It is the custom of some gentlemen to wet a corner of the napkin; but the hostess, whose behaviour will set the tone to all the ladies present, will merely wet the tips of her fingers, which will serve all the purposes required. The French and other continentals have a habit of gargling the mouth; but it is a custom which no English gentlewoman should, in the slightest degree, imitate.

In private parties, a lady is not to refuse the invitation of a gentleman to dance, unless she is previously engaged. The hostess must be supposed to have asked to her house only those persons whom she knows to be perfectly respectable and of unblemished character, as well as pretty equal in position; and thus, to decline the offer of any gentleman present, would be a tactic reflection on the master and mistress of the house.

It may be mentioned here, more especially for the young who will read this book, that introductions at balls and evening parties cease with the occasion which calls them forth, no introduction, at these times, giving a gentleman a right to address, afterwards, a lady. She is, consequently, free, next morning, to pass her partner at a ball of the previous evening without the slightest recognition.

Etiquette amongst the servants was just as important in a well-regulated home, and in her list of duties of a housekeeper Isabella set out rules for her mode of conduct. She had, of course, to be "above suspicion, and her honesty and sobriety unquestionable; for there are many temptations to which she is exposed. In a physical point of view, a housekeeper should be healthy and strong, and be particularly clean in her person, and her hands, although they may show a degree of roughness, from the nature of some of her employments, yet should have a nice inviting appearance. In her dealings with the various tradesmen, and in her behaviour to the domestics under her, the demeanour and conduct of the housekeeper should be such as, in neither case, to diminish, by an undue familiarity, her authority or influence."

Each of the various categories of servants had their proper station, and the caste system which prevailed was a mirror image of society above stairs:

The daily duties of a housekeeper are regulated, in great measure, by the extent of the establishment she superintends. She should, however, rise early, and see that all the domestics are duly performing their work, and that everything is progressing satisfactorily for the preparation of the breakfast for the household and family.

After breakfast, which, in large establishments, she will take in the "housekeeper's room" with the lady's-maid, butler, and valet, and where they will be waited on by the still-room maid, she will, on various days set apart for each purpose, carefully examine the household linen, with a view to its being repaired. . . . The housekeeper's room is generally made use of by the lady's-maid, butler, and valet, who take there their breakfast, tea, and supper. The lady's-maid will also use this apartment as a sitting-room, when not engaged with her lady, or with some other duties which would call her elsewhere. In different establishments, according to the size and rank of the family, different rules, of course, prevail. For instance, in the mansions of those of very high rank, and where there is a house steward, there are two distinct tables kept, one in the steward's room for the principal members of the household, the other in the servants' hall, for the domestics. At the steward's dinner-table, the steward and housekeeper preside; and here, also, are present the lady's-maid, butler, valet, and head gardener. Should any visitors be staying with the family, their servants, generally the valet and lady's-maid, will be admitted to the steward's table.

Later, Isabella deplores the fact that "the introduction of cheap silks and cottons, and, still more recently, those ambiguous 'materials' and tweeds, have removed the landmarks between the mistress and her maid, between master and his man." Also, ". . . there is a conviction of 'Society' that the race of good servants has died out, at least in England, although they do order these things better in France; that there is neither honesty, conscientiousness, nor the careful and industrious habits which distinguished the servants of our grandmothers and great-grandmothers; that domestics no longer know their place . . ." But, she told her readers, she resolutely refused to despair:

The great masses of society among us are not thus deserted; there are few families of respectability, from the shopkeeper in the next street to the nobleman whose mansion dignifies the next square, which do not contain among their dependents attached and useful servants; and where these are absent altogether, there are good reasons for it. The sensible master and the kind mistress know, that if servants depend on them for their means of living, in their turn they are dependent on the servants for very many of the comforts of life; and that, with a proper amount of care in choosing servants, and treating them like reasonable beings, and making slight excuses for the shortcomings of human nature, they will, save in exceptional cases, be tolerably well served, and in most instances, surround themselves with attached domestics.

It is the chapters devoted to cookery in all its branches which form by far the greater part of the book, and the author was at great pains to tell her readers that the format she has chosen was the result of a great deal of thought and not a few sleepless nights:

I have attempted to give, under the chapters devoted to cookery, an intelligible arrangement to every recipe, a list of the *ingredients,* a plain statement of the *mode* of preparing each dish, and a careful estimate of its *cost,* the *number of people* for whom it is *sufficient,* and the time when it is *seasonable* . . . But in the department belonging to the Cook I have striven, too, to make my book

The first edition of Mrs. Beeton's famous cookery book, published in 1861. Clean and complete copies in the original publisher's cloth binding (as shown) are of the utmost rarity.

something more than a Cookery Book, and have, therefore, on the best authority I could obtain, given an account of the natural history of the animals and vegetables which we use as food.

I have followed the animal from his birth to his appearance on the table; have described the manner of feeding him and of slaying him, the position of his various joints, and after giving the recipes, have described the modes of carving Meat, poultry, and Game.

In order that the duties of the Cook may be properly performed, and that he may be able to reproduce esteemed dishes with certainty, all terms of indecision should be banished from his art. Accordingly, what is known only to him, will, in these pages, be made known to others.

In them all the indecisive terms expressed by a bit of this, some of that, a small piece of that, and a handful of the others, shall never be made use of, but all quantities be precisely and explicitly stated. With a desire, also, that all ignorance of this most essential part of the culinary art should disappear, and that a uniform system of weights and measures should be adopted, we give an account of the weights which answer to certain measures.

A table is then given of liquid weights and measures, with the amounts a tablespoon, dessertspoon, and teaspoon, hold translated into liquid ounces, etc. Thus, for the first time, much of the element of chance was removed from domestic cook books, and all her imitators and followers made haste to follow the same procedure.

To choose a representative section of recipes from a book with so wide a scope is almost impossible; but the few I am able to print here will enable the reader to discern the methods Isabella Beeton used and the clarity of instruction which accompanied every one of her dishes:

ROAST SADDLE OF MUTTON

Ingredients: Saddle of mutton; a little salt.

Mode: To insure this joint being tender, let it hang for ten days or a fortnight, if the weather permits. Cut off the tail and flaps, and trim away every part that has not indisputable pretensions to be eaten, and have the skin taken off and skewered on again.

Put it down to a bright, clear fire, and, when the joint has been cooking for an hour, remove the skin and dredge it with flour. It should not be placed too near the fire, as the fat should not be in the slightest degree burnt.

Keep constantly basting, both before and after the skin is removed; sprinkle some salt over the joint.

Make a little gravy in the dripping pan; pour it over the meat, which send to table with a tureen of made gravy and red-currant jelly.

Time: A saddle of mutton weighing 10 lbs., 2½ hours; 14 lbs., 3¼ hours. When liked underdone, allow rather less time.

Average cost: 10d. per lb.

Sufficient: A moderate-sized saddle of 10 lbs. for 7 or 8 persons.

Seasonable: All the year; not so good when lamb is in full season.

PORK CHOPS

Ingredients: Loin of pork, pepper and salt to taste.
Mode: Cut the chops from a delicate loin of pork, bone and trim them neatly, and cut away the greater portion of the fat. Season them with pepper; place the gridiron on the fire; when quite hot, lay on the chops and broil them for about ¼ hour, turning them 3 or 4 times; and be particular that they are *thoroughly* done, but not dry.

Dish them, sprinkle over a little fine salt, and serve plain, or with tomato sauce, sauce piquante, or pickled gherkins, a few of which should be laid round the dish as a garnish.
Time: About ¼ hour.
Average cost: 10d. per lb. for chops.
Sufficient: Allow 6 for 4 persons.
Seasonable: From October to March.

VEAL À LA BOURGEOISE

Ingredients: 2 to 3 lbs. of the loin or neck of veal; 10 or 12 young carrots; a bunch of green onions; 2 slices of lean bacon; 2 blades of pounded mace; 1 bunch of savoury herbs; pepper and salt to taste; a few new potatoes; 1 pint of green peas.
Mode: Cut the veal into cutlets, trim them, and put the trimmings into a stewpan with a little butter. Lay in the cutlets and fry them a nice brown colour on both sides. Add the bacon, carrots, onions, spice, herbs, and seasoning; pour in about a pint of boiling water, and stew gently for 2 hours on a slow fire. When done, skim off the fat, take out the herbs, and flavour the gravy with a little tomato sauce and ketchup.

Have ready the peas and potatoes, boiled *separately*. Put them with the veal, and serve.
Time: 2 hours.
Average cost: 2s.9d.
Sufficient: 5 or 6 persons.
Seasonable: From June to August with peas; rather earlier when these are omitted.

LARK PIE

Ingredients: A few thin slices of beef, the same of bacon, 9 larks, flour. For stuffing, 1 teacupful of bread crumbs, ½ teaspoonful of minced lemon-peel, 1 teaspoonful of minced parsley, 1 egg, salt and pepper to taste, 1 teaspoonful of chopped shallot, ½ pint of weak stock or water, puff-paste.
Mode: Make a stuffing of bread crumbs, minced lemon-peel, parsley, and the yolk of an egg, all of which should be well mixed together. Roll the larks in flour and stuff them.

Line the bottom of a pie-dish with a few slices of beef and bacon; over these place the larks, and season with salt and pepper, minced parsley, and chopped shallot, in the above proportion. Pour in the stock or water, cover with crust, and bake for an hour in a moderate oven.

During the time the pie is baking, shake it two or three times, to assist in thickening the gravy. Serve very hot.

Time: 1 hour.

Average cost: 1s.6d. a dozen.

Sufficient: 5 or 6 persons.

Seasonable: In full season in November.

PIGEON PIE
(Epsom Grand-Stand Recipe)

Ingredients: 1½ lb. of rump-steak; 2 or 3 pigeons; 3 slices of ham; pepper and salt to taste; 2 oz. of butter; 4 eggs; puff crust.

Mode: Cut the steak into pieces about 3 inches square, and with it line the bottom of a pie-dish, seasoning it well with pepper and salt.

Clean the pigeons, rub them with pepper and salt inside and out, and put into the body of each rather more than ½ oz. of butter. Lay them on the steak, and a piece of ham on each pigeon.

Add the yolks of 4 eggs, and half fill the dish with stock; place a border of puff paste round the edge of the dish, put on the cover, and ornament it in any way that may be preferred.

Clean three of the feet, and place them in a hole made in the crust at the top; this shows what kind of a pie it is.

Glaze the crust—that is to say, brush it over with the yolk of an egg—and bake it in a well-heated oven for about 1¼ hour. When liked, a seasoning of pounded mace may be added.

Time: 1¼ hour, or rather less.

Average cost: 5s.3d.

Sufficient: 5 or 6 persons.

Seasonable: Any time.

LOBSTER SALAD

Ingredients: 1 hen lobster; lettuces; endive; small salad (whatever is in season); a little chopped beetroot; 2 hard-boiled eggs; a few slices of cucumber.

For dressing, equal quantities of oil and vinegar, 1 teaspoonful of made mustard, the yolks of 2 eggs; cayenne and salt to taste; ¼ teaspoonful of anchovy sauce. These ingredients should be mixed perfectly smooth, and form a creamy-looking sauce.

Mode: Wash the salad, and thoroughly dry it by shaking it in a cloth. Cut up the lettuces and endive, pour the dressing on them, and lightly throw in the small salad. Mix all well together with the pickings from the body of the lobster; pick the meat from the shell, cut it up into nice square pieces, put half in the salad, the other half reserve for garnishing.

Separate the yolks from the whites of 2 hard-boiled eggs; chop the whites very fine, and rub the yolks through a sieve, and afterward the coral from the inside of the lobster.

Arrange the salad lightly on a glass dish, and garnish, first with a row of sliced cucumber, then with the pieces of lobster, the yolks and whites of the eggs, coral, and beetroot placed alternately, and arranged in small separate bunches, so that the colours contrast nicely.

Average cost: 3s.6d.

Sufficient: 4 or 5 persons.

Seasonable: From April to October; may be had all the year, but salad is scarce and expensive in winter.

Note: A few crayfish make a pretty garnishing to lobster salad.

FORCEMEAT
(For Veal, Turkeys, Fowls, Hare, &c)

Ingredients: 2 oz. of ham or lean bacon; ¼ lb. of suet; the rind of half a lemon; 1 teaspoonful of minced parsley; 1 teaspoonful of minced sweet herbs; salt, cayenne, and pounded mace to taste; 6 oz. of bread crumbs; 2 eggs.

Mode: Shred the ham or bacon, chop the suet, lemon-peel, and herbs, taking particular care that all be very finely minced. Add a seasoning to taste, of salt, cayenne, and mace, and blend all thoroughly together with the bread crumbs, before wetting.

Now beat and strain the eggs, work these up with the other ingredients, and the forcemeat will be ready for use.

When it is made into balls, fry to a nice brown in boiling lard, or put them on a tin and bake for ½ hour in a moderate oven.

As we have stated before, no one flavour should predominate greatly, and the forcemeat should be of sufficient body to cut with a knife, and yet not dry and heavy. For very delicate forcemeat, it is advisable to pound the ingredients together before binding with the egg; but for ordinary cooking, mincing very finely answers the purpose.

Note: In forcemeat for HARE, the liver of the animal is sometimes added. Boil for 5 minutes, mince it very small, and mix it with the other ingredients. If it should be in an unsound state, it must be on no account made use of.

Average cost: 8d.

Sufficient: For a turkey, a moderately-sized fillet of veal or a hare.

TOAD-IN-THE-HOLE

Ingredients: 1½ lbs. of rump-steak, 1 sheep's kidney; pepper and salt to taste. For the batter, 3 eggs; 1 pint of milk; 4 tablespoonfuls of flour; ½ saltspoonful of salt.

Mode: Cut up the steak and kidney into convenient-sized pieces, and put them into a pie-dish with a good seasoning of salt and pepper. Mix the flour with a small quantity of milk at first, to prevent its being lumpy. Add the remainder, and the 3 eggs, which should be well beaten. Put in the salt, stir the batter for about 5 minutes, and pour it over the steak.

Place in a tolerably brisk oven immediately, and bake for 1½ hours.

Time: 1½ hours.

Average cost: 1s.9d.

Sufficient: 4 or 5 persons.

Seasonable: Any time.

BEEF-STEAK AND KIDNEY PUDDING

Ingredients: 2 lbs. of rump-steak, 2 kidneys; seasoning to taste of salt and black pepper; suet crust made with milk (see Pastry), in the proportion of 6 oz. of suet to each 1 lb. of flour.

Mode: Procure some tender rump steak (that which has been hung a little time), and divide it into pieces about an inch square, and cut each kidney into 8 pieces.

Line the dish with crust made with suet and flour in the above proportion, leaving a small piece of crust to overlap the edge. Then cover the bottom with a proportion of the steak and a few pieces of kidney. Season with salt and pepper (some add a little flour to thicken the gravy, but it is not necessary), and then add another layer of steak, kidney, and seasoning.

Proceed in this manner until the dish is full, then pour in sufficient water to come within 2 inches of the top of the basin. Moisten the edges of the crust, cover the pudding over, press the two crusts together, that the gravy may not escape, and turn up the overhanging paste. Wring out a cloth in hot water, flour it, and tie up the pudding. Put it in boiling water, and let it boil for at least 4 hours. If the water diminishes, always replenish it with hot water from a jug, as the pudding should be kept covered all the time and not allowed to stop boiling.

When the cloth is removed, cut out a round piece of the top of the crust to prevent the pudding bursting, and send it to table in the basin, either in an ornamental dish, or with a napkin around it. Serve quickly.

Time: For a pudding with 2 lbs. of steak and 2 kidneys allow 4 hours.

Average cost: 2s.8d.

Sufficient: 6 persons.

Seasonable: All the year, but more suitable in winter, especially after a hard day's hunting.

HOW TO BOIL A HAM TO GIVE
IT AN EXCELLENT FLAVOUR

Ingredients: Vinegar and water; 2 heads of celery; 2 turnips; 3 onions; a large bunch of savoury herbs; a fine ham about 10 lbs. weight.

Mode: In choosing a ham, ascertain that it is perfectly sweet by running a sharp knife into it, close to the bone; and if, when withdrawn, it has an agreeable smell, the ham is good. If, on the contrary, the blade has a greasy appearance and offensive smell, the ham is bad. If it has been long hung, and is very dry and salt, let it remain in soak for 24 hours, changing the water frequently. This length of time is only necessary in the case of its being very hard: from 8 to 12 hours would be sufficient for a Yorkshire or Westmoreland ham. Wash it thoroughly clean, and trim away from the under-side all the rusty and smoked parts, which would spoil the appearance.

Let it now soak for a few minutes in vinegar and water. Put it in a large stew-pot in cold water, after first rinsing it well in a change of water. Bring to the boil, and add the vegetables and herbs. Simmer very gently until tender, which will take about 4 hours. Take it out, strip off the skin, cover with bread-raspings, and put on a paper ruche or frill round the knuckle.

When the ham is boiling, be careful to skim off the scum as it rises.

Time: A ham weighing 10 lbs., 4 hours.

Average cost: 8d. to 10d. per pound, by the whole ham.

Seasonable: At any time.

TO MELT LARD

Melt the inner fat of a pig by putting it in a stone jar, and placing it in a saucepan of boiling water, previously stripping off the skin.

Let it simmer gently over a bright fire, and as it melts, pour it carefully from the sediment. Put it in small jars or bladders for use, and keep it in a cool place.

The flead or inside fat of the pig, before it is melted, makes exceedingly light crust, and is particularly wholesome.

TRUFFLES WITH CHAMPAGNE

Ingredients: 12 fine black truffles; a few slices of fat bacon; 1 carrot; 1 turnip; 2 onions; a bunch of savoury herbs; a sprig of parsley; 1 bay-leaf; 2 cloves, 1 blade of pounded mace; 2 glasses of champagne; ½ pint of stock.

Mode: Carefully select the truffles, reject those that have a musty smell, and wash them well with a brush in cold water only until perfectly clean.

Put the bacon into a stewpan with the truffles and the remaining ingredients. Simmer these gently for an hour, and let the whole cool in the stewpan.

When to be served, rewarm them, and drain them on a clean cloth; then arrange them on a delicately-white napkin, that it may contrast as strongly as possible with the truffles, and serve.

The trimmings of truffles are used to flavour gravies, stock, sauces, &c., and are an excellent addition to ragoûts, made dishes of fowl, &c.

Time: 1 hour.
Average cost: Not often bought in this country.
Seasonable: From November to March.

AUNT NELLY'S PUDDING

Ingredients: ½ lb. of flour; ½ lb. of treacle; ½ lb. of suet; the rind and juice of 1 lemon; a few strips of candied lemon-peel; 3 tablespoonfuls of cream; 2 eggs.
Mode: Chop the suet finely; mix it with the flour, treacle, lemon-peel minced, and candied lemon-peel. Add the cream, lemon-juice, and 2 well-beaten eggs.

Beat the pudding well, put it into a buttered basin, tie it down with a cloth, and boil from 3½ to 4 hours.
Time: 3½ to 4 hours.
Average cost: 1s.2d.
Sufficient: 5 or 6 persons.
Seasonable: Any time, but more suitable for a winter pudding.

BAKED APPLE PUDDING

Ingredients: 5 moderately-sized apples; 2 tablespoonfuls of finely-chopped suet; 3 eggs; 3 tablespoonfuls of flour; 1 pint of milk; a little grated nutmeg.
Mode: Mix the flour to a smooth batter with the milk; add the eggs, which should be well whisked, and put this batter into a well-buttered pie-dish.

Wipe the apples clean, but do not pare them. Cut them in halves, and take out the cores. Lay them in the batter, rind uppermost; shake the suet on the top, over which also grate a little nutmeg. Bake in a moderate oven for an hour, and cover, when served, with sifted loaf sugar.

This pudding is also very good with the apples pared, sliced, and mixed with the batter.
Time: 1 hour.
Average cost: 9d.
Sufficient: 5 or 6 persons.

GERMAN PUDDING

Ingredients: 2 teaspoonfuls of flour; 1 teaspoonful of arrow-root; 1 pint of milk; 2 oz. of butter; sugar to taste; the rind of ½ lemon; 4 eggs; 3 tablespoonfuls of brandy.
Mode: Boil the milk with the lemon-rind until well-flavoured; then strain it and mix with the flour, arrowroot, butter, and sugar. Boil these ingredients for a few minutes, keeping them well stirred. Then take them off the fire and mix with them the eggs, yolks, and whites, beaten separately and added separately.

Boil some sugar to candy; line a mould with this, put in the brandy, then the mixture. Tie down with a cloth, and boil for rather more than 1 hour.

When turned out, the brandy and sugar make a nice sauce.
Time: Rather more than an hour.
Average cost: 1s.
Sufficient: 4 or 5 persons.
Seasonable: At any time.

MANCHESTER PUDDING
(To eat cold)

Ingredients: 3 oz. of grated bread; ½ pint of milk; a strip of lemon-peel; 4 eggs; sugar to taste; puff-paste; jam; 3 tablespoonfuls of brandy.
Mode: Flavour the milk with lemon-peel by infusing it in the milk for ½ hour; then strain it on to the bread crumbs, and boil it for 2 or 3 minutes.

Add the eggs, leaving out the whites of 2; the butter, sugar, and brandy. Stir all these ingredients well together.

Cover a pie-dish with puff-paste, and at the bottom put a thick layer of any kind of jam. Pour the above mixture, cold, on the jam, and bake the pudding for an hour.

Serve cold, with a little sifted sugar sprinkled over.
Time: 1 hour.
Average cost: 1s.
Sufficient: 5 or 6 persons.
Seasonable: At any time.

YORKSHIRE PUDDING
(To serve with hot roast beef)

Ingredients: 1½ pints of milk; 6 *large* tablespoonfuls of flour; 3 eggs, 1 saltspoonful of salt.
Mode: Put the flour into a basin with the salt, and stir gradually to this enough milk to make a stiff batter. When this is perfectly smooth and all the lumps are well rubbed down, add the remainder of the milk and the eggs, which should be well beaten.

Beat the mixture for a few minutes, and pour it into a shallow tin which has previously been well-rubbed with beef dripping. Put the pudding into the oven, and bake it for an hour; then, for another ½ hour, place it under the meat to catch a little of the gravy which flows from it.

Cut the pudding into small square pieces, put them on a hot dish, and serve.

If the meat is baked, rather than being before the fire on a turning-spit, the pudding may at once be placed under it, resting the meat above it on a small three-cornered stand.

Time: 1½ hours.
Average cost: 7d.
Sufficient: 5 or 6 persons.
Seasonable: At any time.

APRICOT CREAM

Ingredients: 12 to 16 ripe apricots; ½ lb. of sugar; 1½ pints of milk; the yolks of 8 eggs; 1 oz. of isinglass.
Mode: Divide the apricots, take out the stones, and boil them in a syrup made with ¼ lb. of sugar and ¼ pint of water, until they form a thin marmalade, which rub through a sieve.

Boil the milk with the other ¼ lb. of sugar, let it cool a little, then mix with it the yolks of eggs which have been previously well beaten. Put this mixture into a jug, place this jug in boiling water, and stir it one way over the fire until it thickens; but on no account let it boil. Strain through a sieve, add the isinglass previously boiled with a small quantity of water, and keep stirring it till nearly cold. Then mix the cream with the apricots, stir well, put into an oiled mould, and, if convenient, set it on ice; at any rate, in a very cool place. It should turn out on the dish without any difficulty.

Time: From 20 to 30 minutes to boil the apricots.
Average cost: 2s.
Sufficient: To fill a quart mold.
Seasonable: In August, September, and October.

THE HIDDEN MOUNTAIN
(A pretty supper dish)

Ingredients: 6 eggs; a few slices of citron; sugar to taste; ¼ pint of cream; a layer of any kind of jam.
Mode: Beat the whites and the yolks of the eggs separately; then mix them and beat them well again adding a few thin slices of citron, the cream, and sufficient pounded sugar to sweeten it nicely. When the mixture is well beaten, put it into a buttered pan, and fry the same as a pancake; but it should be three times the thickness of an ordinary pancake.

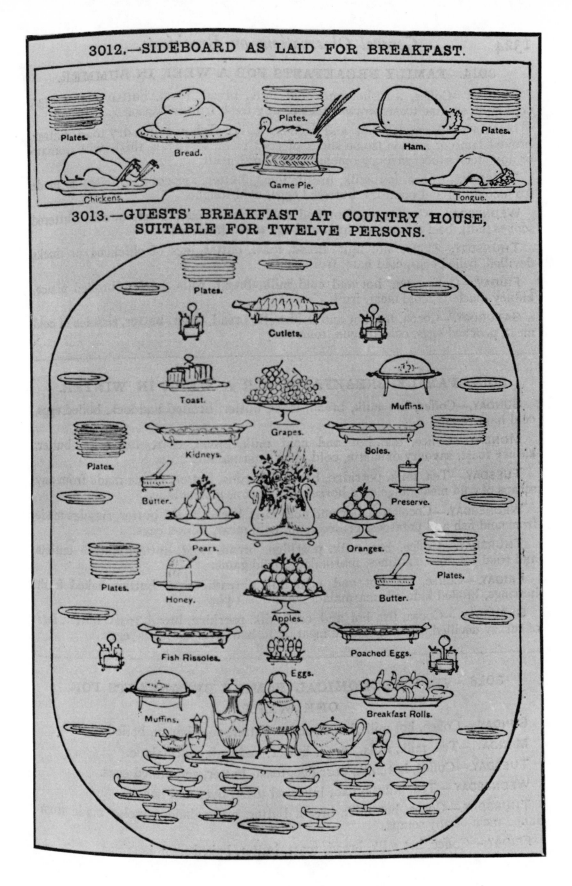

Breakfast in the country. An illustration from the 1889 edition of *The Book of Household Managment* by Isabella Beeton.

Cover it with jam, and garnish with slices of citron and holly-leaves.

This dish is served cold.

Time: About 10 minutes to fry the mixture.

Average cost: With the jam, 1s.4d.

Sufficient: 3 or 4 persons.

Seasonable: At any time.

PLAIN OMELET

Ingredients: 6 eggs; a saltspoonful of salt; ½ saltspoonful of pepper; ¼ lb. of butter.

Mode: Break the eggs into a basin, omitting the whites of 3, and beat them up with the salt and pepper until extremely light. Then add 2 oz. of butter broken into small pieces, and stir this into the mixture.

Put the other 2 oz. of butter in to a frying-pan, make it quite hot, and, as soon as it begins to bubble, whisk the eggs, &c., very briskly for a minute or two, and pour them into the pan. Stir the omelet with a spoon one way until the mixture thickens and becomes firm, and when the whole is set, fold the edges over, so that the omelet assumes a semi oval form. When it is nicely brown on one side, and quite firm, it is done. To take off the rawness on the upper side, hold the pan before the fire for a minute or two, and brown it with a salamander or hot shovel.

Serve very expeditiously on a very hot dish, and never cook it until it is just wanted.

The flavour of this omelet may be very much enhanced by adding minced parsley, minced onion, or grated cheese, allowing 1 tablespoonful of the former, and half the quantity of the latter, to the above proportion of eggs. Shrimps or oysters may also be added: the latter should be scalded in their liquor, and then bearded and cut into small pieces.

In making an omelet, be particularly careful that it is not too thin, and, to avoid this, do not make it in too large a frying-pan as the mixture would then spread too much and taste of the outside. It should also not be greasy, burnt, or too much done, and should be cooked over a gentle fire, that the whole of the substance may be heated without drying up the outside.

Omelets are sometimes served with gravy, but *this should never be poured over them,* but served in a tureen, as the liquid causes the omelet to become heavy and flat, instead of eating light and soft. In making the gravy, the flavour should not over-power that of the omelet, and should be thickened with arrowroot or rice flour.

Time: With 6 eggs, in a frying-pan 18 or 20 inches round, 4 to 6 minutes.

Average cost: 9d.

Sufficient: 4 persons.

Seasonable: At any time.

RICH PANCAKES

Ingredients: 6 eggs; 1 pint of cream; ¼ lb. of loaf sugar; 1 glass of sherry; ½ teaspoonful of grated nutmeg; flour.

Mode: Ascertain that the eggs are extremely fresh, beat them well, strain and mix with the cream, pounded sugar, wine, nutmeg, and as much flour as will make the batter nearly as thick as that for ordinary pancakes. Make the frying-pan hot, wipe it with a clean cloth, pour in sufficient batter to make a thin pancake, and fry it for about 5 minutes. Dish the pancakes piled one above the other, strew sifted sugar between each, and serve.

Time: About 5 minutes.

Average cost: With cream, at 1s. a pint, 2s.3d.

Sufficient: To make 8 pancakes.

Seasonable: At any time, but especially served on Shrove Tuesday.

TIPSY CAKE

Ingredients: 1 moulded sponge, or Savoy cake; sufficient sweet wine or sherry to soak it; 6 tablespoons of brandy; 2 oz. of sweet almonds; 1 pint of rich custard.

Mode: Procure a cake that is three or four days old—either sponge or Savoy, or rice-cake, answering the purpose of a tipsy cake. Cut the bottom of the cake level, to make it stand firm in the dish. Make a small hole in the centre, and pour in and over the cake sufficient sweet wine or sherry, mixed with the above proportion of brandy, to soak it nicely.

When the cake is well soaked, blanch and cut the almonds into strips, stick them all over the cake, and pour round it a good custard, made rich and palatable. For this, allow 8 eggs instead of 5 to the pint of milk. The cakes are sometimes crumbled and soaked, and a whipped cream heaped over them, the same as for trifles.

Time: About 2 hours to soak the cake.

Average cost: 4s. 6d.

Sufficient: For 1 dish.

Seasonable: At any time.

It was when Isabella came to give the recipe for what she had named "The Curé's Omelet" that she was unable to resist giving a translation of Brillat-Savarin's anecdote respecting the quiet *tête-à-tête* during which this delicacy was gratifyingly consumed:

"Every one knows," says Brillat-Savarin, in his *Physiology of Taste,* "that for twenty years Madame Récamier was the most beautiful woman in Paris. It is also well known that she was exceedingly charitable, and took a great interest in every benevolent work. Wishing to consult the Curé of —— respecting the working of an institution, she went to his home at five o'clock in the afternoon, and was much astonished at finding him already at his dinner-table.

"Madame Récamier wished to retire, but the Curé would not hear of it. A neat white cloth covered the table; some good old wine sparkled in a crystal decanter; the porcelain was of the best; the plates had heaters of boiling water beneath them; a neatly-costumed maid-servant was in attendance. The crawfish-soup had just been removed, and there was on the table a salmon-trout, an omelet, and a salad.

" 'My dinner will tell you,' said the worthy Curé, with a smile, 'that it is fast-day, according to our Church's regulations.'

"Madame Récamier and her host attacked the trout, the sauce served with which betrayed a skillful hand, the countenance of the Curé the while showing satisfaction.

"And now they fell upon the omelet, which was round, sufficiently thick, and cooked, so to speak, to a hair's-breadth.

"As the spoon entered the omelet, a thick rich juice issued from it, pleasant to the eye as well as to the smell; the dish became full of it; and our fair friend owns that, between the perfume and the sight, it made her mouth water.

" 'It is an *omelette au thon*' (that is to say, a tunny omelet), said the Curé, noticing, with the greatest delight, the emotion of Madame Récamier, 'and few people taste it without lavishing praises on it.' "

The latest in oil-fired cooking stoves. An advertisement from the 1880s showing the most modern of labor-saving domestic inventions.

Then came the salad, which Savarin recommends to all who place confidence in him. It refreshes without exciting; and he has a theory that it makes people younger.

Amidst pleasant conversation the dessert arrived. It consisted of three apples, cheese, and a plate of preserves; and then upon a little round table was served Mocha coffee, for which France has been, and is, justly famous.

OMELETTE AU THON

Take for 6 persons, the roes of 2 carp (pike or shad would do as well, and any other fish, indeed, may be used with success). Bleach the roes by putting them for 5 minutes in boiling water slightly salted.

Take a piece of fresh tunny about the size of a hen's egg, to which add a small shallot already chopped. Hash up together the roe and the tunny so as to mix them well, and throw the whole into a saucepan with a sufficient quantity of very good butter. Whip it up until the butter is melted. This constitutes the speciality of this omelet.

Take a second piece of butter, the size to be at your own discretion, mix it with parsley and herbs, place it in a long-shaped dish destined to receive the omelet. Squeeze the juice of a lemon over it, and place it on hot embers.

Beat up 12 eggs (the fresher the better); throw up the sauté of roe and tunny, stirring it so as to mix all well together; then make your omelet in the usual manner, endeavouring to turn it out long, thick, and soft.

Spread it carefully on the dish prepared for it, and serve at once.

This dish ought to be reserved for *recherché déjeuners*, or for assemblies where amateurs meet who know how to eat well. Washed down with good old wine, it will work wonders.

Note: The roe and the tunny must be beaten up (sauté) without allowing them to boil, to prevent their hardening, which would prevent them mixing well with the eggs. Your dish should be hollowed towards its centre, to allow the gravy to concentrate, that it may be helped out with a spoon. The dish must be heated, otherwise the cold china will extract all the heat from the omelet.

The final chapters in *The Book of Household Management* were devoted to such matters as "Invalid Cookery"; "The Duties of a Butler," and those of all other ranks of servants; "The Bearing and Rearing of Children"; "The Doctor"; "Legal Memoranda"; etc., etc. There was still space for a recipe or two, but these were confined to the ordering of dinner parties, weekend parties, and bills-of-fare for Christmas and holidays. The last of these dealt with the catering for that favorite Victorian outdoor excursion, the picnic, and, perhaps with memories of Derby Day on Epsom Heath, Isabella set out a menu that today would have satisfied the inner cravings of a regiment of hungry marines:

BILL OF FARE FOR A PICNIC

The following bill of fare will ensure enough food being available for a large family party, perhaps consisting of as many as forty persons.

A joint of cold roast beef; a joint of cold boiled beef; 2 ribs of lamb; 2 shoulders of lamb; 4 roast fowls; 2 roast ducks; 1 ham; 2 veal-and-ham pies; 2 pigeon pies; 6 medium-sized lobsters; 1 piece of collared calf's head; 18 lettuces; 6 cucumbers.

1 stick of horseradish; a bottle of mint-sauce well corked; a bottle of salad dressing; a bottle of vinegar; made mustard, pepper, salt, good oil, and pounded sugar. If it can be managed, take a little ice.

Stewed fruit, well sweetened, and put into glass bottles well corked; 3 or 4 dozen plain pastry biscuits to eat with the stewed fruit; 2 dozen fruit turnovers; 4 dozen cheesecakes; 2 cold cabinet puddings in moulds; 2 blancmanges in moulds; a few jam puffs; 1 large cold plum-pudding (this *must* be good); a few baskets of fresh fruit; 3 dozen plain biscuits; a piece of cheese; 6 lbs. of butter (this, of course, includes the butter for tea); 4 quartered loaves of household bread; 3 dozen rolls; 6 loaves of tin bread (for tea); 2 plain plum cakes; 2 pound cakes; 2 sponge cakes; a tin of mixed biscuits; ½ lb. of tea. Coffee is not suitable for a picnic, being difficult to take.

Beverages: 3 dozen quart bottles of ale, packed in hampers; ginger-beer, soda-water, and lemonade, of each 2 dozen bottles; 6 bottles of sherry; 6 bottles of claret; champagne and other light wine at the discretion of the host; and 2 bottles of brandy. Water can usually be obtained; so it is useless to take it.

It is scarcely necessary to say that plates, tumblers, wine-glasses, knives, forks, spoons, etc., must not be forgotten; as also teacups and saucers, 3 or 4 teapots, some lump sugar, and milk, if this last article cannot be obtained in the neighbourhood. Take 3 corkscrews.

The success of *The Book of Household Management* was assured long before the work was issued in book form in October, 1861, and Samuel Beeton in the meantime had moved to more modern and more commodious premises in the Strand. It was from here that *The Englishwoman's Domestic Magazine* continued to be published; but in May, 1860, made bold by its success, the format was increased to a paper-wrapped issue of 8¾" x 5½", each of some forty-eight pages, and, in the words of its editor: ". . . on Demy 8vo paper of excellent quality, beautifully printed in various types, from new founts expressly purchased for the magazine, and richly illustrated with wood cuts." But it was the new innovation of a large-sized fashion-plate, colored by hand, showing the latest feminine fashions direct from Paris, together with "patterns from Berlin Wool Work, printed in from ten to twenty colours, from original Berlin designs . . ." that filled Isabella's

Isabella Beeton, aged twenty-eight.

heart with pride. The price had been advanced to sixpence a copy, and, with a sufficiently large cirnulation, this would more than enable the venture to pay its way.

With financial success seemingly assured, she accompanied her husband on business and sightseeing trips to Germany, Ireland, and Paris, each time returning to London to take over an increasing share of the responsibility of running the Beeton publishing business. Samuel's health had been giving both of them cause for concern for several months, and the stubborn cough that plagued him was enough to make them fearful enough to move house to what they believed was a more salubrious situation at Greenhithe in the Thames Valley.

Christmas, 1864, was spent happily in their new home, while they awaited the birth of Isabella's fourth child. Young Orchart romped around as a thoroughly healthy baby, and, as their neighbor Mrs. Browne put it, they hoped for another son ". . . so as to have two little boys playing together."

During the weeks preceding her confinement, Isabella was kept busy correcting the proofs of a shortened version of her cookery book, to be issued as *The Dictionary of Every-Day Cookery*. Still in her late twenties, she was a strong and healthy young woman fretting to be able to return to the literary and commercial world of the Strand, and chafing in the semi-idleness forced on her during the final few days of her pregnancy.

On January 29, 1865, Isabella gave birth to a son. The midwife who attended her pronounced mother and child perfectly well, and at first all seemed to be in order. The little boy thrived from the start, but after a day or two Isabella complained of feeling unwell, was found to be running a high temperature, and within forty-eight hours had relapsed into a coma. The doctor diagnosed puerperal fever, child-bed fever as it was known, the scourge of lying-in hospitals and from which very few mothers indeed recovered. Isabella was not one of the fortunate few, and on February 6th, just over a week after the birth of her son, she died. She was not yet twenty-nine.

The blow which deprived the ailing Samuel Beeton of a wife he treasured was a stunning one. It was felt the more as being entirely unexpected, and for a time he was inconsolable. "My agony is excessive," he wrote to his close friend William Stagg, "but I have hours of calm and quiet which refresh me and enable me to meet the dreadful grief that well nigh overpowers me, and renders me unable to move or stir. . . ." But an effort had to be made to keep his several monthly magazines and periodicals in full production. It was only when he attempted to take over full control that he realized how much he had owed to his wife's unobtrusive assistance and intelligent collaboration.

Within months Beeton was in difficulty. Some of his magazines were disposed of to other publishing houses, while his own brainchild, *Beeton's Illuminated Family Bible,* which he himself later described as "a literary white elephant" lay piled up unsold in his warehouse. The final blow came with the failure of Overend, Gurney & Co., in May 1866, one of London's largest banking houses. S. O. Beeton was amongst the thousands who lost heavily by its failure, and, with bankruptcy staring him in the face, he was forced to dispose of his remaining copyrights to the rival firm Ward, Lock and Tyler, of Paternoster Row. With them went the copyright of his most valuable remaining asset, *The Book of Household Management.*

Without his Isabella to guide him, Samuel Beeton lost much of the commercial acumen she had once so carefully nurtured, and with it the consuming desire he once had of making his way to the top in the world of publishing. At first he worked for Ward, Lock; but a quarrel leading to writs and injunctions severed his connection with the firm. In his declining years, he attempted to build another publishing business of his own; but without Isabella all the old drive seemed to be gone. Only his sons, Orchart and Mayson, brought him any consolation; his desire for their well-being driving him repeatedly to his offices in the City, ill as he was. He died June 6, 1877, age forty-six, and was buried in his wife's grave in Norwood Cemetery.

With hindsight, it becomes obvious that the copyright of Mrs. Beeton's monumental work could scarcely have fallen into better hands. Ward, Lock and Tyler could have had little idea, back in 1866, the bargain they acquired when they offered the all-but bankrupt S. O. Beeton a regular salary of £400 a year, plus one-sixth of any profits made on his side of the business, in exchange for the copyrights of the publications issued under his name. In time, several of these periodicals fell by the wayside, but *The Book of Household Management* went from strength to strength.

By 1868, "Mrs. Beeton's Cookery Book" as the public now affectionately called it, had become the standard British work on culinary affairs and domestic economy. By the early 1870s the demand often outstripped supply, a new edition of some 20,000 copies being oversold within weeks of publication, In 1877, Ward, Lock and Company, as the firm was now called, issued the first of many companion volumes to *Household Management,* a thick octavo of 1,056 pages, complete with many full-page color-printed plates. Entitled *Beeton's Housewife's Treasury of Domestic Information.* This bulky volume of domestic tidbits of information, published in a binding of quarter-roan, stained brightly-red, and with a heavily gilt spine, contained no recipes or hints on cookery, but covered almost every other aspect of life in the home and out-of-doors. It was the first of many such companion volumes, some of which continue in modern format to the present day.

By 1890, over half a million copies of *The Book of Household Management* had been sold, yet there was still no sign of the demand abating. As the years went by, the book's popularity steadily increased: it became an almost standard wedding present, and one of the most acceptable gifts for Christmas and anniversaries from husband to wife. New and "entirely revised" editions made their appearance every few years, but still with the vast majority of Isabella Beeton's original recipes remaining almost exactly as she compiled them way back in the late-1850s.

Ward, Lock and Company soon recognized the book as one of their greatest assets. With the passage of time the work was gradually brought up to date to accord with modern ideas. Gas, electric, and oil-fired cookery techniques took their places in its pages, and the thousand-and-one labor-saving appliances shouldered out the black-leaded grates, the open fires, candle-lit kitchens, brass turnspits, salamanders, capped and aproned cooks and scullery-maids that were part of Isabella Beeton's everyday life when she compiled the classic that has immortalized her name.

Every year, well over a hundred brand-new cookery books make their appearance in the bookshops of Britain, devoted to every conceivable aspect of the art. Lavishly illustrated and beautifully produced, each strives to command attention and the respect of the tens of thousand of sophisticated housewives it tries so hard to please. Yet not one of them has ever come within striking distance of a single year's sales of that continuing phenomenon of culinary history, the close-packed encyclopedia of domestic economy Isabella Beeton bequeathed to the women of Britain well over a hundred years ago.

As the compiler of what is universally acknowledged to be the best cook book ever written, she will continue to be read as avidly into the twenty-first century as she has been in the nineteenth and twentieth. There must be a basic reason for her ageless popularity, and George Meredith long ago supplied the answer:

Kissing don't last: cookery do!

Dressing for dinner in the 1890s.

BIBLIOGRAPHY

The bibliographical works listed below form a selective reference background that a collector of early cook books will need to consult. A few of the best-known compilers of cook books have their own individual bibliographies which can be bought and consulted separately as your interest dictates, and these are not included in this general list.

AMERICAN HERITAGE COOKBOOK (New York: American Heritage Publishing Co., 1964)

BABEES BOOK by F. J. Furnivall (London: Early English Text Society, 1868)

BIBLIOGRAPHIE GASTRONOMIQUE by Georges Vicaire (Paris: Rouquette et Fils, 1890)

BIBLIOGRAPHY OF AMERICAN COOK BOOKS by W. Lincoln (American Antiquarian Society Proceedings, vol. 38, 1928)

BIBLIOTHECA GASTRONOMICA by André L. Simon (London: Wine & Food Society, 1953)

BOOK-AUCTION RECORDS (London: Dawsons Ltd., Pall Mall, 1902 to present day) 74 annual vols.

COLLECTOR'S BOOK OF BOOKS by Eric Quayle (London: Studio Vista, 1971)

CONCISE DICTIONARY OF AMERICAN BIOGRAPHY (New York: Charles Scribner's Sons, 1964)

COOKERY BOOKS, 1500–1954: AN EXHIBITION (London: Times Bookshop, catalogue, 1954)

ENGLISH COOKERY BOOKS TO THE YEAR 1850 by A. W. Oxford (Oxford: Oxford University Press, 1913)

ENGLISH TABLE IN HISTORY AND LITERATURE by Charles Cooper (London: Sampson, Low, Marston & Co., 1929)

FIRST CATCH YOUR HARE by Mary Aylett and Olive Ordish (London: Macdonald, 1965)

FOOD AND DRINK THROUGH THE AGES: 1500 B.C.–1937 A.D. (London: Maggs Bros, catalogue of books, 1937)

GASTRONOMIC BIBLIOGRAPHY by K. G. Bitting (San Francisco: 1939)

GEIST DER KOCHKUNST by C. F. von Rumohr, but published as by "Joseph König" (Germany: Stuttgart & Tübingen, 1822)

ISABELLA AND SAM—THE STORY OF MRS. BEETON by Sarah Freeman (London: Victor Gollancz Ltd., 1977)

NEW CAMBRIDGE BIBLIOGRAPHY OF ENGLISH LITERATURE, edited by George Watson (Cambridge: Cambridge University Press, 1969–1977), 5 vols.

OLD COOKERY BOOKS AND ANCIENT CUISINE by W. C. Hazlitt (1866)

PHYSIOLOGIE DU GOUT by J. A. Brillat-Savarin (Paris: A. Sautelet & Cie, 1826), 2 vols.

PORTRAIT OF A CHEF by Helen Morris (Cambridge: Cambridge University Press, 1938)

ROMAN COOKERY BOOK by Barbara Flower and Elisabeth Rosenbaum (London: George G. Harrap & Co., 1958)

INDEX TO RECIPES

GENERAL INDEX